Tropics of History

TROPICS OF HISTORY

Cuba Imagined

ALAN WEST

BERGIN & GARVEY
Westport, Connecticut • London

Library of Congress Cataloging-in-Publication Data

West, Alan, 1953–
    Tropics of history : Cuba imagined / Alan West.
      p. cm.
    Includes bibliographical references (p.) and index.
    ISBN 0–89789–338–7 (alk. paper)
    1. Cuban literature—20th century—History and criticism.
  2. Cuba—In literature. 3. Literature and history—Cuba. 4. Cuba—
History. I. Title.
PQ7378.W4   1997
860.9'97291'0904—dc21   96–47628

British Library Cataloguing in Publication Data is available.

Library of Congress Catalog Card Number: 96–47628
ISBN: 0–89789–338–7

First published in 1997

Bergin & Garvey, 88 Post Road West, Westport, CT 06881
An imprint of Greenwood Publishing Group, Inc.

Printed in the United States of America

The paper used in this book complies with the
Permanent Paper Standard issued by the National
Information Standards Organization (Z39.48–1984).

10 9 8 7 6 5 4 3 2 1

Copyright Acknowledgments

The author and the publisher are grateful to the following for granting permission to reprint from their materials:

Passages from Nancy Morejón's poems "Ana Mendieta" and "Before a Mirror" (Summer 1994, pp. 618–22); Lourdes Casal's "For Anna Veldford" (Summer 1994, pp. 415–16); and Dulce María Loynaz's "Eternity" (translations by Davide Frye) appear courtesy of *The Michigan Quarterly Review*.

Translations by Alan West from Dulce María Loynaz in *These Are Not Sweet Girls*, edited by Marjorie Agosín (1994), appear courtesy of White Pine Press.

Excerpts taken from the works of Dulce María Loynaz appear courtesy of Dulce María Loynaz.

Excerpts taken from the works of Nancy Morejón appear courtesy of Nancy Morejón.

Translations by Kathleen Weaver of Nancy Morejón's "Amo a mi Amo," "Piedra Pulida," "Madre," "Los ojos de Elegguá," and "Elogio de Nieves Fresneda," in *Where the Island Sleeps Like a Wing* by Nancy Morejón, appear courtesy of Black Scholar Press.

Excerpts from Alan West's historical essays on Cuba printed in the CD-ROM "American Journey: The Hispanic American Experience" appear courtesy of Primary Source Media, Inc.

Translations by Alan West of Elías Miguel Muñoz's "Vaticinios" appear courtesy of Elías Miguel Muñoz.

Contents

A Suggestion for the Reader

If you have little or no prior knowledge of Cuba before reading this book, I strongly recommend reading the Appendix first, since it is a basic outline of Cuban history from pre-Columbian times to the present. Even readers somewhat familiar with Cuban history should find it helpful in refreshing their memories. The Appendix, however, is no substitute for more complete studies on Cuban history, and following the Appendix there is a list of selected readings so that readers can pursue lengthier, more detailed, and complete studies on the subject.

Each chapter on individual writers begins with an introduction that gives an overall evaluation of the author and places him or her within the wider context of Cuban literature and history. This should be helpful to the reader, particularly where a small part of the author's work is discussed, as is the case with Alejo Carpentier, Virgilio Piñera, José Lezama Lima, and Severo Sarduy.

Acknowledgments

This book owes a debt of gratitude to Hayden White, who in turn is equally indebted to Vico and Kenneth Burke. His books *Tropics of Discourse* (which contains a chapter on Vico called "Tropics of History") and *Metahistory: The Historical Imagination in Nineteenth Century Europe* have been valuable in helping me understand the rhetorical strategies underlying the narratives of history. Vico, Burke, and White have been equally important in bringing clarity to some of my readings of José Lezama Lima (none of them, especially Vico, has read Lezama), whose highly metaphorical historical essay *La expresión americana* has shaped this book in many unexpected ways. Perhaps my greatest debt is to Antonio Benítez Rojo and his work *The Repeating Island*. Even if I have not quoted extensively from it, the audacity and scope of its imagining and questioning have made this book possible. César Salgado was extremely helpful in making some ideas take on greater shape. I am grateful to Pío Serrano for providing valuable information on the Nancy Morejón chapter.

Finally, I am grateful to Ester Shapiro, who has been a loving and rigorous editor and an extraordinary companion. With her inimitable Cuban *chutzpah*, she has stimulated the creative and critical faculties that have made this book become a reality.

Tropics of History

INTRODUCTION

Tropics of History: Cuba Imagined

History is the most dangerous product evolved from the chemistry of the intellect. Its properties are well known. It causes dreams, it intoxicates whole peoples, gives them false memories, quickens their reflexes, keeps their old wounds open, torments them in their repose, leads them into delusions either of grandeur or persecution, and makes nations bitter, arrogant, insufferable, and vain.

History will justify anything. It teaches precisely nothing, for it contains everything and furnishes examples of everything.

—Paul Valéry

We comfort ourselves by reliving memories of protection. Something closed must retain our memories, while leaving them their original values as images. Memories of the outside world will never have the same tonality as those of home and, by recalling these memories, we add to our store of dreams. We are never real historians, but always near poets, and our emotion is perhaps nothing but an expression of poetry that was lost.

—Gaston Bachelard

Cuba and its history are continuously being imagined. Both from within and afar, by its own people and by interested foreigners, the island has exercised a fascination that spans continents and centuries. Abetted by its strategic geographical location, Cuba has been at different times a focal point for Europe, North America, Africa, and Asia. The island has been a magnet for conquerors, profiteers, dreamers, and artists. This kind of

attraction is combustible material, so eloquently expressed by Carlos Franqui, who says that "Cuba is an island of immigrants and emigrés. In
constant movement and danger. Coveted by the great powers. Invaded by
buccaneers and pirates. Occupied by Spaniards, Britons, North Americans.
An island of sugar and tobacco, of misery and slavery: rebellion itself"
(Brenner et al., 1989, p. xxxv). Franqui, himself a Castroite revolutionary
turned critic of fidelismo, goes on to add that in that rebellious spirit there
is a willingness to take on great challenges: "Cuba is an adventure without
fear of the unexpected, the magical, the impossible, of the unknown" (ibid.,
p. xxxiii).

The unexpected derives precisely from Franqui's migrant island description. The dynamic tensions of Cuban history as an immigrant nation are a
grounding for that rebelliousness. Perhaps the very rootlessness of the
immigrant, who has given up a measure of security for the ultimate act of
imagination, reinventing the self in a new land, is a stimulus for different
kinds of defiance. Not all, of course, immigrated freely, as was the case with
Africans or Chinese indentured laborers in the nineteenth century; however, this makes their experience acquire a double-leveled resistance. If we
accept Franqui's definition, Cuba, far from being a melting pot, is an
alchemist's forge: the transmutation of elements (race, culture, nature, and
myth) that becomes a transcultured identity, an exploration of the Cuban
historical unconscious with its deepest fears, images, and dreams.

This rebellious spirit has sought out the island's independence, be it in
economic, political, or cultural terms. That these three factors are inextricably linked was perhaps best expressed by José Martí when he said that there
would be no Latin American culture without Latin America. What he meant
was that an entity with a shared political vision, economy, and language
had to exist before a truly Latin American identity could flourish. The words
are equally applicable to Cuba: only its political and economic independence could allow Cubans to claim their own culture. Martí well understood the cost of imperial imagery imposed on the island from outside.
From other shores, the island has been imagined and expressed in a series
of more familiar discourses with a plethora of images: Pearl of the Antilles,
tropical paradise, whorehouse of the Caribbean, Cuba as gold mine, cane
field (slave trade), military outpost (strategic location/geopolitical pawn),
tourist haven/exotic folkloric locale (flesh depot, fun in the sun, shed your
inhibitions), investment opportunity (source of cheap labor), showcase for
third world liberation movements (under USSR aegis), or revolutionary
menace/terrorist haven (as U.S. nightmare). Cuba's images of "otherness"
come from outside observers or covetous foreign powers. What happens
when we look at Cuba from within, as imagined by its own best poetic
historians? A fountain of images will gush forth, perhaps not as obvious,
contesting many of these more well-known yet exploitative and constrain-
ing images.

Martí's quest for sovereignty at every level was inclusive. His nationalism embraced an internationalist perspective which artfully mixed in the ideas, cosmologies, religions, science, and art of Latin America, Europe, North America, Africa, and Asia. In his vivid poetic parlance he has set a standard for all Cuban writers, the poet-warrior, one which will probably never again be embodied in one person. For Martí, creating a free nation meant you had to act like a soldier and imagine as a writer.

To construct a nation implies a narrative (na[rra]tion) of what is being built, and usually the narrative is an epic tale. Epics depict heroic deeds, conquests, victorious wars. Their heroes can be human or divine, but even when human they must perform divine deeds. They are the foundational tales or myths of a nation or a culture, and these narratives are central(izing) definitions of a country or a people. Homi Bhabha reminds us that nation building involves a "syntax of forgetting." The written sentence of nation narrative is a way of sentencing other histories to oblivion. The formulaic aspect of epic/nation narrative requires suppressing many aspects of a country's history: not only complex political forces but also its class divisions, racial divides, or sexual differences. Cuban poet and narrator Rolando Sánchez Mejías, rejecting formulaic heroism, echoes his own doubts by saying his work does not form part of the "epico-sentimental guild" that characterizes much Cuban writing. Poets and writers speak to the hidden nation—a truly independent clause?—that the "syntax of forgetting" would sentence to silence.

Martí's greatness derived from his ability to offer an image or dream of nationhood that wholly embraced a complex, multidimensional people and body politic. His death (1895) before the nominal achievement of independence (1902) no doubt helped make his subsequent iconization an even more potent rallying point. By welding together an empowering political discourse with an imaginative poetics, Martí founded a unique kind of subjectivity, as well as a more inclusive definition of nationhood. Martí viewed politics as an art form, poetry as a kind of Edenic adventure naming/creating the world. His generosity of spirit viewed the human subject as a crossroads engaged in an Emersonian cosmic dialogue. Poetry as an aesthetic creative language is a nonmanipulative corrective to the desiring, acquisitive, pragmatic exhortation of politics and science. Poetry's way of thinking avails itself of relatedness, ethical questioning with no ready-made answers, and a knowledge derived from wonder, and steers away from the realm of utility, moral certitude, and narrow cognition. Elias Canetti said, "There should be a description of the way thoughts grow *between* people." For Martí this desire to express not only the "hope of thought," but the thought of hope, is perfectly embodied in the inclusiveness of his thinking as it grows between people in an impassioned friendship from which imagination, ethics, and nationhood are collaboratively built. Martí's inclusiveness was expressed in these words: "not [wanting] to be a soldier in only one side of a battle." Moreover, these traits create conditions for intersubjectivity (of vulnerability and giving) which allow Martí and his conversational partners (readers) to overcome internalized modes of domination creatively, in both the literary and political fields.

The "island of the unexpected" has produced both the first mulatto cosmonaut and almost nuclear armageddon. The magical has brought forth Santería and the poetry of José Lezama Lima. The impossible has been incarnated by both José Martí at a sublime level and by an array of politicians at the level of Grand Guignol. The headlong rush into the unknown often confounds our received notions about human conduct or what is possible in the realm of action and thought. Categories become fuzzy, definitions elusive: it becomes too difficult to discern when the rumba ends and the funeral march begins (or is it the other way around?). In Cuba's recent history, liberation and terror become intertwined, offering a situation which is both entangling and stupefying. In fighting adversity, acts of selflessness can literally become acts of suicide. In the thick of harsh and often brutal reversals, heroism can become meaningless. To understand some of these feats of historical imagination, this book explores different dimensions of the island's "sociocultural imaginary," that is, the myths, narratives, discourses, or fictions that constitute the foundational symbols of Cuban identity.

This book provides a look at Cuba's history through the minds and images of some of its most perspicacious writers and artists. The artistic realm offers us a distinctive way of understanding both present and latent meanings of Cuban reality and history. The greater freedom in the aesthetic realm means that fiction, myth, folktales, popular music, and poetry can be brought to bear on the historical as a "dialogue between intentional subjects," as originating thought. And like Wilson Harris, I agree that "a philosophy of history may well lie buried in the arts of the imagination."

The rationales for the selections are as varied as the authors, but a common thread unites them all: an audacious willingness to produce images which take us beyond past and current dead-ends of historical discourse. In the meaning they attach to Cuban history through their various tropes, they question or subvert the images expressed by both imperial outsiders and totalizing insiders. Through the prism of race, gender, sexuality, power relationships, and notions of heroism, they fashion their own "animistic counterpoint," as Lezama said, speaking to the kind of ingenuity needed to follow and interpret history, Latin American or Cuban. Some of the authors are considered "canonical," like Alejo Carpentier (and Lezama to a lesser degree), or champions of "postmodernism" (Severo Sarduy). Still others have been scandalously ignored outside of Cuba (Virgilio Piñera). All six writers selected for this book achieve their own distinctively Cuban tropes by both deep immersion and skeptical emergence from the island's history, a "homecoming through otherness."

While some of the authors spent a great deal of their adult lives outside Cuba (Sarduy, Piñera, Carpentier), and others literally never left the island (Lezama Lima), all six in their own way have come to understand Cuba intimately from "afar." The way these writers manage their closeness and distance from the island, in itself, is used tacitly or overtly to question notions central to Cuban nationhood and identity.

The authors' comprehension of the island's history is crafted through metaphor and image. The title *Tropics of History: Cuba Imagined* offers an examination of this tropical isle's tropes of history. The sources of these tropes are many, but to assist the reader we can distinguish four main areas: history (Cuban and otherwise); religious/mystical thought (or its antithesis, atheism, Marxism); literature (both Cuban and world); and landscape. The sources are refracted through a poetic and personal memory, through which, as Gaston Bachelard's words at the beginning of this book suggest, we make a house in history. By virtue of being poetic and personal, memory functions not as a vehicle for nostalgia but by exploring the past through constructed images that free us from the constraints of past and present. The image, as in Lezama, is not a representation (an effect) but a generative matrix. It is both original and originating. But more important, we need to recognize that tropes are not merely artistic fantasies, not just products of strong-willed creators, pure individualistic expressiveness. Tropes are an intersubjective phenomenology tied to collective reality, with a lived historicity. As Richard Kearney says of Bachelard: "This phenomenological emphasis on the *originality* of images leads in turn to the discovery of their *trans-subjectivity*. Unlike Sartre, who saw the intentional uniqueness of each image as implying self-enclosure, Bachelard marvelled at the mystery that the image can be both *unique* to the originating consciousness, and yet *common* to different subjects. . . . For Bachelard the image was revealed as a world of dialogue *between* intentional subjects" (Kearney, 1991, p. 92). Maybe the image is that hope of thought (Canetti, Martí) growing between people, which in history is positioned from race/gender/class. This generative phenomenology of the image will allow us to explore themes such as anti- or post-colonialism, revolution, independence, and national identity as the distinctive domain where each writer as an individual expresses his or her common ground with Cuban history. All of the writers in this book have lived or are still living with a direct and personal contact with the Cuban Revolution. In many cases the work discussed does not directly deal with the Cuban Revolution (as with Lezama, Dulce María Loynaz, and Piñera), but nonetheless, what these authors have to say eventually intersects with post–1959 events on the island. For all the writers in this volume, history is not some remote object of study or a kind of intellectual protein consumed to pump up the muscles of curiosity. History is a lived experience that shapes a writer's thoughts and art, but equally history is fashioned through the artist's work by virtue of its own interpretations, by the meanings it suggests which speak to the hopes, dreams, and frustrations of a nation's course in time.

Cuba's history is extraordinary in so many ways, but just its more recent past is convulsive enough. First, there is dictatorship under Fulgencio Batista and armed struggle through a popular guerrilla movement (1952–59). The revolution (1959) led to the creation of the first socialist country in the western hemisphere (1961–present), Cuba's becoming a major player in the cold war, and the October Missile Crisis (1962) that almost brought a nuclear showdown between the United States and the USSR. Just before that, the United States had invaded the island at the Bay of Pigs (1961). Cuba's revolutionary enthusiasm transcended its national borders, leading to involvement in African liberation struggles (1975–89). The dramatic ideological tensions of building a socialist/communist society produced the Mariel Exodus (1980) and most recently the Rafter Crisis of 1994. (See the Appendix for a historical narrative.) Any one of these events highlights issues of sovereignty, superpower politics, the image of Cuba as a player on a Caribbean, continental, or world stage. Why has Cuba played this large role? As we said before, its geopolitical reality has kept it as a crossroads (and sometimes battleground) where major powers converge. As the largest Caribbean island it has developed a lively, transcultured society, having been blessed with extraordinary talents such as poet/soldier/politician José Martí, anthropologist/writer Fernando Ortiz, poet/novelist/essayist José Lezama Lima, painter Wifredo Lam, bassist/composer Israel "Cachao" López, and pianist/composer Ernesto Lecuona. This transcultured society is a product of those convergences. And, more recently, Cuba took on a "mini-superpower" status of its own (when it was funded by the USSR), which further highlighted the nature of North-South power relationships.

Cuba's recent history could be presented in a more dramatic, if not biblical vein: a small, poor, third world country (David) stands up to a superpower nation (Goliath), with ensuing miscomprehension from both parties. This scenario has been documented and analyzed by historians, political scientists, and policy analysts (see the suggested readings list following the Appendix), and it is not my intention to repeat their efforts. Instead, I will explore images of the island generated by its writers as they struggle with the same forces that shape Cuba's history. Many metaphors will issue forth in the chapters of this book, none of which can be called a central or guiding image with greater importance or "truth" than the others. Cuba's history, particularly since 1959, has been marked by having one (and only one) interpretation of its history (Marxian), with the accompanying suppression of dissident historical poetics toward an overriding central political goal of building a classless society. If these essays are to have any merit, they must contribute to a plurality of interpretations about its history, without exclusions. The Marxist project is neither completely rejected nor accepted, since it has important things to say about social justice, inequality, and power that are central to all aspects of Cuban history. Interpretation has an ethical dimension (as does the imagination) and is a recognition of a contested terrain, the shape and meaning of Cuban history, which will acquire its truest expression through plurality. That Cuba's history is still (and will be) contested terrain should not be so surprising, given that the French are still discussing the relative merits of Danton, Robespierre, and their revolution some two hundred years after its occurrence and demise. The following chapters make a case for different authors and thinkers as to why their metaphors offer thought-provoking images that make us want to explore their work or thinking more thoroughly, and through that exploration arrive at a more complex view of Cuban history.

How are tropes useful in understanding this complexity? Through metaphor we see thought striving to bring together two seemingly disparate elements, a unity-in-difference which is extremely helpful in understanding history, a discipline fraught (and fought) with many contradictions, aims at odds with each other, and bewildering if not murderous passions. This implies seeing metaphor as fundamentally conceptual and not linguistic. Metaphors and images are not just tricks or embellishments of speech, but are integral to consciousness and knowledge. They are crucial elements of speculative thought, in the Hegelian sense, of something positive that can unite opposites (like the poetic imagination) by transcending the merely sensory toward understanding. Speculative thought through metaphor will be present throughout this book, as a way of making the history of Cuba reveal its latent images.

A Hegelian tension between layers of meaning characterizes the use of the word *image* as well. In German, *bild* is the word used for *image*, with other associated meanings of portrait, illustration, idea, symbol, representation, metaphor. Used in certain compound words, it can mean sculptor, hieroglyph, or the face of a coin. The verb *bilden* means to form, shape, cultivate, educate, or fashion, from where *bildung* (education, culture) comes. Images and metaphor are (in)formative; they help shape, represent, and configure the movements of history. They contain, by definition, dynamic forces of tension and reconciliation. The tropic inventiveness of Cuba's artists and writers helps us to understand or demystify certain "foundational symbols of Cuban identity," or offers alternative tropes.

Hegel's integrative act of interpretation (speculative thought, imagistic thinking) underlies Paul Ricoeur's analysis of metaphor. Ricoeur points out, "It is the conflict between these two interpretations [literal and figurative] that sustains the metaphor." Ricoeur says that there is an absurdity involved here if we see it from the point of view of literal meaning, but it is surpassed as the "conflict of interpretations" is worked through and worked out. "Thus a metaphor does not exist in itself, but in and through an interpretation. The metaphorical interpretation presupposes a literal interpretation which self-destructs in a significant contradiction. It is this process of self-destruction or transformation which imposes a sort of twist on the words, an extension of meaning thanks to which we can make sense where a literal interpretation would be literally nonsensical" (Ricoeur, 1976, p. 50).

This self-destruction, or transformation, is part of the movement of metaphor already suggested etymologically (meta-*phora*). Metaphor's movement or displacement of meaning from one signification to another, or its ability to borrow meaning from one domain of "original belonging" to a new one, might allow it to be best understood as personal and historical problem-solving. This movement mirrors not only the movement of thought, but suggests other kinds of movements and displacements in Cuban history: migrations, exiles, the pendulum of political movements and allegiances, the rhythms of Cuban nature and culture (and not just its music), the counterpoint of event and context. The movements, rhythms, and migrations of Cuban metaphorical discourse are nurtured by sources other than the historical.

The religious sources of the tropes are varied, ranging from Catholicism and Santería to Taoism, Buddhism, and Sufism. In none of the authors to be discussed will any of these beliefs be presented in an orthodox fashion, that is, merely offering the content of religious beliefs or systems. These sources' ability to evoke the sacred, the power of its imagery, work themselves into the writings and thoughts with eloquent persuasiveness, as is the case with Lezama, Sarduy, Nancy Morejón, and Loynaz. Religion serves as a ground for seeing the origins of Cuban history, as a lively conversant with the secular and the social, as a combustive element in the crafting of personal or collective narratives, and as a key factor in defining the shifting parameters of Cuban identity.

The literary-philosophical sources are too vast to be discussed here, but will come up in each chapter. They range from Cuban writers and historians (José Martí, Fernando Ortiz, Julián del Casal, Juan Clemente Zenea, Nicolás Guillén, Manuel Moreno Fraginals) and Latin American intellectuals, all the way to Heraclitus, Heidegger, Samuel Beckett, James Joyce, and Thomas Mann. The international sources are made to function in a Cuban context, often with remarkable ease and humor, adding a new beat or voice to a vastly complex Cuban chorus. They nourish the Cuban imagination, especially if we remember Bachelard's definition: "Imagination is the faculty of forming images, which go beyond reality, which *sing* reality."

Landscape is a crossroads of nature, culture, myth, and history. We will be seeing the island from within and from afar, as homeland and myth, from the point of view of the traveler who achieves "a homecoming through otherness," as well as the homebound writer who turns a garden into an entire world. Other writers examine the island's beauty as a source of peace, a spiritual source, an affirmation of national sovereignty, or as creatively powerful as culture itself. All the writers draw on these four sources—

history, religion, literature, and landscape—to fashion their tropes, trying to sing reality, or history.

This book works at two metaphoric levels which are often indistinguishable. One level is the artists' and writers' own work, where they fashion their own figurative language from the ashes of literalness (absurdity), creating new metaphors with which to understand Cuban history. The second level is the reworking or deconstruction of previous authors and metaphors. Severo Sarduy is a vibrant example of both levels: his neo-baroque aesthetic and language have yielded unique metaphors, which I have grouped under the rubric of "cross-dressing as transculturation." At the second level, though, Sarduy's work implies an engagement (as expansion, refutation, reworking) with previous authors such as José Lezama Lima, Alejo Carpentier, and Fernando Ortiz, all of whom explored issues of Cuban national identity from exceptionally different perspectives.

The authors discussed in this book have created important metaphors which have generated significant insight into Cuba's history. They are not glib, flashy images which titillate and then fade away, but are constantly recreating that tension so crucial to good metaphor. That is, the tension which constantly creates its own meaning, by virtue of the "conflict of interpretation," so that when these new metaphors are used to comment on the foundational symbols, they find the latter often coming up short. If you prefer, these symbols have become "dead metaphors."

Symbols bear an affinity with metaphor but create no "semantic impertinence" between the primary (literal) meaning and the secondary (figurative) meaning. The figurative significance happens *through* the literal meaning, as *the* meaning between many (Ricoeur). It is more "bound" than metaphor, usually forging a direct link to cosmic/natural forces, as when Cuba is referred to as the Pearl of the Antilles or the land of royal palms. Metaphor, being more "bound" to discourse, is freer and more inventive, but perhaps without the lasting power that potent symbols have (flags, anthems, certain images). This has led some to say that metaphors die, while symbols become transformed.

After the Cuban Revolution, for example, to be considered a "Cuban" you had to reside on the island. Those who left were considered counter-revolutionary. Implicit in this label is a symbol about personal identity and worth, one's patriotism, as well as one's ideological commitment, given a final touch by geography. The United States' hostility to the Cuban Revolution, its various attempts to assassinate its leaders, as well as the royal welcome it offered any Cuban who wanted to emigrate, exarcebated those feelings and identities. This "patriotic" symbol was manipulated with great skill and passion by the Cuban Revolution, most notably by its ruler, Fidel Castro. However, as the following chapters will reveal, many Cuban authors and artists have questioned the limitations and legitimacy of such a narrowly defined viewpoint, expressed more directly in Sarduy, Cuban-

American authors, and Morejón, or indirectly as is the case with Lezama and Piñera. Despite a wearing down of this "patriotic symbol" and recent political events, this emblem of national identity still holds an enormous emotional resonance for many Cubans.

If language works as symbolic action, then the relationship between metaphor and history becomes more coherent and Ricoeur's observations ring even truer: "A metaphor tells us something new about reality" or about "the capacity of language to open up new worlds." If we follow Ricoeur, then words are not just talk or merely descriptive tags which aspire to photographic verisimilitude, but also shape, define, and create reality and history; not *ex nihilo*, but based in history, myth, lived experience, where meaning is explored, contested, and revised by different agents (e.g., classes, institutions, individuals, the media). A frightening example of this ability of language to shape reality is racist or anti-Semitic propaganda, which through stereotyping, slander, euphemism, and outright lying, can systematically deny the humanity and rights of entire groups of people. George Orwell's "newspeak" is another well-known example.

Opening up new worlds with language or metaphor requires both the creativity and the courage of imagination. This is a book about the poetics of the Cuban historical imagination, keeping in mind the ancient meaning of *poiesis*: to act, to produce, to make, to create. To make or do, one must make decisions, weigh consequences, face limitations or obstacles, which entails seeing the imagination's functions as not merely having the power to create fantasies. What unites many of the concerns of the writers discussed in this book is what Richard Kearney called the ethical powers of the imagination: the utopian, the empathic, and the testimonial (discussed in the final chapter). None of this implies that the artists/authors are "moralists" in the pejorative sense of the word. Quite the contrary, they are all concerned with justice and nationhood, but in distinctive ways that bypass the certainties of ideology and engage their readers with great verve, wit, and intelligence. As they share their doubts and their self-assertiveness with equal passion, they create the shared exploratory dialogic space within which the reader can construct her or his own ethics of imagination.

Our most common way of understanding history is as narrative, as the biography of a nation. Severo Sarduy's *From Cuba with a Song* is probably the only work discussed which offers a wide panoramic sweep of Cuban history, albeit in a highly parodic and entirely unorthodox form. Sarduy's narrative interrupts itself, contradicts itself, questioning the epistemological validity of narrative as a way of comprehending history or of making it coherent. The other works discussed are more bound by specific historical eras or moments, with the exception of Lezama Lima, whose *La expresión americana* speaks more directly to Latin American history over four centuries. However, Lezama's essay still sheds much insight on Cuban history. The others offer a small slice of Cuban history, bringing it under intense scrutiny, suggesting that the neat flow of events must be stopped and magnified so as to be better understood and appreciated. If we were to use a corporeal image reminiscent of Orphic myth, we could say that these explorations are the limbs of a body that need to be detached before the body can become whole again.

In the following chapters we will witness the figurative act of tolerance, voices that imagine Cuba in many inclusive ways, by "creating the imaginative province where no one owns the truth and everyone has the right to be understood" (Milan Kundera). This imaginative province will conjure up metaphors that pertain to the following: national identity and personal identity as seen through class, race, and sexual difference (Sarduy, Morejón); gender roles (Loynaz, Morejón, Sarduy, Piñera); national liberation and anti-imperialism (Carpentier); modernity/postmodernity; the production of historical meaning (Sarduy, Carpentier, Lezama); religious or sacred dimensions of lived experience (Lezama, Loynaz); notions of power and political control (Piñera); and the manipulation of images and symbols for the purpose of domination (Piñera, Morejón). The voices of these writers are original, not preachy, and avoid rigid didacticism, even though they express strongly held views, political and otherwise.

This tolerance might seem confusing, if only because it recognizes that the past is neither an unassailable fortress with one entrance or a comforting place of repose under a shady tree. Through art the dead are made to speak again, and they are likely to tell us things that are perplexing, what we don't want to hear. Or, if a narrative explanation is preferred, it means that either a different story is to be told, or the same story with a different plot and characters. The art of memory, of recollection, will always yield more than we expected, perhaps in the spirit of these words of Elias Canetti: "The past grows in all directions through its depiction. Wouldn't the same hold for history? Or is historiography reductive, in contrast to memory accumulated and shaped?" This accumulation and shaping is the *bildung*, the gallery of images, the formation of history through images, and the power of those images to shape history.

Many of the issues, themes or tropes discussed here will lend credence to the words of Paul Valéry. History does cause dreams, and often the dreams do turn into nightmares. But that does not mean that dreams are to be avoided or are without meaning. History does indeed "intoxicate whole peoples and give them false memories," the most brutal example in our century being the Third Reich or Kampuchea under Pol Pot. But history is impossible without memory, especially if we consider history a people's memory. The "delusions of grandeur or persecution" that make nations "bitter, arrogant, insufferable, and vain" can be brought into perspective thanks to history. The temporal distance inherent in historical discourse allows us to look at those passions, if not with total objectivity, at least with a measure of compassion and, if need be, irony. We must distinguish between history as an organizing narrative of political mobilization and history as personal counternarrative that interprets past events without the primary purpose being political action. This does not mean that the latter definition cannot inform or motivate political action, since the writing of history is neither disinterested nor innocent; but its primary function is not to become an instrument of control, ideological or otherwise.

There is a saying attributed to Epictetus that "it is not deeds that shock humanity, but the words describing them." This statement offers a eulogy to the power and conscience of words. At the same time one has to admit that certain horrors are impossible to put into words (torture, genocide, mass repression, and slaughter). It is a cliché to say that these atrocities are "unspeakable acts," for several reasons: they defy definition, they are meant to silence and intimidate, and their only language is death. And yet words, those most human of creations, are one of the few bridges that allow us to see, remember, create a shared and lived history. Butchers rarely document their atrocities; it is through the words of Rigoberta Menchú, Primo Levy, Jacobo Timmerman, and many others that the true horror of deeds is known to the world, but the shock is no less real to the protagonists who suffered if the story is not told.

There are other events that do not shock humanity, either in deed or word. Some are on a grand scale; others are quite humble and modest— gestures of defiance, hope, solidarity, or compassion. It is a cautious hope, evocative of these words: "Only one thing is incontrovertible: the course of history defies prediction. It remains open at every point. No one acts according to its inner logic, because no one knows it. Probably this logic doesn't even exist. If that is the case, then history, in its openness, is always subject to influence; it is so to speak, always in our hands. Perhaps our hands are too weak to accomplish anything. But since we don't even know that for sure, we should at least try" (Canetti, 1994, p. 213).

The authors selected for this book, with their bare hands, offer their readers an interpretative framework for Cuba's history. For Cuban readers on the island, these writers offer a lost self that had been banished in the pursuit of a dream; for Cubans in exile a rediscovery of a legacy that is still new, controversial, and fresh. For U.S. readers, in a land where "the syntax of forgetting" is structured as the amnesia of acculturation (versus the historical memory of transculturation), these authors bring forth a historical self-knowledge through the "other." Through image and word, memory and dream, our tropes hand us understanding, if not hope.

ONE

Nancy Morejón: Poet of Cultural Crossroads

Nancy Morejón is the human and poetic embodiment of the word *transculturation*. Firmly rooted in the hybridity of her mulatto family, nourished by Spanish and African ancestries, Morejón is a keen observer of Havana street life, with all its rhythms and nuances. Her life and work are also closely intertwined with the course of the Cuban Revolution. Born in 1944, she was fifteen when the Cuban Revolution triumphed, but in many ways she is a "child" of that social upheaval. Her first book of poems, *Mutismos* (Silences), was published in 1962, soon followed by *Amor, ciudad atribuida* (Love, Attributed City) in 1964. She studied French language and literature at the University of Havana and is a specialist in Francophone literature of the Caribbean. She has translated the work of Aimé Cesaire (Martinique), Jacques Roumain (Haiti), and René Depestre (Haiti) from French to Spanish.

Richard trajo su flauta (1967; Richard Brought His Flute) was her third book of poetry. Morejón's next book of poems, *Parajes de una época* (1979; Parameters of an Epoch), took twelve years to appear, though she did a testimonial book co-authored with Carmen Gonce in 1971, *Lengua de pájaro*, as well as editing a volume of criticism on the work of Nicolás Guillén in 1974 (*Recopilación de textos sobre Nicolás Guillén*). Morejón was wrongly associated with a group of poets from El Puente (The Bridge), from the literary magazine *Ediciones el Puente*. They had invited U.S. poet Allen Ginsberg to the island, but Ginsberg's open expression of gayness (he publicly declared he'd like to sleep with Che Guevara) earned him an invitation to leave as quickly as possible. From that moment on, the poets and artists of El Puente were considered ideologically suspect. Some of the members of the group, such as José

Mario and Pío Serrano (1941–), eventually left Cuba. Others, such as Miguel Barnet and Luis Rogelio Nogueras, stayed on. But various authors from the group, in the post-1968 ideological hardening within Cuba, were marginalized from cultural life, most significantly in not having their own creative work published. Morejón was obviously affected by not having her poetry published, but with the waning of a hard-line policy by the late 1970s, her *Parajes de una época* finally appeared, with poems (in some cases) that were nearly a decade old. In 1982 she published a book-length study of the work of Cuba's "national poet" called *Nación y mestizaje en Nicolás Guillén* (Nation and Mestizaje in the Work of Nicolás Guillén).

Since then Morejón's work has been published often: *Octubre impre-scindible* (1983; Essential October); *Cuaderno de Granada* (1984; Grenada Notebook); and *Piedra pulida* (1986; Polished Stone), one of her best books and a source for many translations of her work. Most recently *Paisaje célebre* (1993; Famed Landscape) was published in Venezuela, after having won the finalist award in the Pérez Bonalde International Poetry Prize.

Over the years, Morejón has worked with Casa de las Américas as a journalist, theater critic, and more recently with the Pablo Milanés Foundation, which was the first cultural organization formed after the revolution not directly financed or administered by the Cuban state. However, the foundation closed in June 1995 because of problems with the Ministry of Culture, which had placed many material obstacles to the publishing of its magazine *Proposiciones*, as well as the overall functioning of the foundation.

Morejón's poetry has shown different interests that have a close relationship with the recent history of Cuba. In the 1960s and 1970s her themes often ran to the political, with well-known poems such as "Mujer Negra" (Black Woman), "Freedom Now," and "Manzano de Oakland" (Apple Tree in Oakland), this last poem dedicated to Angela Davis. Fortunately, it was political poetry that never forgot it was poetry, that is, it never used the language of poetry in a one-dimensional, crudely didactic way. Certain political or social themes are grappled with in *Piedra pulida* but are linked more to issues of gender and are found mostly in the last third of the book. Her *Paisaje célebre*, which brings together poems from 1987 to 1992, raises such themes in a very indirect fashion, if at all. This should not be surprising, since by the mid-1980s Cuban literature had drifted away from overtly social commentary and/or exhortation. This was partly due to a certain stability of the Cuban Revolution, which by 1984 was a quarter of a century old, and was in part a rejection of a socially committed aesthetic of the 1970s which had had a deadening effect on literary culture. It has often been called the "gray decade of Cuban letters." Morejón, whose poetry kept an intense lyrical element even when it drew on historical or political subjects, was able to evolve in a calm or measured way, avoiding sudden turns or crises that beset other authors.

Nancy Morejón's poetry and persona are direct, vibrant, and intimate. She is able to capture the minute details of everyday life and imbue them with the light of the Caribbean, yet filtered through her poetic and historical sensibility. Drawing on her life growing up in a working-class Havana family, imbibing the country's rich history, myth, and Afro-Cuban beliefs, Morejón's work is inspired by diverse literary traditions, as well as oral and folk cultures: "I believe in the oral tradition as a loving source of dispersed identities spread out among territories and seas of the Gulf. My own literary creations have drawn from that oral tradition." In Morejón's embracing of that orality, we sense a reverent listener attuned to Cuba's living culture, a poet who is popular and erudite, funny and philosophical, feminist and freewheeling.

THE STONE AND ITS IMAGES

Roads are like dreams, their invitation to journey filled with the lusty air of freedom, but also with wonderfully strange and sometimes dark auguries. A crossroads both centers outdoor space in a system of coordinates and yet opens up onto vastness, the universe. A kind of expansive optimism overpowers one as it did Walt Whitman: "Afoot and lighthearted I take to the open road, /Healthy, free, the world before me, /The long brown path before me leading wherever I choose" (Whitman, 1902, p. 177). But roads have a long history, secrets, hidden paths: "You road I enter upon and look around, I believe you are not all that is here, /I believe that much unseen is also here" (Whitman, 1950, p. 178). In Cuba, roads and crossroads must begin with the Afro-Cuban orisha (deity) Elegguá. Elegguá is the beginning—not the beginning of creation, but the point of departure of an imaginative faith that is one of the main sources of Cuban culture and history.

Nancy Morejón's poem "Los ojos de Elegguá" (The Eyes of Elegguá) is a rich reworking of Cuban transcultured identity. The author recalls seeing the eyes of Elegguá at nighttime. Morejón recalls it dancing, like all the Santería orishas: "bursting out in shrieks /Elegguá leaps /imagines songs /grazes space with a copper dagger" (Morejón, 1985, p. 67). Elegguá is the orisha of destiny and of crossroads, and so is the orisha invoked before all others, because he is the messenger of all the gods. Elegguá is also vitally linked to the unexpected, twists of fate, and death. In part this is due to his story, or *pattakí*. One day he found a coconut (*obi*) in the road giving off a blinding light from its three eyes. He picked it up and took it home to his mother and father. But the eyes didn't shine (in another version of the tale, the eyes kept shining behind the door, but it was forgotten). He threw the coconut behind a door. Three days later he died. Soon disaster hit the kingdom, and finally they looked for the *obi* behind the door; it was empty and crawling with bugs. In its place they put an *otá*, a sacred stone, which is the origin of Elegguá, and that is why it is said, "The dead one gave birth to the saint." Morejón is evoking this *pattakí* with the eyes for a reason: she is hoping to enlist his all-seeing capabilities. Because of this, Elegguá is known as the personification of justice, and by knowing what is best for humankind, he symbolizes perfect balance in nature. But the poem has an Elegguá who might be needing the powers of Olofi to keep his orientation. This is not so strange since Olofi is the personification of the Creator and his forces. According to one of the *pattakís*, it was Olofi who created the orishas by projecting his *aché* (power, energy) into the *otanes* or stones. Still, there is a moment if not of doubt, at least of precaution: the last stanza begins, "If Elegguá's eyes were to return /they would come crossing the vigorous river / where the gods drew off in the distance, where there used to be fish" (ibid., p. 67). Morejón's poem seems to be caught between belief and the power of *aché*: is it the eyes of Elegguá that give her faith, or is it the faith that makes her see Elegguá's eyes? Possibly a little of both, because to see things along the dark road of life, there's nothing better than to have Elegguá's eyes lighting the way, as if you were being protected by the orisha's headlights.

Though Morejón makes no overt references to Catholic saints, Elegguá's Christian counterpart is St. Anthony of Padua. The orisha is also linked to St. Martin of Porres and El Niño de Atocha. An orisha has many *caminos* (roads) or avatars, sometimes twenty, thirty, or more. St. Anthony was noted for performing miracles and was a charismatic preacher. It is said that he even delivered a sermon to fish, who listened in rapt attention. He is often represented with the child Jesus in his arms, which explains his association with Elegguá, who is often presented as mischievous and playful, like a child. St. Martin of Porres is perhaps more consistent with Cuban culture. St. Martin is the saint of racial harmony and social justice, since he was so committed to helping the poor and particularly slaves. He was a mulatto who had been rejected by his white father.

El Niño de Atocha goes back to the time when Spain was still occupied by the Moors, who were holding many Christian prisoners in what the Spaniards call the War of Reconquest. In the town of Atocha a child was sent in with food (bread and water) for a few prisoners, and yet was able to feed hundreds. According to legend, it was Christ himself that had appeared in the form of a child, in order to provide the prisoners with material and spiritual nourishment.

It is also possible to read certain historical references being made here, although they are indirect. Elegguá's colors are red and black, which are also the colors of the July 26th Movement led by Fidel Castro. Elegguá is a warrior and is considered the first in a trio of holy warriors that also includes Ogún and Ochosi. Again, Cuba since 1959 has often espoused a self-definition of itself as a guerrilla society, traits that include warrior values such as courage, determination, skill, and strength. Furthermore, the Niño de Atocha's day is January 1st, the New Year, which is also the date of the triumph of the Cuban Revolution (1959). Should we stretch things further by pointing out that one of Cuba's "sacred warriors of independence," Antonio Maceo (born on June 14), was named for St. Anthony (June 13)? Che Guevara, born on the same date as Maceo, might be considered one of the "sacred warriors of the Cuban Revolution." Whether Morejón had these allusions in mind or not when she wrote the poem is not the point. What is significant is how her poetry draws on different traditions, histories, literatures, and images to fashion a uniquely Cuban work. They are part of the many *caminos* (roads, avatars) that feed her work, evoking Whitman's "the world before me," the "much unseen," and "the long brown road before me leading wherever I choose."

In a brief poem to Elegguá, Morejón has brought together a true example of Cuban transculturation: a Yoruba orisha, symbol of destiny, chance, and justice, merges with the power of faith and miracles (St. Anthony), racial harmony and social justice (St. Martin of Porres), and the total nourishment of El Niño de Atocha. Time, *mestizaje*, social justice, fate, faith, and utopian fulfillment (through faith and revolution) come together in the vigorous imagery of this powerful poem.

In a poem dedicated to Nieves Fresneda, an extraordinarily gifted dancer in the Cuban folkloric tradition who died in 1981, the author builds on the images of another orisha, Yemayá. With consummate skill, Morejón brings together history and myth, invoking the powers of fertility and the imagination. Yemayá is one of the principle orishas, goddess of the ocean, fertility, and life that Fresneda often danced in her performances.

Elegy for Nieves Fresneda

Like a flying fish: Nieves Fresneda.

Sea waves, galley slaves
blue algae petals
close over her days and hours
reborn at her feet.

A whisper of Benin
bore her to the depth of this land.

There dwelt
her snakes,
her circles,
her shells,
her petticoats,
seeking out the brush,
blazing paths
toward Olokún.
Her ocean feet
finally,
were lodes of salt,
perpetual flickering feet,
aloft like moons for Yemayá.

And in space,
later,
over the sea foam
Nieves
whirling over the sea,
Nieves
deep in immemorial

song of dream
Nieves
in Cuban seas
Nieves.
(Morejón, 1985, p. 69; trans. Weaver)

Morejón begins with a concrete image of Nieves that both unites her to her Yemayá but still retains her individuality. The first verse begins with "like a flying fish," and seems to be inspired by Manuel Mendive's floating Santería-based figures. This verse not only refers to her dancing ability but already brings her into the realm of Yemayá, for in Yoruba, *Yeyeomo eja* means "the Mother whose children are the fish." The verse ends with her whole name, as if to underline her uniqueness as a human being.

After establishing a mythic but individual presence, Morejón immediately gives historical weight to the first images. With sea waves she mentions galley slaves and then "A whisper of Benin" that brings her to the depths of Cuba. The beauty of the Yoruba cosmology is grafted onto the deep pain of historical reality: slavery. The author makes one more historical reference in the poem when she says "seeking out the brush" (*buscando la manigua*). *Manigua* is a Taíno (indigenous) word referring to a place with dense vegetation, consisting of shrubs, bushes, lianas; a kind of natural profusion of confusion. Curiously, it also refers to illegal card games, dice, and other forms of gambling. Taking advantage of both profusion and confusion, many slaves escaped into the *manigua* to begin a new life (gambling with freedom?), free from the oppressive eyes of their masters. In the nineteenth century, the expression *coger la manigua* (take to the *manigua*) meant to take up arms against Spain and join the revolution for independence.

Morejón deftly builds a transition from the *manigua* that goes to Olokún with the verse "blazing paths." It looks back at the *manigua* and goes toward the depths of the ocean, where Olokún, one of the major orishas, is to be found. Olokún is a mysterious and powerful orisha. Her energy can be destructive, which is why it is said that Obatalá had her tied to the bottom of the ocean. Olokún's image is presented as a woman (or siren) with arms outstretched, one holding a snake, the other a mask. She is also visualized as a hermaphrodite. Olokún is the frightening mix of the origin (the ocean floor, and of Yemayá), the generative principle, and the awesome power of wrath and destructiveness. All the orishas, and particularly Yemayá, must make sure that she is treated with the utmost respect.

The final part of the poem focuses on Nieves attaining an almost mythic presence or substance, dancing over the water. The water imagery is central to Morejón's poetics, and this poem in particular draws on the many resonances of water, as we have seen. The Atlantic passage, fertility, and the source of life, which is part of the Afro-Cuban (Santería) tradition, derived from Western and Yoruba beliefs. Undoubtedly other images come to mind:

purity, the waters of the feminine and of reverie (Bachelard). Feminist critics point out that water is synonymous with women's eroticism, as it is concerned with a blurring of rigid boundaries of hierarchy and gender, just as water runs over, flooding distinctions with a kind of plenitude (Ostriker, 1986). Water's mysterious depth and infinity, its movement, its enveloping "warmth" and strangeness, bring it close to a dream state. Morejón's poem conjures up these forces.

Fresneda dancing over the waves maintains both the flow of water (since she is dancing Yemayá's steps) as well as the lightness of air. More important, both air and water convey the sense of movement, which is a key ingredient of the imagination. "We always think of the imagination as the faculty that *forms* images. On the contrary, it *deforms* what we perceive; it is, above all, the faculty that frees us from immediate images and *changes* them. If there is no change, or unexpected fusion of images, there is no imagination; there is no imaginative act. If the image that is present does not make us think of one that is absent, if an image does not determine an abundance—an explosion—of unusual images, then there is no imagination" (Bachelard, 1988, p. 1). This creates both a mobility of images and, to borrow a well-known phrase, an "invitation to the voyage," or, as Bachelard says: "Perceiving and imagining are as antithetical as presence and absence. To imagine is to absent oneself, to launch out toward a new life" (ibid., p. 3). Morejón echoes this play of absences and presences in her poem, through both the content (the past, Olokún, Fresneda herself who has died) and the rhythms and pacing of the words, which stream toward the reader in little waves. For Helene Cixous, poetry means traveling on foot: "Walking, dancing, pleasure: these accompany the poetic act. . . . So perhaps dreaming and writing have to do with traversing the forest, journeying through the world, using all available means of transport, using your body as a form of transport" (Cixous, 1991, p. 63). Why is the imagination a voyage, a movement of images? Because it entails a kind of pursuit: of a transformation of the real, traveling to the *manigua* of meaning, the domain of the imaginary. In a recent talk, Morejón spoke of García Lorca's definition of poetry as "penetrating a jungle at night in order to hunt precious animals, otherwise known as words" (Morejón, 1995b). This magical and perilous hunting expedition will have the author equating dancing and writing: "dancing with the feet, with ideas, with words, and need I add that one must also be able to dance with the pen—that one must learn how to write?" (Nietzsche, 1990, p. 76). In this dance, Morejón choreographs the juncture of myth, history, and the imagination of the artist.

The author has spoken eloquently about the gestation of poems such as "Eleggguá's Eyes" and "Elegy for Nieves Fresneda" as being the humble Havana neighborhood she grew up in. Her statement is worth quoting at length because it offers the "lived experience" of historical and mythical themes:

I was born and raised in a Havana neighborhood known as Los Sitios, where I learned early on to relate to my city—a constant theme in my poems. Life put me in touch with songs and rhythms which were of an anonymous character, this being the essential root of its power. Voices in the late morning would bring a sad melody, evoking the death of a loved one. They were the moving *coros de clave* (chorus with clave rhythm), so much part of Havana, so eroded by the dust of roads and seas, since that singing had been passed on from mouth to mouth, coming from faraway lands. It was a wandering music and we had no idea if it was from a patio in Andalucía or a *museke* from Luanda. Truly it was a kind of combustible magic, whose smoke rose from the plaza Antón Recio all the way to the corners of Peñalver and Manrique. My childhood was marked by these nomadic musicians who went from neighborhood to neighborhood sharing their music generously, out of the simple pleasure of making themselves happy or to brighten up the threadbare night of poverty-stricken neighbors.

There I heard ancient rumbas performed with the hands and muscles (making the sound of drums) of those *rumberos* who never needed a percussion instrument. These were the *rumbas de cajón* (rumbas played on a box). The beats or strokes—hand against hand, hands against the chest or legs, filled with a blessed, loving African energy, would validate the flamenco spirit which lay dormant in the rhythms of the nation. The sounding of those *rumbas* were born of those skins and improvised instruments played to accompany the *ñáñigo diablitos* (little devils of the Abakuá religion) or *íremes* that appeared on the street on Three Kings Day or during funeral ceremonies. The energy of those sounds throbs in poems of mine like "Elegy for Nieves Fresneda," "The Eyes of Elegguá," among others. (Morejón, 1995b)

The author's reference to the rumba is important because it is a central element in Cuban popular culture. As her remembrance states, they were (and are) fairly spontaneous and celebratory moments. People gather in the streets, some with instruments or boxes, the singing begins (often with call and response), and people begin to dance, forming a chain of feeling from the feet up. Unlike the music of Santería, the rumba's Afro-Cuban roots are not religious. It is important to recall that the influence of the rumba on Morejón's poetry is not a mimetic one. She does not try to imitate it rhythmically but instead incorporate "the energy of those sounds." And, of course, the poems, despite the freewheeling, spontaneous feel they might have, are anything but improvised.

"The *monte* (bush, thicket, brush), the sea become an integral part of mythic poetry. In the Caribbean, there is always a voyage, always a ship" (Morejón, 1995a). These poles form the title of her poem "Montes y mares," from *Piedra pulida* (Polished Stone). *El monte* and the sea: two geographic spaces marked by nature and history. But in this long poem, Morejón is more allusive, using a continuous metaphoric stream that expands the mystery it seems to offer us. She plays with the reader, giving clues that slip away, like an elusive lover. At first reading, it seems like a love poem, and there is no reason to abandon this view. But greater delights await the reader. In the second stanza she mentions the eyes of someone that cause great peace, eyes that are "the legitimate children of this song" (Morejón, 1986, p. 66). Quickly she begins a "new scene": "The crops return to source. It is the time / of the peacock. What slowness in supplication. / A woodcutter breathes / the hollow of the valleys / And you take me away with those eyes of unscathed water / to the *monte*" (p. 66). What is the time of the peacock? Morejón seems to be indicating a profound temporal change, even sacred. The peacock, of course, has a long association with immortality, longevity, resurrection, as well as love. (Could this be an oblique reference to St.-Pol-Roux's "Le Paon" [The Peacock]?) The peacock's feather is the sign of St. Barbara, the supplication referred to (*preces* in Spanish) are entreaties to God. In Santería, St. Barbara is syncretized as Changó, who is often shown with a hatchet or ax, like the woodcutter. The poet is not affixing labels, however; it is still the magic of love being awakened in someone that is being described. But Morejón is taking the mystery and wonder of love and linking them up to a wider net of meaning: nature, religious sentiment (Christian and Afro-Cuban), the mesmerizing eyes that enchant or bewitch, plus going to *el monte*.

The poem's use of language is curious, combining rich, sensual details with words that, if not arcane, are still not very common. They are by no means disruptive or out of place, but they have a glow that is reminiscent of a precious stone, this no small feat in a poem brimming with luminous images. The words have a strong Castilian ring to them, which contrasts with the island nature of the poem (sea, sand, coral). It helps contribute to a certain lively tension that the poem has throughout, giving it a strange atmosphere. There is an almost lazy drift of images, followed by vigorous brushstrokes and energetic tableaux. It even evokes previous poems by Morejón: "mar de nostalgia como mares poblándose" ("sea of nostalgia like seas being peopled") brings to mind the verse "el agua sin fin de la memoria" ("the endless water of memory") from "Nubario," as well as her poem about the movie "Solaris." Despite the shafts of light that fall on many passages, there is a feel of a "sombre, voluptuous dream," which is how Debussy's *Pelléas et Mélisande* has been described. This might seem farfetched, but it is not, and the end of the poem even sounds like Mélisande talking: "and an inspired enigma throws me into your arms / so as to live with you in a star." Debussy and Maeterlinck (whose play the opera is based on) were both enthralled by the work of Edgar Allan Poe.

And it is Poe that Morejón quotes in a recent talk about her own poetry, titled simply "Poetics." After discussing García Lorca's metaphor of hunting words like precious animals in a jungle at night, she turns to the master of the macabre tale.

The other concept of poetry or of composing poetry to which I'm close to, is, strangely enough, that of Edgar Allan Poe. I say strangely because he's so apparently distant from me in terms of language, race, gender, and social milieu, and yet, his brief and extraordinary essay that accompanies his famous poem "The Raven" moves me. It's not by chance that Poe entitled these reflections "The Philosophy of Composition," whose pedagogical luminosity should serve as the guide for all teaching on the writing vocation. I was able to distinguish two phenomena he mentions as integral to my own creativity: the originality that flows from ecstasy as well as a unique sense of the beautiful. According to Poe: "Most writers, poets in especial (sic), prefer having it understood that they compose by a species of fine frenzy, an ecstatic intuition." Later he adds the following: "The point, I mean, that beauty is the sole legitimate province of the poem (. . .) My first object, as usual, was originality." (Morejón, 1995b)

This apparently surprising admission is not so striking, as we shall see. It is important to recall what Poe meant by beauty as being something that transcends the physical, echoing perhaps Plato in this regard. "That pleasure which is at once the most intense, the most elevating, and the most pure, is, I believe, found in the contemplation of the beautiful. When, indeed, men speak of Beauty, they mean, precisely, not a quality, as is supposed, but an effect—they refer, in short, just to that intense and pure elevation of *soul*— not of intellect, or of heart—upon which I have commented, and which is experienced in consequence of 'contemplating the beautiful' " (Poe in Bradley, et al., 1967, p. 890). The key word in Poe's definition is *effect*, and how he distinguishes it from a quality, a distinction which is crucial for Morejón as well. Beauty is not just a proportioned array of attractive traits and shapes, but a state of resonance between people induced by the power of imagery and rhythm, by the flow of events and words capable of eliciting the movement of the imagination, "the elevation of the soul." Poe's choice of the word *ecstasy* is even more revealing, as it literally means to be out of the body. Perhaps that is the greatest tension, then, that lies in the poem "Montes y mares." On the one hand, it is most definitely a poem about the body and the senses, yet as it progresses, it seeks to transcend them, stake out the "province of beauty." As it does, it draws a perimeter, a map of chasms, perhaps exemplifying the words of Simone Weil: "Distance is the soul of beauty."

Morejón's historical understanding and insight, as well as her generosity, are poignantly evident from these observations on Poe. In the same essay, "The Philosophy of Composition," Poe speaks about the importance of melancholy as a universally poetic state that can move readers or listeners. Nothing is better for inducing melancholy than death, but for Poe death must be linked to beauty: "The death, then, of a beautiful woman is, unquestionably, the most poetical topic in the world—and equally is it beyond doubt that the lips best suited for such topic are those of a bereaved lover" (Poe in Bradley et al., 1967, p. 892). Morejón, inspired by Poe's insight, creates her own image of the beautiful, which, of course, does not mean that the death of a beautiful woman cannot be a poetic topic, nor its effectiveness diminished by writing it from the point of view of a bereaved lover. Her sympathy for Poe is not naive, nor does her critical stance make her unable to see his important contributions to aesthetic theory. This is not a trivial point since at different moments during the Cuban Revolution (and in our own literary-ideological wars), a certain one-dimensional Marxist cultural theory would either ignore crucial elements of an author's work (like the religious dimension of César Vallejo's poetry) or dismiss the work on political grounds (Paz, Sarduy, Borges, Cabrera Infante, Arenas).

In another poem from *Piedra pulida* called "Mundos" (Worlds), Morejón seems to be carrying on a conversation with Dulce María Loynaz. As in the latter's *Ultimos días de una casa* (1958), both are centered on images of a house or home. But the younger poet's version is radically different; its optimism, though tempered, radiates throughout the poem. The comparison brings out what the Cuban Revolution meant for two different women: one older, upper class, white, and professional; the other young, black, and working class. Though I make a direct historical reference here, it is not as overt in the poem, but nonetheless, this history underlies its imagery. This said, the reader must proceed with caution since this is not an openly political poem, at least not in a partisan sense.

The poem's principal refrain is "Mi casa es un gran barco" ("My house is a grand ship"); perhaps "venerable vessel" would give it the more exalted image that *gran barco* implies. It is also a suggestive metaphor for the island itself, in expressing the desire to go away and return, of a "homecoming through otherness" (discussed further in Chapter 5 on Lezama). Every stanza of the poem begins repeating this verse, and stanza 6 repeats it again within the body of that section. So what does the author tell us about her "ark"? Morejón begins with an apparent contradiction: the house is a ship, but it does not want to embark on its journey; its masts and riggings become roots. It ends with three powerful and vexing verses: "can I say the sea / watched over by the son / or by the fetid gold of the ransacked galleon?" The image is deliriously baroque, as if some all-seeing Polyphemus was ready to devour the sea. But the delirium is reigned in by the historical reference: "the fetid gold of the ransacked galleon." The act of theft and violence makes it doubly fetid: colonial plunder and pirates pillaging. The gold described as fetid adds a psychoanalytic layer to its meaning as well (money as filth or excrement).

The second stanza maintains the ocular elements that the poem begins with, ending with "Oh the furtive eyes of the mortal past." Here the author seems to establish the closest of affinities with Loynaz's poem, but in Morejón the shadow of the past is not the anchor of the poem, as is the case with Loynaz. Morejón's *barco/casa* is like a sponge that seeks to absorb everything: "Old world that I love, /new world that I love, /worlds, worlds the two, my worlds: /Oh the sacred tortoises; /ah the algae /ah the name of the coastal woman /anchored in the center of the world." Loynaz's poem is one of loneliness, silence, solitude, and dark forebodings; Morejón, despite retrieving certain dark moments of the past, displays an optimism about the future which is entirely absent from Loynaz.

The house/vessel is almost free of demons because she has threatened them into retreat, she wants a house where "good fortune reigns supreme." In the last stanza, she reiterates the ship or house as something that protects her and ends: "I live in my ship live /sheltered from thunder and lightning /My house is that grand ship [venerable vessel] /I say /over the golden island /in which I will die" (Morejón, 1986, p. 108). The sheltering images of the house are not merely an inward phenomenon or a place to flee the outside world; in Morejón's house they are the starting point to embrace the world, to meet it head on. This is most evident in the stanza where she refers to a slave who tells her, "Vamos a andar" (Let us stride together) and "we both plant our legs in the earth /like unscathed tree trunks, like built nests /embracing beneath the tempest" (Morejón, 1986, p. 107). Right after this she says, "I think of the time of polished stone," which is the title of the book, an image taken up again in the final poem, also called "Piedra pulida" (Polished Stone).

This last poem is brief and worth quoting in its entirety:

A new book,
a new day,
another brand-new city
more summers, more flowers,
that perpetual sea,
and I, now,
on polished stone,
I search for your lips,
for your eyes.

(Morejón, 1985, p. 49; trans. Weaver)

The mood of this poem is even more upbeat than the previous one, but it retains a sense of longing, of renewed desire. Stones have a strong cosmic resonance, as we saw in discussing "The Eyes of Elegguá." The *otá* or *otán* (sacred stone) is where an orisha's *aché* is gathered in the Afro-Cuban tradition. Their solidity has always been associated with immortality, imperishability, the indestructible element of ultimate reality. But Morejón goes a little farther, since polished stone, aside from evoking an archaeological term (neolithic age), also denotes something worked on, perfected, changed, or transformed, like the poem or the aesthetic object, which can also be polished but must be made to endure. The ending of the poem reinforces this view, recalling the famous "stones that speak" from which the divine oracle at Delphi would issue forth. Morejón's poem also seems to evoke that extraordinary interview of Lezama Lima where he says: "I remember that phrase by Nietzsche: 'Wherever there's a stone there will be an image' " (CILCA, 1971, p. 70). And yet Morejón delivers the lines with the intimacy that one would use in addressing a lover. The mere nine verses achieve a synthesis of wonder, hymn to simple pleasures, self-reflexive meditation, and love poem.

While in much of Morejón's work race and gender are implicit sources of resonance, they also appear more overtly in her images. Two poems in particular illustrate this more explicitly gendered and racial historical view: "Amo a mi amo" (I Love My Master) and "Mujer negra" (Black Woman). "I Love My Master," also from *Piedra pulida* (p. 100), is steeped in history, and the poet puts herself in the shoes of a black woman slave talking about her master. It is constructed as a paradigmatic situation, since neither the master nor the slave is named as an individual. Morejón's poem is laced with enormous irony which begins from the first verse. Unfortunately, the English does not retain the richness of the Spanish "Amo a mi amo," which feels like a palindrome. The echo effect further underlines the irony between the verb *amar* (love) and the noun *amo* (master). Love is in this context an act of submission. Morejón's poem deftly exploits all the contradictions of the situation: "I love his roving pirate's feet /that have pillaged foreign lands. /[. . .] he strummed his *vihuela* [ancient guitar] and /melodious couplets soared, /as though from Manrique's throat. /I longed to hear a marímbula sound. /I love his fine red mouth, /that speaks words I can't understand. /The language I speak to him /still isn't his own" (Morejón, 1985, p. 75). The body, music, language, everything reflects the colonial and slave relationship, but the poem deals with gender-specific oppression as well. Morejón's poem has close affinities with Adrienne Rich's analysis of male power over women, that range from the denial of sexuality to exploitation of labor, to objectification and stifling of creativity and knowledge-seeking; but her approach is always embedded in a Cuban or Caribbean perspective.

Morejón has the slave questioning her plight: "What's he going to say to me? /Why do I live in this hole not fit for a bat? / Why do I wait on him hand and foot? / Where does he go in his lavish coach /drawn by horses that are luckier than me?" (Morejón, 1985, pp. 75–77). And further, she dreams of rebellion, of freedom: "I love my master but every night /When I cross the blossoming path to the canefield / the secret place of our acts of love, /I see myself knife in hand, /flaying him like an innocent animal /" (ibid., p. 77). But the ending of the poem leaves the female slave at a crossroads. Of course one's sympathies are with the slave's yearning for freedom, but the poet has the dream of freedom rudely interrupted: "Bewitched drumbeats /now drown his cries, his sufferings. /The bells of the sugar-mill call . . ." (ibid., p. 77). This is the bell that calls the slaves back to work. Will the dream become a reality? Will she heed the calling of the bells or become a *cimarrona* (runaway slave)? Morejón does not take the easy way out by producing an obvious outcome: she leaves it up to the reader to imagine. Despite the ironic nature of the poem, the frequent "I loves" of the slave should be taken seriously: they indicate an identification and/or love of the master which is commonplace in the oppressor/oppressed relation. Of course, it is a twisted love, deformed by male domination and (self)-de-valuation of women, but the author significantly chooses to make it have weight within the overall context of the historical situation depicted. More-jón seems to be issuing a warning: liberation from oppression does not mean that the past vanishes. It is a long process, an ongoing dialogue with the forces of the past, and if we ignore it, we continue to run the risk of bringing it back, sometimes in even deadlier forms.

In "Mujer negra" (Black Woman), Morejón revisits history again, but in a much more rebellious spirit. Although there are references to the Middle Passage, to back-breaking work and injustice, the poem focuses on the resistance to the iniquities of race and class. It even draws a historical affinity between Maceo and the Cuban revolutionaries of the nineteenth century and the July 26th Movement led by Fidel Castro's guerrilla army. And it ends with considerable optimism concerning the goals and achievements of the Cuban Revolution, with great enthusiasm about the future. Despite the rational and thought-out nature of the poem, the poet reminds us that writing a poem is not the same as documentary history or the elaboration of a political manifesto. Speaking of this poem, she says:

> Writing, however, is an act of absolute irrationality. A perfect example of this is found in my poem "Mujer negra" ("Black Woman"), so well-known and received by my readers. I remember perfectly that I was sleeping and was awakened by the image of a black woman behind the bars of the small common room which I shared with my parents. She was an ample woman and wouldn't let me sleep. I looked at her quite intently, wanting her to let me keep sleeping, until she went away. The next morning the first thing that came into my mind was the memory of that image. The black woman returned and dictated the poem to me. I struggled a lot with the end. It wasn't easy finding it because the "I" of that woman was an epic "we," which was all mixed up with my personal experience of living in Cuba in the 1970s. (Morejón, 1995b)

In this same University of Missouri presentation, Morejón recognizes that her contribution to Cuban letters resides in the fact that she is a woman and black. As a woman she quotes Virginia Woolf's "We think back through our mothers, if we are women." She always begins her poetry readings with the same poem, "Madre" (Mother), from *Piedra pulida* (1986):

My mother had no patio garden
but rocky islands
floating in delicate corals
under the sun.
Her eyes mirrored no clear-edged branch
but countless garrottes.
What days, when she ran barefoot
on the lime of the orphanages
and didn't know how to laugh
and she couldn't even look at the horizon.
She had no ivory-inlaid bedroom,
no drawing room with wicker chairs
and none of that hushed tropical stained-glass.
My mother had the handkerchief and the song
to cradle my body's deepest faith,
and hold,
banished queen—
She gave us her hands, like precious stones,
before the cold remains of the enemy.

(Morejón, 1985, p. 3; trans. Weaver)

This extraordinary poem, heartfelt and tender, is also hard as nails. There is no sentimentality at any moment, but instead a spirited and quiet heroism that is nothing less than inspirational. Morejón comments on this poem: "Virginia Woolf lived convinced that behind each woman writer fluttered the ghost of her mother. I'm no exception to this. So it's not just that my mother is a symbol of my poetry because she engendered me, but because, without any resources, she raised me, she gave me an education, she instilled in me the longing for independence, and she showed me forms of refinement to which I am still grateful" (Morejón, 1995b). Clearly her mother has taught the author much about life, a life in the New World, quite different from the mothers and daughters of Virginia Woolf's imagination, yet still recognizing a womanly solidarity in a world run by men. In an interview she explains: "Women also have a special vision that is born of pain, and pain smartens one up a great deal" (Behar and Suárez, 1994, p. 629).

Morejón clearly admits that her specificity as a writer derives from being a woman and black, but she interjects a note of caution: "This doesn't mean I'm a strident feminist. I don't tend to be strident about anything" (Behar and Suárez, 1994, pp. 628–29). Morejón's feminism is not dogmatic; it is transcultured, where there is room for Yemayá and Kristeva, Poe and García Lorca, Woolf and Angela Davis. It is born from the loving and stern example of her mother, given impulse by her friendship with Cuban artists like Ana Mendieta, and nurtured by the inclusiveneess of a host of women who have tried to build bridges between the island and its diasporic community (Lourdes Casal, Ruth Behar). Morejón's words must also be understood in the Cuban context of a revolutionary society under assault from a powerful

adversary, where ideological debate is often strident. Because of her formation within the Cuban Revolution, Morejón uses political consciousness for
its liberating possibilities, while being careful of the doors that ideology can
close on the creative process. For example, if someone chooses to leave Cuba
and emigrate to the United States, they are called a counterrevolutionary at
best, a *gusano* (worm) or *escoria* (scum, dregs) at worst. Now, *gusano* is a
loaded word in Cuba: the epithet is not only a personal insult but calls into
question a whole series of other attributes. The motive does not have to be
overtly political (family reunification, desire to travel, work, or study);
leaving cannot be an individual choice, but a political statement tantamount
to treason. It means you have abandoned your patriotic duty to defend the
Cuban Revolution, and by extension the sacred territory of the Cuban nation.
From one moment to the next you become an outlaw to *cubanidad*, or
Cubanness. This example might be considered exceptional, but it really is not:
the nature of different types of ideological stridency permeates the Cuban
system that runs through its politics, education, sexuality, and culture.

Morejón is equally cautious about issues of race. Though she points out
her blackness as a factor that has shaped her political and cultural sensibility, she is keenly aware of how that can be used against her, either because
of racism, trivialization, superficial exoticism, and tokenism: "Race in the
Caribbean has been a fountain of events, a catalyst, an incentive, an act of
faith, and more often than not, a narcotic. But if closed in on itself, racial
attitudes, negritude can become a dead end. Nicolás Guillén addressed this
admirably when he said, 'It's like trying to find a black cat in a dark room.'
Or Wole Soyinka, who with a certain irony, speaks of tigers defending their
tiger-tude" (Morejón, 1995a). Morejón in this regard practices and embodies
a transculturated aesthetic. In this she is indebted to Fernando Ortiz (1881–
1969) and Nicolás Guillén (1902–89), two Cuban authors who sought to
explore the racial, economic, religious, and cultural complexities of Cuban
identity as a unique amalgam of European, African, Chinese, and other
ethnicities.

For Morejón the concept of transculturation does imply *mestizaje* (racial
mixing), but it is not necessarily the only or even the most important
component, ultimately. It involves a dynamic interaction at every level:
food, dress, music, folklore, religious belief (Santería), and community
interaction. "Transculturation signifies constant interaction, transmutation
between two or more cultural components whose unconscious end is the
creation of a third cultural whole—that is, culture—new and independent,
although its bases, its roots, rest on preceding elements. The reciprocal
influence is determining. No element is superimposed on the other; on the
contrary, each one becomes a third entity. One remains immutable. All
change and grow in a give and take which engenders a new texture"
(Morejón in Pérez Sarduy and Stubbs, 1993, p. 229). These new textures are
what we have discussed in Morejón's poetry; not only in the poems with

obvious Afro-Cuban themes like "The Eyes of Élegguá" and "Elegy to Nieves Fresneda," but in ones that seem more "universal," like "Montes y mares," "Mundos," or "Polished Stone" or in "city" poems like "Amor, ciudad atribuida." But like any good Caribbean poet, Morejón appropriates and transforms all the traditions when she creates her verses. She goes from the world of the orishas to quoting Paul Eluard or Rilke; she draws on Cuban authors like Martí, Lezama, or Eliseo Diego, and on Havana street scenes. When she describes the ocean, she casts her net even wider, evoking popular ballads or songs, Rimbaud, as well as Yoruba and Greek mythology. Perhaps, because "there is always a ship, always a voyage," as the author says, the Caribbean is always adding new layers of culture, meaning, and identity. By being the crossroads of so many interests and cultures (European, indigenous, African, and Asian), every work of art is also an epic, a journey, a new cosmology, a creation myth. Maybe this is what Alejo Carpentier meant when he said, "America is a long way from having exhausted its mythologies." Transculturation always implies an unfinished subject, something constantly evolving, changing, adding new elements, witnessing new births, and so in the realm of culture it calls for renewed attempts at new definitions. Each new definition becomes a creation myth.

Some new textures to her own work are seen in her most recent book, *Paisaje célebre* (1993; Famed Landscape). This short book of poems is more philosophical and rueful than her previous work, with a greater concern expressed about time and the nature of absence. The author's personal circumstances changed: she traveled, several times to the United States. A rarity among Cuban families, Morejón's family had all remained in Cuba after the revolution. She had never directly lived (or suffered) the experience of being almost totally cut off from family. By traveling to the United States and having to take letters back or by meeting Cuban-Americans like Lourdes Casal, Ana Mendieta, Sonia Rivera, and others, who traveled to Cuba exploring their own personal and political turmoil, Morejón has been able to witness one of the saddest dimensions of Cuban family life, one of the many human tolls of the revolution.

Paisaje célebre has at least three poems that deal with this issue specifically: "A Chronicle That Swoons before the Immigrant Tree," "Before a Mirror," and "Ana Mendieta." "Before a Mirror" is dedicated to Sonia Rivera Valdés, a Cuban-born professor at York College. It is a hauntingly beautiful poem about how the city you were born in continues to pursue you no matter how far away you are. Its phantasmatic presence is more real than all the shapes and cities that surround you. The poem ends:

> Wherever you might move
> you'll hear the same streetcry every morning,
> be on the same boat crossing the same route,
> the route of eternal emigrants.

Nothing will put you in place, anywhere.
Though you scavenge the world over,
from castle to castle,
from market to market,
this will always be the city of your phantoms.
You will have spent your life rather fruitlessly
and when you are an old woman
before a mirror, as in Cinderella,
you will smile half-sadly
and in your dry pupils
will be two faithful rocks
and a resonant corner of your city.

(trans. David Frye in Behar and Suárez, 1994, p. 622)

The structure of the poem is built around looking into a mirror: that of an exile looking at new cities and countries, trying to see if they will mirror their reality or identity. Naturally, there is a frustration, because that reflection is interfered with by the very disruption and displacement of exile. As the poem says: "No other country, no other city is possible" (Behar and Suárez, 1994, p. 621). The poem is in dialogue with another poem by Lourdes Casal entitled "For Ana Veldford," from her book *Palabras juntan revolución* (1981). Casal, a writer-scholar, was one of the first Cubans in exile who attempted to build bridges to her homeland, where she had lived the first twenty-odd years of her life. As evidenced in this poem, it was no easy task:

This is why I will always remain on the margins,
a stranger among the stones,
even beneath the friendly sun of this summer's day,
just as I will remain forever a foreigner,
even when I return to the city of my childhood
I carry this marginality, immune to all turning back,
too *habanera* to be *newyorkina*,
too *newyorkina* to be
—even to become again—
anything else.

(trans. David Frye in Behar and Suárez, 1994, p. 416)

This (n)either (n)or dynamic is not strange to exile reality, and it has been a constant preoccupation of Cuban exile writers such as Cristina García, Elías Miguel Muñoz, José Kozer, and many others. However, it is refreshing to see it taken up by a poet "from the other side," that is, a writer still living in Cuba. But even more important is that Morejón avoids the stereotyped "revolutionary" view that they are uprooted Cubans who are on their way to becoming deracinated Anglos with an accent. The Cuban cultural establishment did not even view this literature as Cuban for many years; this has changed, but more out of political opportunism than anything else. Morejón sees this writing and its concerns as important to Cuban literature because it forms part of a Cuban reality, even if it is not confined to the physical geography of the island.

In "Ana Mendieta" (1948–85), Morejón offers a heartfelt remembrance of the Cuban artist exiled in the United States, who met a terrible death when she fell from the thirty-fourth floor of her apartment building. Many claim she was shoved by her artist husband, Carl André, but he was acquitted. Mendieta emigrated at thirteen, living for five years in an orphanage, an experience that marked her for life. In 1980 she returned to Cuba and began making a series of rupestrian sculptures in the rock formations of Jaruco. Before that she had been doing "earth sculptures," silhouettes of her body imprinted on soil, similar to the corpse drawings she had done even earlier (all this work was documented in photos or videos). At the risk of simplifying, it was clear that Mendieta's art had a strong link to her search for identity, that rock, earth, and soil were literally dug into in order to affirm her identity, to combat the sense of displacement and uprootedness. Morejón admirably deals with these themes in the poem. She begins the poem in New York, where Mendieta lived: "Ana was fragile as lightning in the sky. /She was the most fragile girl in Manhattan." Soon after, she mentions her awful demise: "Ana cast into space. Ana, our lady of despair, /yourself sculpted in the hostile cement of Broadway. /A desert, like the desert /you found in the orphanages, /a desert, yellow and gray, reaches you /and holds you tight, through the air." (trans. D. Frye in Behar and Suárez, 1994, p. 618). But the entire rest of the poem is dedicated to images of flying, floating, birds, and kites, as if to suggest that Ana's art, the most terrestrial of work, actually defied gravity, and, of course, death. Morejón, consistent with that imagery, ends the poem in like fashion, with a splendid mood of reconciliation, of Ana returning not only to earth but also returning to her homeland. In her journey she was able to recuperate her lost country and childhood.

> Ana, gliding like a kite
> [...]
> Your silhouettes, sleepy, calm,
> tip up the multicolored kite
> which flees Iowa, skirting indigenous cypresses,
> and comes to rest on the sure clouds
> of the mountains of Jaruco, in whose humid land
> you have been reborn again, wrapped in a celestial moss
> that dominates the rock and caves of the place,
> yours now, more than ever.
>
> (trans. David Frye in Behar and Suárez, 1994, p. 620)

Morejón, as can be seen from this brief view of her work, is a poet with a vast and powerful range of themes and modes of expression. As she herself has expressed it: "There's no poetics of Nancy Morejón as such, but several of them. The ones that I'm aware of have been forged over forty years. What's important for you to know is that I started to be abducted by poetry since I was nine" (Morejón, 1995b). The opening poem of *Paisaje célebre* offers a glimpse of the nature of that abduction. It begins with a simple description: "To see the fall of Icarus from a harbor of /blues and greens of Alamar." The second stanza is cryptic, speaking of "a misanthrope wearing a hood" and a "small man, by himself, toiling above fruit trees /until he joins a rainbow in the sky." The poem ends with a reference to painting and then Icarus again.

> That little man
> is a relative of Brueghel, the Elder, dear brother,
> who paints the solitude of the soul
> surrounded by splendid laborers.
>
> It's dusk and I need the wings of Icarus.
>
> (trans. Alan West, in Morejón, 1993, p. 11)

Morejón is taking the famed (celebrated) landscape and examining its exalted and praised history. First she situates it in a mythic landscape by beginning with the fall of Icarus, along with the blue-greens of the harbor or sea. Even the word Alamar is an interesting choice. At a pedestrian level, it is a reference to a modern housing project about twenty minutes from Havana, near the sea, where Morejón lives. But the name itself is made up of *ala* and *mar* (wing and sea), which works as a kind of indirect refrain of Icarus.

The second stanza seems a bit more mysterious, particularly with its "hooded misanthrope." Visually one thinks of Zurbarán's monks, but the idea behind it seems a throwback to medieval theology or the iniquities of the inquisition. The following image of the little man plowing above fruit trees and water seems like one of the flying figures of Mendive, part winged horse or cow, part fish, and part human. Only in the third stanza is the reference brought back to something more familiar: Brueghel the Elder. Although the final references evoke his paintings that have dozens of figures, such as "The Netherland Proverbs" or "The Battle between Carnaval and Lent," there is a painting attributed to him called "Landscape with the Fall of Icarus" (c. 1555). It is a curious work, with a green sea, someone plowing in the foreground, with a shepherd further below as one's sight goes down rightward toward the ocean. Near a ship there are two legs, sticking out of the water, as if capturing the moment of impact of Icarus's body hitting the water. It is sundown. You have to strain to see the two legs and only the brightly lit sky hints at Icarus's travail. Everything else in the painting seems like a quiet landscape, very matter-of-fact.

Morejón's ending has a Promethean ring to it. Despite Icarus's failure, she wants the wings back to attempt the flight into the unknown, reminiscent of Paul Claudel when he said: "We lack wings, but we always have enough strength to fall." What are these wings for Morejón? The wings of freedom and creation, those of eros, or the four wings of Cronus? Maybe the wings that allow us to "deform what we perceive" (imagination), as we saw with Bachelard when discussing the poem "Elegy for Nieves Fresneda." In twelve verses the poet has brought together a vast web of images and cultures to bear on a beautiful Caribbean sundown, in a magnificent abduction of the reader.

It would be inaccurate to say that *Paisaje célebre* synthesizes all of Nancy Morejón's political, historical, and aesthetic concerns. But it does reveal an extraordinary amount about history, aesthetics, and politics through the voice of a masterful poet. In *Paisaje célebre*, as in her poetic oeuvre in general, Nancy Morejón weaves together nature, politics, myth, creation, and personal testimony so adroitly that they gleam like "the precious stones that are her mother's hands," like the sacred stones that contain an orisha's *aché*, the rough-edged rock of history, or the polished stone of poetry.

Note

A version of this essay was published in *Studies in Twentieth Century Literature* 20, no. 1 (Winter 1996): 181–205.

TWO

Alejo Carpentier: Symphonist of History's Emblems

Alejo Carpentier (1904–80), one of the great Latin American novelists of the twentieth century, was born in Havana of a French father and a Russian mother. He grew up bilingually (French and Spanish) and from an early age showed a voracious appetite for reading, as well as a keen interest in music, architecture, philosophy, and art. He was politically active against the Machado dictatorship, for which he was thrown in jail. When he was released he went to Paris (1928–39), where he became familiar with the French avant-garde scene and the surrealists, befriending the likes of Robert Desnos, André Breton, Picasso, Varese, and Braque. Carpentier returned to Cuba, but in 1945 he moved to Caracas, where he lived until the triumph of the Cuban Revolution (1959). He was involved in several cultural endeavors, until 1966, when he was named minister for cultural affairs at the Cuban embassy in Paris, a position he held until his death. Carpentier won many awards, but the most important was the Cervantes Literary Prize in 1978.

Many of Carpentier's novels are considered classics, such as *The Kingdom of This World* (1949; trans. 1957), *The Chase* (1956; trans. 1990), *Explosion in a Cathedral* (1962; trans. 1962), and *Reasons of State* (1974; trans. 1976). His erudition, baroque language, and heady mix of politics, philosophy, myth, and history are an exhilarating challenge for any reader. Though not the first person to use the term, Carpentier made the phrase *realismo mágico* (magical or marvelous realism) stick. It grew out of his research in Haiti for his first successful novel, *El reino de este mundo* (*The Kingdom of This World*). In the novel's preface, Carpentier speaks about magical realism as a style of writing that was founded in history and the beliefs of local peoples rather than a literary imposition (or embellishment) grafted onto indigenous cultures. In Spanish, the term evokes many associations: strangeness, unpredictability, amazement. And because magical realism—unlike Surrealism, in his view—originated in the people's faith and daily experience of reality, he believed it could inspire them to social action, to seek freedom.

Whatever the successes of these political ambitions for his work, and however diluted and imprecise the term has become, Carpentier's influence on the Latin American novel and on the generation that came after him has been immense. His erudite, richly textured, and discursive novels made their mark on writers as varied as García Márquez, Fuentes, Vargas Llosa, Cortázar, and Valenzuela. Only Borges (short story) and Neruda (poetry) can claim a similar stature and influence in Latin America.

Carpentier was a tireless essayist and writer of chronicles and an excellent researcher/writer on music. His book *La música en Cuba* (1946; Music in Cuba) is still much used and quoted, and his three-volume *Esa música que llevo dentro* (That Music within My Soul) brings together his music articles from the Caracas daily *El Nacional* (for which he wrote during fourteen years) as well as other articles and essays on Latin American and classical music. But as in his fiction he proposes a fierce, incendiary dialogue between the cultures of Europe and Latin America.

Only in his next-to-last major novel did Carpentier openly write about the Cuban Revolution in a fictional context (*La consagración de la primavera* (1978; The Consecration of Spring), which has not been translated and has received mixed reviews. Whatever reservations Carpentier might have had about the Cuban Revolution, he never made them known, either in his novels or in public statements. Some later writers (born after the revolution) see Carpentier as an "official writer" because he was much admired and given prizes by the Cuban state. But that would be too simplistic a view of the matter, as we shall see in our discussion of Carpentier's view of revolution in *Explosion in a Cathedral*. To his credit, even in *La consagración de la primavera*, he presents the revolution as a process, as something unfinished, and as a complex, evolving phenomena, not a terrestrial paradise.

Throughout his mature work, Carpentier sought to elucidate a Latin American perspective on history's complexities and horrors. He believed that an epic scope was crucial for a twentieth-century novelist. As he said in a lecture in 1967: "To concern yourself with this world, this tiny world, this enormous world, is the task of novelists nowadays. To understand it, with people who struggle, and criticize it, exalt it, paint it, love it, try and have it make sense, try and talk to it, talk about it, to show it, to show in its innermost depths, the errors, the grandeur, the misery." There are few writers of any time who were able to do this with the passion, intelligence, and rigor of Alejo Carpentier.

HISTORY AS STEPPING RAZOR: TRAGEDY AND REVOLUTION IN EXPLOSION IN A CATHEDRAL

Alejo Carpentier's fifth novel, *El siglo de las luces* (1962; *Explosion in a Cathedral*, 1963) is a work of immense scope. Set against the backdrop of the French Revolution, it begins in Havana, goes to Haiti, France, Spain, Guadeloupe, French Guyana, and ends in Spain at the time of the Napoleonic invasion. It features wars, revolutions, jailings, exile, torrid love affairs, scenes of great natural beauty, and rousing philosophical and political discussions. More broadly, it speaks to the issue of violence and social change, with important insights on twentieth-century revolutions.

Carpentier was fascinated with history. *Explosion in a Cathedral* is an elaborate, sometimes dense exploration of the historical impact of the French Revolution on the Caribbean. Through a human, emotional, and historical triangle, Carpentier examines the relationship between art and politics. In a rich, allegorically baroque style, the Cuban novelist traces the lives of Víctor Hugues, a French entrepreneur and revolutionary, two Cuban cousins, Esteban and Sofía (and her brother Carlos). Over time Hugues betrays ideals he had earlier espoused. Sofía, after falling in love with Hugues, abandons him and links up with her cousin Esteban, who, through an act of sacrifice (being jailed) allows Sofía, the true revolutionary of the novel, to escape. Esteban, as an artistic soul, is withdrawn enough from (and disillusioned with) history to have little direct impact, but through his actions in relation to Sofía, he can influence the forces of human emancipation.

Explosion in a Cathedral is probably Carpentier's greatest novel, and it certainly helped put the Latin American novel on the world map before the so-called boom of the mid- to late 1960s. Its interweaving of revolutionary politics, exquisite descriptions of place, emotional turmoil, philosophical musings, and collisions between ideals and stark realities are breathtaking. Though Carpentier seems to stand in the tradition of Balzac, Stendhal, and above all Tolstoy, his modernist and avant-garde leanings give the novel a heterogeneous mix that distance it remarkably from nineteenth-century realism or epics.

At first sight, *Explosion in a Cathedral* is provocative: it causes confusion, irritation, or consternation. In the text we find a combination of elements, genres, and styles. Carpentier goes from minute descriptions with baroque arabesques, to chronicle, exhilarating epic, reflective essay, and the ample freedom of novelistic discourse. At times we find ourselves in an adventure novel, at other times in a romance, later in a Caribbean *Bildungsroman*, and further on we are immersed in a philosophical rumination with traits that belong to the essay or historical research; the author quickly shifts gears and parodies the gothic or romantic novel. The underlying ideological context conjoins the Cabala, freemasonry, Marxism, psychoanalysis, existentialism, the Sublime, and eighteenth-century revolutionary thought. The characters are often unbelievable, the temporal leaps even more so, and the narrative turnarounds are disconcerting. Despite the careful structuring of his novels (using musical or architectural models), Carpentier's fiction fans out in many directions, elusive, always pushing its formal construction to the breaking point.

One of those centripetal elements in *Explosion in a Cathedral* is the tension between political praxis and utopia. Carpentier heightens that tension using the notion of tragedy and theatricality in order to explore the historical phenomenon of revolution.

The novel, with a wealth of detail, describes the French Revolution and its repercussions in the New World as tragedy. But what do we mean by the word *tragedy*? It has been defined traditionally as a gesture of great courage condemned to defeat. This gesture usually is played out on a large scale; it normally is something beyond the everyday, and since its perspective is so extreme, it seems to go beyond history (which is why Nietzsche crucially links myth and tragedy). The rhythm of tragedy is the rhythm of sacrifice. Through the suffering of the protagonist, the tragic hero, there is a disintegration that ends in death. However, death is not just a personal act, but a means to cleanse others or a collective, be it a society or a smaller grouping or community (Williams, 1966, p. 156).

In *Explosion in a Cathedral* some of these elements of the classical definition of the term apply, but other factors make it necessary to introduce new concepts in order to make the notion of tragedy more complete. The very evolution of the words *tragedy* and *revolution* brought about two things: they were viewed as antithetical and as being apart from society. This second point might seem puzzling, but if we look into the history of the words, the apparent paradox will be cleared up.

According to Raymond Williams, Renaissance tragedy or drama (fourteenth–sixteenth centuries) secularized tragedy by predicating tragic action not as a metaphysical fault within a mythical structure, but belonging more to a character's behavior within a moral scheme. The hero, otherwise a good and dignified person, commits a moral error. The human weakness of the protagonist and his or her subsequent "fall" would elicit compassion or pity in the spectator. Suffering was thus a consequence of error, and happiness was the execution of virtue. The problem with this framework, Williams points out, is not that it is superficial, but that morality is conceived in static terms, and, more than a case of redemption (classic drama), tragedy's resolution becomes more of an adjustment in order to return to the natural and moral order of things.

With the triumph of liberal ideas (eighteenth–nineteenth centuries), the issue of individual human values versus the social system becomes central. Liberalism slowly erodes the concept of a permanent and inalterable human nature, and it equally questions a static social order linked to a divine scheme of things. With greater clarity and vigor, the possibility of changing a society is palpable, something a revolution puts into relief dramatically. Liberalism, with its faith in change, progress, and social transformation, distances itself even further from tragedy, where altering the prevailing order is inconceivable.

Romanticism (1780–1840), on the other hand, pushes individual will and human-as-creator-of-self to an extreme. But when Romanticism propounds this will within the context of a criticism of society or out of a desire to build a new social order, there are several blind spots in its conception: the Romantics viewed society's hostility toward the individual with such great concern that their critique of society fell prey to a kind of nihilism. Since for the Romantics the idea of revolution is a total, totalizing, and sublime act, it paradoxically contributed to the idea of revolution as being separate from society. The Romantics saw society as the alienating consequence of reason. It would be unjust, however, to say they were anti-reason. What they criticized was the following: "The alienation of reason from all other activities of man, changed reason from activity to a mechanism, and society from a human process to a machine" (Williams, 1966, p. 72). In their failure to revolutionize all of life, the Romantics alienated themselves in a kind of irrationalism that led them to seek refuge in love, art, and nature. In Carpentier's novel, Esteban's character follows this trajectory of aesthetic refuge. (However, he is able to break away from this kind of alienation when he "sacrifices" his own freedom of movement so Sofía can flee to Cayenne; chap. 41.) For the Romantics, seeking refuge in art and nature further closed the circle, which Williams lucidly summarizes: "Before we could not recognize tragedy as social crisis; now, commonly we cannot recognize social crisis as tragedy" (ibid., p. 77).

With the bankruptcy of liberalism we are faced with two bleak alternatives: first, revolution has been reduced to an impersonal and mechanical process outside of human control. Second, individual rebellion, guided by an ideology of social transformation and the construction of a new order, was futile since human beings were irreparably passionate, irrational, and destructive. In terms of social action, only two paths seemed desirable: modernization, that is, an evolutionary process which differentiated change from the question of values, or flight toward a personal, apolitical, nonsocial liberation.

Carpentier, however, from the vantage point of the shattering experiences of twentieth-century revolutions, is able to bring together tragedy and revolution. In *Explosion in a Cathedral*, revolution is put forth as tragedy, which had been seen as removed from social thought, defeatist, irrational,

and unable to understand social contradictions. But more significantly,
Carpentier captures the inner workings of a colonial society's abjection and
subjugation, along with its longings for freedom. This kind of society,
afflicted by slavery or racial exclusion, poverty, dependency on the Spanish
crown, divided by social rivalries and political fragmentation, will express
its utopian yearnings in a complex and contradictory fashion. Again, Williams underlines key themes for our understanding of the social dimensions
of tragedy:

> The idea of the "total redemption of humanity" has the ultimate cast of
> resolution and order, but in the real world its perspective is inescapably tragic.
> It is born in pity and terror: in the perception of a radical disorder in which
> the humanity of some men is denied and by the fact that the idea of humanity
> itself is denied. It is born in the actual suffering of real men thus exposed, and
> in all of its consequences of this suffering: degeneration, brutalisation, fear,
> hatred, envy. It is born in an experience of evil made the more intolerable by
> the conviction that it is not inevitable, but is the result of particular actions
> and choices.
>
> And if it is tragic in its origins—in the existence of a disorder that cannot
> but move and involve—it is equally tragic in its action, in that it is not against
> gods or inanimate things that its impulse struggles, nor against mere institu-
> tions and social forms, but against other men. This, throughout, has been the
> area of silence, in the development of the idea. What is properly called
> utopianism, or revolutionary romanticism, is the suppression or dilution of
> this inevitable fact. . . .
>
> We have still to attend to the whole action, and to see actual liberation as
> part of the same process as the terror which appalls us. I do not mean that
> liberation cancels the terror; I only mean that they are connected and that this
> connection is tragic. (Williams, 1966, pp. 77, 82)

Carpentier refuses to be part of this "revolutionary romanticism." No
matter how strongly he believed in the importance and impact of the French
Revolution, he does not flee its harsh realities: the ideological hardening,
the cult of the supreme being, the mass executions, the exiles and jailings,
the errors committed in cultural policy, and the ideological regressions
(ultimate restoration of slavery). For social thinkers, as has been pointed
out, revolution cannot be tragic because it would be a cause for disenchant-
ment, disillusionment, and defeatism. For a revolutionary, the revolution is
something constructive, liberating, the road to the future. Revolution can
be described only in epic terms, and to achieve an epic dimension, social
upheaval must be viewed a little more abstractly, with a certain social
determinism. It is precisely the collison of epic and tragic views that is
witnessed in chapter 36 when Esteban argues with Sofía, Carlos, and Jorge
about his bitter personal experiences that have soured his revolutionary
zeal. Sofía eloquently defends the revolution with the following statement:

One could not live without a political ideal; the happiness of a whole people could not be achieved at the first attempt; . . . perhaps he had been the victim of an exaggerated idealism; she admitted that the excesses of the Revolution were deplorable, but great human victories could not be achieved without pain and sacrifice. To sum up: nothing big could be done in this world without blood being shed. (Carpentier, 1963, p. 262)

Esteban lashes back lucidly: "It's the pious believers like you, the deluded, the devourers of humanitarian pamphlets, the Calvinists of the Idea, who erect guillotines" (ibid., p. 262). Esteban sees only tragedy (in the traditional sense); Sofía, true to the epic spirit, sees blood as the sweat of revolutionary freedom.

The most extreme example of the epic orientation is Víctor Hugues, the exemplary man of action and prime mover in the novel. Hugues's political will is so potent that he is capable of roundly negating reality, as is the case with the death of Robespierre: he hangs onto Jacobin doctrine, and, without missing a step, tries to promote the revolution in the New World. The tragedy of Víctor Hugues is his entrapment in the mirage of ideology and power. Even when he is cognizant of this later on, with Esteban (chap. 28), he continues impetuously without knowing how to stop, not unlike Macbeth. Hugues sees society and the revolution as machines, as Hobbes would say. He is only an instrument in the hands of the great force of revolutionary power. He admits as much to Sofía much later, when in Cayenne (French Guyana): "I'm like those automata who play chess, walk, play the fife or beat the drum when they're wound up. There was only one role I hadn't played, a blind man. I'm playing that now" (ibid., p. 333).

Hugues is touching on a fundamental problem of political language and its usefulness in trying to bring about change. Political discourse is exhortative; it needs to initiate or motivate action, and in revolutionary times, language is closely allied with forces that are not easily controlled: power and violence. Even when this language speaks of virtue, reason, honor, and the common good, it must face social forces that will energetically oppose revolutionary ideas. Roland Barthes said that the Stalinist universe defined everything in terms of Good and Evil, that every word uttered implied naming a value (Barthes, 1973, p. 31). The distance between naming and judgment was nil, and therefore all thought became tautological. Carpentier describes a similar situation in the novel. In other words, those who are not with the revolution are counterrevolutionaries, and if you are an enemy of the revolutionary order, you could be sent to the guillotine (or to a work camp, reeducation center, prison). Jean Starobinski, in a book about the French Revolution, describes the hallucinatory spiral which ends in this kind of dementia:

In its attempt to lend principles the force that makes them effective, language lets itself be annexed by the violence it sought to tame. Without losing any of its brilliance, the limpid speech of principle became the trenchant words of action. It was no longer compared with the innocent transparency of crystal but with the cutting edge of steel. To expound the source of the law was no longer enough; now those who opposed it had to be punished. Obviously, there was a risk that this sort of language would wear itself out in an ever-mounting tide of austere vehemence, anathema, and unrelenting abstraction. (Starobinski, 1982, p. 60)

This escalation of verbal vehemence in political language confronts opposing forces in a death struggle, often literally. The same bloody reality makes the rhetorical sources used take on the declamatory power of theater. The revolution is a stage, the *Gran teatro del mundo* (*The Great Theater of the World*, a play by Calderón de la Barca), where the liberating dream of reason and utopia collides with the course of history, made of flesh-and-blood men and women who suffer, struggle, and die. Images linking theater and politics have been longstanding for various reasons: many great tragic works have political themes; drama or comedy often deals with individual-collective conflicts; issues of motivation, will, moral agency, and action have close analogies to the world of politics; or, conversely, political discourse has imitated theatrical conventions. But most significant is that revolutionaries see language as symbolic action, intimately linked to ideology. As Ricoeur says, any group or society needs to "give itself an image of itself, to 'play itself' in the theatrical sense of the word, to put itself at issue and on stage" (Ricoeur, 1991, p. 182). This collective symbol making is how a society constructs a narrative of itself. In revolutionary times a new script is written and enacted, often in the heat of bloody confrontation. The players are new or different: the ruled are now the rulers; the despised have become heroes. "The time is out of joint," Hamlet would say. This theater of revolution is constant throughout Carpentier's novel.

The theatrical space Carpentier constructs is achieved through several devices and discourses. In them he wields historical references, art (painting and drawing), philosophical, and rhetorical strategies, which go toward "building the set." This is done in a variety of ways: first by references to theater made by the author, directly, indirectly, or by the characters; but also by the use of emblems so dear to baroque theatrical practice. Another baroque device is used in the description of the guillotine that begins the novel, which functions as a kind of ironic *loa* (a short verse panegyric that was a kind of prologue to a long drama). Carpentier is extremely deft in handling recognition and reversal (anagnorisis), a frequent technique in the world of theater. Building on the long history of religious and metaphysical theater in the Spanish tradition, Carpentier uses words, particularly nouns, with capital letters, for certain roles or concepts, which is similar to their use in *autos sacramentales* (allegorical or religious plays). The novel's use of allegory in a historical context highlights the signifying levels of the work, and shows its own inner workings, its mise-en-scène. By drawing attention to the "theatricality" of its meaning, *Explosion in a Cathedral* also shows how political language acquires the configuration of theatrical spectacle, converging on vehemence, manipulation, or tautology.

The allusions to theater are plentiful in the novel and begin with Víctor Hugues, who arrives at Sofía's house like a kind of Don Giovanni, except that his initial seduction is at an intellectual and political level. Later, of course, it will be amorous and sexual, at least with Sofía. *Don Giovanni* (1787), Mozart's opera, begins with the death of the Commendatore, Donna Anna's father, similar to the death of Sofía's father in the novel. In 1787 Mozart's father also died. Víctor Hugues, like Don Giovanni, is a figure of the Enlightenment: "But the original and still famous story identified him clearly enough as an atheist and blasphemer, and by the 18th century opinions such as his were taken as signs not only of revolt but of rational and self-justifying revolt. Don Giovanni has clearly concurred in the enlightenment's multiple parricide; and, being a man of the enlightenment, he believes himself in the right and refuses to repent when the statue of the Commendatore threatens him with hell" (Brophy, 1988, p. 83). When Hugues takes over their home (by ideological assault) and finds certain clothes in the wardrobes, they dress up representing different figures of antiquity: Mucius Scaevola, Caius Gracchus, Demosthenes, Inez de Castro, Juana la Loca (chap. 4, pp. 36–37). Unconsciously they (Esteban, his cousin Sofía, her brother Carlos) start to "rehearse" their entry onto the historical stage, which, evidently, will be more alienating and less playful than the farcical skits they enact with Hugues. Further on in the novel (chap. 6, p. 52), Hugues actually performs different scenes from the life of Lycurgus, the great innovator of the Spartan legal system (Díaz-Plaja, 1960, p. 165). Right away he begins creating a political *auto sacramental* with characters such as the Nobility, the Church, the Navy, the Judiciary, and Diplomacy (chap. 6, p. 52). In any case, these scenes take on a savagely ironic premonition, since they are pale simulacra of the bloody events from which they will later suffer.

Víctor Hugues, almost at the end of the novel, defeated and depleted by the forces of history, confesses the following to Sofía: "I thought I was controlling my own destiny, they—the people who always make and unmake us—have made me take so many parts that I no longer know which one I should be playing. I've put on so many costumes I no longer know which is the right one. . . . Baker, trader, mason, anti-mason, Jacobin, military hero, rebel, prisoner, absolved by the men who killed the man that made me, Agent of the Directory, Agent of the Consulate . . ." (chap. 46, p. 333). All of history's costumes (he sounds like a retired diva reminiscing, but without a hint of nostalgia), all of the different roles apportioned, have left him without a hint of authenticity. A few pages later, when they put slices of bloody veal on him to cure him of the Egyptian disease, Sofía reminds Hugues that he looks like Oedipus, a parricide from ancient tragedy (ibid., p. 334). Hugues not only evokes Oedipus, but surely Saturn devouring his son, quite consistent with the references to Goya throughout the text. And like Don Giovanni, he will sink into the depths without repenting.

The guillotine forms one of the theatrical foundations of the novel, and Carpentier sets the stage ingeniously and with lush detail in chapter 21, when the beheading machine is first used in public. The people gather around it in a kind of festive mood to witness a spectacle:

> They had never seen a theater open to all, and, for this reason, the people were now discovering the essence of Tragedy. Fate was present among them, its blade waiting, with inexorable punctuality, for those who had been ill-advised enough to turn their arms against the town. And the spirit of the Chorus was active in every spectator, as strophes and anti-strophes, occurrences and apostrophes were bandied across the stage. (chap. 21, p. 150)

This public, open-air theater, with its bloody tragedy, provokes a reaction: of wanting to shake off the terror and death, and, as a result, another spectacle is created, the public ceremony or carnaval. Later, the guillotine goes on the road, from town to town, like a traveling theater company (ibid., p. 153). When it arrives in a town it centralizes life around its awesome destructiveness, even to the point of being the axis of economic activity (p. 151), as if it were an emblem on the stage of a baroque drama. In Calderón de la Barca's *El gran teatro del mundo* (1633), there are two emblematic globes on stage: on one is the author seated on a throne; on the other, an emblem with two doors on which are painted a crib and a tomb, respectively. (Carpentier's other baroque source for "the world as stage" image [aside from Shakespeare, of course] is Lope de Vega's *Lo fingido verdadero*.) The guillotine announces the birth of a new world, incarnate in two documents: the Declaration of the Rights of Man and the Constitution of 1793. But it also announces judgment, ideological vehemence, and blood. It is this conjunction of the good bathed in blood that makes Robespierre's words comprehensible: "Virtue without Terror is impotent; Terror without Virtue is malignant."

Theater and guillotine are paired up from the start, in a chilling, two-page description that begins the novel. It could be likened to an ironic *loa*, which traditionally has been defined as a brief piece or poem presented before the main play of the evening. Usually it was a panegyric extolling the virtues of an illustrious person or an august event, and it was meant to grab the audience's attention. Its two functions were to establish a relationship between the performers and the public and to "highlight the fictitious nature of the upcoming dramatic representation" (Rodríguez and Tordera, 1983, p. 32). Carpentier, with this *loa*, sets the tone for one of the principal themes of the novel: the apotheosis of political reason and its murderous consequences. Furthermore, he also draws attention to the allegorical discourse which he will employ in his novel as a means with which to meditate on history (more will be said about allegory later on). And by placing this narrative fragment out of chronological order—if he had followed a strict realist approach, the *loa* would go just before the beginning of chapter 17—Carpentier underlines the materiality of the writing process and his own insertion into the text as author (again, echoing the beginning of *El gran teatro del mundo*). The novelist accentuates a technique, a method, that he has adopted from the dramatic and lyric literature of the sixteenth and seventeenth centuries—the emblem. In *Explosion in a Cathedral*, the guillotine as emblem is counterposed to another emblem: the seashell that Esteban admires, conjuring up images of the Sublime (chap. 24).

The birth of the emblem in literature is usually attributed to the publication in 1531 of Andrea Alciato's *Emblematum liber* (Alciato, 1985). The influence of emblems on the literary arts was immense, and its visual, didactic strengths were highly valued by preachers and teachers (Daly, 1979). In his study of Alciato, critic S. Sebastián defines the emblem as follows:

> If in the origins of culture, letter and image went together, the sixteenth century fostered a dialectic between the two, creating the illusion of correspondences that also appealed to the traditional harmonic reationship between microcosms and macrocosms. The internal harmony of the emblem is established between its components. The *emblema triplex* . . . is distinguished from other icono-verbal forms by virtue of its three differentiated parts: (1) the *inscriptio* or motto, which is the emblem's title; (2) the *pictura* or symbolic image; and (3) the *subscriptio*, a statement or epigram at the foot of the image. Alciato and other, later emblematists conceived the image as the body, and the texts as the soul of the emblem; therefore, any attempt at clarification or analysis of the emblem must take into account its representation (*res picta*) and its formulation (*res significans*). (Alciato, 1985, pp. 8–9)

In Carpentier's case the *subscriptio* is not always directly related to the *pictura*, or the relationship is expressed indirectly in the very text of the novel. The important thing is that the author does establish a relationship between literature and painting, representation and signification, image and idea. Carpentier is able to achieve this with great skill and subtlety, using a modern (novelistic) emblematic construction.

In *Explosion in a Cathedral* there are various clusters of emblems. Two already mentioned are the guillotine and the seashell. If we turn to Alciato, we find "El término" (emblem 157), which symbolizes death. The inscription says *Nulli cedo* (I yield before no one), an apt description of the guillotine or of Hugues's political positions if there ever was one. The "El término" emblem represents an obstacle for men, the day that cannot be changed, the prearranged time of fate, in which the last things judge what came before. There are two emblems that use the shell, both relating to

Esteban: the emblem that reads "Acquiring immortality by the study of letters" (132) and another called "Sudden terror" (122). These relate to Esteban's artistic nature and his being witness to the Revolutionary Terror in France. These are not only analogies between Alciato's work and Carpentier's novel, but bring into relief the influence or relationship between emblem and literature, as well as how the text puts into practice its own theatricality through the emblem.

The other emblematic clusters in the novel are the epigraphs taken from Goya's *Los desastres de la guerra* (The Disasters of War), the painting *Explosion in a Cathedral* by Desiderio Monsú (François Nomé), and a painting by Goya, perhaps his best-known work, *May 3, 1808*. The latter, though never mentioned overtly, is the subtext of the last chapter. Carpentier refers to Goya twelve times, always in key chapters. At times, the Goya quotation, the drawing it is associated with, and the novel's chapter are complementary. Such is the case with *Los estragos de la guerra* (Devastations of War), which blends perfectly with chapter 17 of the novel and describes the cruel battle with the English in order to recapture the island of Guadeloupe for the French. But on other occasions such symmetry is not found (chap. 24, with the shell, linked up with *Desastre 16*, "Se aprovechan"—they take advantage). Goya's *Disaster 16* shows Spanish soldiers stripping French soldiers of their uniforms and materiel. Maybe Carpentier, with a certain malevolent humor, is alluding to what Esteban had told Hugues in chapter 17 when he said: "Beware of the intoxication of the uniform!" Maybe the chapter with the shell (the wonders and sublimity of nature) is an indirect "undressing" of Hugues, at a symbolic level (Nature vs. Society).

The important point is that the "emblems" frame key moments in the novel, drawing attention to the process of how history is (re)presented within the novel's discourse. To begin, *The Disasters of War* alludes to events in Spain's history that occur after the death of Esteban and Sofía, so there is a kind of temporal cut (incision) in the chronological flow of the narration, a *tableau* that stops or slows down the action, inciting one to think *across* different historical moments.

The emblems bear an affinity with Diderot's theatrical aesthetic. For the French philosopher, theater had to forget words and accede immediately to the image, and proceed from truth to evidence, from reason to rapture (de Azúa, 1983, pp. 236–47). Visual (and mute) signification is what predominates, and the minimal element is the *tableau*: "One unforeseen incident that occurs in the action and changes the state of the characters is a theatrical jolt (*coup de théâtre*). A scenic composition, so natural and authentic, which is faithfully executed by a painter, which I would like on canvas, is the painting (*tableau*)" (ibid., p. 236). In other words, Diderot devalues the *coup de théâtre* and substitutes for it a mute and natural gesture, a signifying emblem. De Azúa further draws out the pictorial emphasis in Diderot: "Personally, I think that, if a dramatic work were well staged, the set would offer the spectator real paintings (*tableaux*) as favorable to a painter as the action allows" (ibid., p. 237). For Diderot, then, drama would be a succession of highly emotional *tableaux*, which elicit this emotion through an ability to present stirring emblems. Carpentier, through the use of the Goya drawings, achieves a similar result, but inversely, in that he uses the verbal element (the *subscriptio*, if you will) to bring out the visual (*tableau* or *pictura*), which is impossible to present literally in the novel. Diderot favors the *tableau* at the expense of the verbal or discursive. (Diderot also recognizes the narrative relevance of the *tableau* and that the difference between the dramatic and the narrative *tableau* is one of degree. The former, the novel, "follows the gesture and pantomime in all of its details"; the latter [a work of theater] "only lets a word drop on the run.")

The most radical example of the use of the *tableau* is a scene where Víctor Hugues is in his office, with a painting of Robespierre hanging on the wall. Here everything comes together: the image (of power, the will of the people), the social role of Hugues (including his uniform), and the petrification of political language. The utopian impulse has hardened into ideology, an ideology transformed into formula or judgment. It has become so abstract that it freezes history; ideology has turned into ahistorical ritual, an image of its own dissolution. It is the *tableau* of the revolution exhausted by its fury of blood, even while it still promises a new future.

Carpentier uses the *tableau* (and the *coup de théâtre*) in order to construct his pictorial scenes, his living and thinking emblems, verbal feasts which shimmer; but the way scenes are articulated, with the use of anachronisms, his baroquely chiseled images, his humor and irony, the relationship between emblem and narration, call into question the issue of representation (of history, ideas, revolution) to the point where the author turns his language into spectacle. This language takes on a corporeal density; it begins to perform the discourse, to make the text gesture, to become a *tableau*. This gesture and performance point to the work's different levels, particularly the examination of history through the use of allegory.

Many have commented on the use of allegory in Carpentier's work, but most of the discussion has been limited to finding out the "hidden messages" of this allegorical discourse. What has generally been left unsaid is the nature of allegorical discourse and how it is used to demystify historical narration (González Echevarría, 1983, pp. 60–65).

"We have allegory when the events of a narrative obviously and continuously refer to another simultaneous structure of events or ideas, whether historical events, moral or philosophical ideas, or natural phenomena" (Preminger, 1974, p. 12). The emphasis here is on the obvious and the continuous, with an implicit rigidity, abstraction, and, at times, difficulty. It is counterposed to the symbol, which is the perfect fusion of signifier and signified, the particular and the general, and is the result of a direct, instantaneous perception.

As González Echevarría points out, following Paul de Man, allegory connotes a temporal dimension, something outside of itself and "from the point of view of the individual, it always says more than it pretends to, or only a part of what is meant; it is a kind of surplus value of signification, in which the individual has no control over the surplus, outside of and not belonging to him" (González-Echevarría, 1983, p. 61).

Allegory, then, is a mode of literary discourse which recognizes the impossibility of that perfect fusion of the empirical and the eternal and thus demystifies the symbolic relationship by underlining the separation between the two levels. The union of the two levels (empirical and eternal) is possible for only a moment, against a backdrop of nonassociation, making the union even more arbitrary; allegory makes this connection a self-conscious, questioning process. Allegorical meaning exhibits a metonymic movement; it is goaded on by a ferocious displacement mechanism in a kind of looting of the empirical (Eagleton, 1981). Terry Eagleton quotes Walter Benjamin's *The Origin of German Tragic Drama*: "In the context of allegory, the image is only a signature, only the monogram of essence, not the essence itself in a mask" (Benjamin, 1977, p. 214). The emblematic image of baroque drama points to a crucial feature: the passage from classical to baroque tragedy, which also marks the shift from myth to history. This historical realignment is even truer if we accept Lezama Lima's baroque aesthetics of rebellion as a baroque of Counter-Conquest (as opposed to the European baroque of Counter-Reformation).

In *Explosion in a Cathedral*, Carpentier manipulates allegory with a supreme and ironic mastery. At the same time that he "describes" the French Revolution, the first great bourgeois revolution, he evokes many other events: the theatricality of political discourse, its impact on the Romantic movement, its degeneration which leads to the invasion of Spain (which, in turn, precipitates Latin American independence struggles), analogies with Stalinism and the literary feuds that centered around the Brecht-Lukacs debates. Going back in time, the French Revolution adopted a neo-classical model in order to dress up its actions as a continuation of those "great and enduring aspirations" of Greek and Roman antiquity. The revolution enacted a mise-en-scène of this classicism armed with the ideas of Jean-Jacques Rousseau; the revolutionaries used the emblems of antiquity to hide perhaps the true poverty of the social content of their ideas, as Eagleton has suggested, following the lead of Marx's *18th Brumaire of Louis Bonaparte* (Eagleton, 1990, p. 213). Carpentier, whether visually, theatrically, even operatically, shuffles about discourses, concepts, ideas, images, emblems, piecing together a profound meditation about history and modernity.

Most notably, Carpentier rejects any kind of linearity in history. The notion that history can be narrated with a kind of luminous transparency collapses in this novel, as does the essentialist trap of history having a subject. Through allegory Carpentier shows that this vision is idealist, presupposing a close relationship between signifier and signified. Allegory in Carpentier "stages" interpretation; it makes language function with all its arbitrariness and makes the signifying process a spectacle, a theater where the most abject and sublime coalesce in that tragedy which is revolution. The only utopia, Carpentier seems to be saying, is language itself. Every utopia is a dream, but it is a dream that beckons to be put into practice. To accomplish that, the dream must confront the true nature of power. And in that war between utopia and power, reason and terror, praxis and representation, Carpentier constructs his verbal edifice, where words will not fall into a vacuum.

This last sentence refers not only to the quotation that begins the novel, but to Carpentier's own words about *Explosion in a Cathedral*. The book commences with the following words from the Zohar: "Words do not fall into a vacuum." This quotation from an ancient cabalistic text might have more recent and Cuban connotations as well. José Martí once said, "Trincheras de palabras valen más que trincheras de piedras" ("Trenches made of words are better than those of stone"). All of this is consistent with what Carpentier said about the novel in an interview: "The underlying principle of the book? It could be summed up in this phrase: Human beings might weaken and give up, but ideas follow their own path and finally are put into practice" (Carpentier, 1989, p. 52). Again, this seems to resonate with Julio Antonio Mella's phrase, "Hasta después de muertos somos útiles" ("Even in death we are useful"). Mella, a founder of the Cuban Communist Party (1925), assassinated before his twenty-sixth birthday, in both life and thought had his prophetic optimism redeemed by Fidel Castro and the Cuban Revolution, according to Carpentier.

While the French Revolution drew on antiquity, twentieth-century revolutions seem to draw on the French example, with its use of language such as right and left, Jacobins, terror, and the will of the people. Carpentier, however, wrote his novel between 1956 and 1958, while he was living in Venezuela, so it is difficult to impute to him a *roman à clef* about the Cuban Revolution, even though the novel was not published until 1962, apparently with some substantial modifications to the 1958 version. The writing and rewriting process of the novel reveals the historical density of Caribbean reality. No doubt many references in the novel allude to the Bolshevik Revolution, and Víctor Hugues's megalomania is unequivocally reminiscent of Stalin's. The period of the novel's gestation was an extraordinarily difficult moment in the history of the communist movement, with the Soviet invasion of Hungary as well as the famous speech of Khrushchev to the twentieth Party Congress (both in 1956) denouncing the abuses of the Stalin era.

Despite the savage history of many revolutions, Carpentier was not totally inimical to their contributions to humanity, and he went to great pains to indicate that his novel did not have in mind the revolutionary transformation of his native Cuba. Here are his words in an interview published in 1983 (after his death):

> I'm not in agreement with the statement that says I have a "Saturnian" concept of history. And I differ from the idea that no revolution has delivered on its promises. If, in a certain way, the French Revolution failed, I couldn't, histori-cally speaking, show great optimism towards it. History is what it is, and can't be any other way. But in reference to revolutions in general, it's enough for me to see the results of the Cuban Revolution, its great achievements, the magnificent changes it has brought about in the life of my compatriots, so that I become aware that not all revolutions have to defraud those who have made it. (Carpentier, 1989, p. 54)

These words might seem quaint and ironic to many at this stage in Cuba's history (reflecting how rapidly things shift), but they must be understood within a certain context (before 1980), when Cuba was living in greater economic prosperity and with certain social gains (health, education, close to zero unemployment) that had universally been achieved.

Carpentier's "method" of trying to represent revolution is a vast in-tertextual drama placed and performed on the stage of history. It is a conversation with Greek tragedy, baroque theater, Spanish painting and history, Caribbean voodoo, French politics and thought, African-based religions, German aesthetic theory and philosophy, and Cuban historians. This intoxicating dialogue with the dead, the living (and the future) could be called transcultured historiography. Like Severo Sarduy's idea of *retom-bée*, sometimes the echo precedes the voice. This approach to history re-quires the determination of an archivist, the rigorous logic of a scientist, the insight of a philosopher, the creative architectonics of a composer, and the imagination of a poet. Perhaps this explains Carpentier's generous mixing of genres under the novelistic umbrella. Antillean (Cuban) realities require a fluid, inclusive manner, aspiring to the liquid alchemy characteristic of the Caribbean Sea.

But although we cannot attribute to Carpentier, or to his novel, a view of the Cuban Revolution, his interpretive and historical approach in the novel can invite such thoughts in current readers. Indeed, Carpentier's method of moving across vast stretches of time (from the Zohar to Stalin, from Goya to Brecht, from Rousseau to Lenin) incites those very associa-tions. The idea is not so simple, though, because it is not just a question of linking up Robespierre or Saint-Just with, say, Fidel Castro, or perhaps Esteban with Lezama Lima. That could be a fruitful and interesting exercise, but Carpentier had larger issues in mind, such as the role of violence in revolutionary change, or the idea of beginning anew by transforming a society from the bottom up, or the relationship between freedom and necessity.

The hope for a new beginning, a new society, has driven revolutionaries for the last two centuries. The French Revolution went so far as changing the calendar, giving different names to the months. In Cuba one constantly hears "antes" and "después" (before and after), with the implicit understanding that it refers to the revolution. It is as if Cuba became another country on January 1, 1959. To a certain extent this is true; the revolution made a radical break with the past in terms of class relations, unemployment, racism, education, health, and economic policy, not to mention a vast reorientation of its foreign policy. But this newness harks back to biblical times, with the Judeo-Christian messianistic impulse. But differently, it was not a divine act which would interrupt and give a new course to secular history, but instead an act (or acts) of men and women that would give history a new dimension, and society a new set of rules, defined by freedom. It is as if the revolutionary process had tried to abolish or wipe away society's original sin by seeking a new start and attempting to build a utopian future. This new start must reckon, however, with the so-called "social question."

Hannah Arendt, in her incisive book of essays *On Revolution*, has traced the inner tension of revolutionary movements since the French Revolution. She defines as crucial the conflict between freedom and necessity, defining the latter as a social issue (and, of course, economic, as well). Moreover, the step from freedom to necessity becomes a crucial element in the valoration of the necessity of violence. Says Arendt: "Thus the role of revolution was no longer to liberate men from the oppression of their fellow men, let alone to found freedom, but to liberate the life process of society from the fetters of scarcity so that it could swell into a stream of abundance. Not freedom but abundance became now the aim of revolution" (Arendt, 1990, p. 64). To "liberate the life process," at least in the Marxist revolutionary tradition, means the violent overthrow of a corrupt and shallow society, because that society will not change peacefully nor give up its privileges without a fight. Alain Touraine adds that Marx believed in the liberation of nature, that a classless society would be the triumph (or return) of nature (Touraine, 1995, pp. 80–81). But this comes about through "an obsession with totality" which does not "make allowance for the appearance within civil society of the social actor" (ibid., p. 82). Liberating the life process leads to the corruption or elimination of civil society, a destructive feature for any society.

Curiously, though, violence, despite its relationship to revolutions and historical events, falls outside of politics, in the strict sense. If, as Aristotle said, humans are political beings endowed with human speech (and both are necessary to transact politics), violence is the exhaustion of the political, the reign of silence. As a result, a revolutionary justification for violence must expend time (and words) to invade or cover this silence: "a theory of revolution, therefore, can only deal with the justification of violence because this justification constitutes its political limitation; if instead, it arrives at a glorification or justification of violence as such, it is no longer political but antipolitical" (Arendt, 1990, p. 19). Carpentier's novel treads this line of the justification of violence for political ends, always keeping in mind, perhaps, Saint-Just's remark, "Nothing resembles virtue so much as a great crime." Not surprisingly, Carpentier has the ship that brings the guillotine to the New World accompanied by a written document of great political significance: the Declaration of the Rights of Man.

Once, however, the idea of necessity is established—be it history, the indivisible will of the people, the glory of the invincible Reich, the will of God, the dictates of the class struggle, or the engine of progress—the groundwork is laid on which it becomes possible to commit enormous crimes with impunity draped in the cloak of virtue. There has scarcely been a revolution in this century that has not followed this pattern to a greater or lesser extent. Does this invalidate the political and economic importance of revolution? According to Carpentier, no. The end of his novel bears this out. The French Revolution has run its course and failed. The bourgeoisie has put its faith in Napoleon, who subsequently invades Spain, and by this action enables the Latin American independence movements to advance and eventually defeat Spanish colonialism in the Americas (except for Cuba and Puerto Rico). Esteban and Sofía die in the streets of Madrid defending the sovereignty of Spain, even though the most "progressive" political force in this battle are the French. In history, Carpentier seems to tell us, ideas triumph in indirect, often unexpected ways.

It will take many years for historical analysts to sort out the triumphs and reversals of revolutions in the Caribbean. In recent history there have been only two: Cuba and Grenada. The latter was destroyed by those who put necessity before freedom, crushing the new and innovative government of Maurice Bishop and the New Jewel Movement by giving the U.S. government a flimsy pretext for direct military intervention. Cuba's social experiment has lasted thirty-six years, battered and struggling. One could say, with reasonable certainty, that the Cuban Revolution has failed. To make that claim is not a simple statement: it does not mean that the last thirty-six years of Cuban history are meaningless. The nature of what was achieved and what has failed is by no means an open and shut case: it will require all the intertextual skill and imaginative insight that Carpentier brought to *Explosion in a Cathedral* to sort out lucidly. To a degree, then, it is not "over," and Carpentier's allegorical method, with its distantiation (temporal and otherwise), suggests that "the monogram of essence" that Benjamin spoke of will continue to be reinscribed, contested, become an evolving palimpsest of images.

For two generations now Cuba has represented the hope of the down-trodden in many parts of the world. Yet in its attention to necessity over freedom, it reveals severe weaknesses which are compounded in its current economic crisis. Arendt has said that compassion for the poor has led to pity, and "Pity, taken as the spring of virtue, has proved to possess a greater capacity for cruelty than cruelty itself" (ibid., p. 89). Behind the selfless devotion to "the people" can lie a vicious inclination to persecute. The problem with this pity is its boundlessness, Arendt says of Robespierre, so "that the evil of his virtue was that it did not accept any limitations" (ibid., p. 90). This limitless nature of revolution, its words and deeds, its vicious virtue, its passion for freedom and justice, do not fall into a vacuum. They continue to beset our century's dreams, no matter how skeptical postmodernists may be of these "grand narrative" schemes. They form the emblems of Carpentier's theater of history that have haunted the twentieth century with passionate hope and bloody intolerance, revealing that if man is "a tattered coat upon a stick" (Yeats), from its meager threads are woven the opposites "with which there is no progress: attraction and repulsion, reason and energy, love and hate . . . [so] necessary for human existence."

THREE

Virgilio Piñera: History to the Bone

Virgilio Piñera (1912–1979) was born in Cárdenas, Cuba. He is not only one of the major writers to come out of Cuba, but Latin America as well. His work has unjustly been neglected, except for a handful of Cuban, Puerto Rican, and Argentinian writers/critics. His early reputation was made in theater with *Electra Garrigó* (1943), *Jesús* (1948), and *Falsa alarma* (1948), the latter two being the first works of absurdist theater and precursors to Beckett, Ionesco, and others. Had he been living in Paris at the time (1940s), he might be a staple of the college literary reading lists. Equally gifted as a short story writer, novelist, and poet, Piñera published four collections of stories, three novels, and three books of poems, as well as having written thirty plays. Piñera's oeuvre emphasizes the fate of the human body as a focal point for the relationships between power, discourse, and sexuality. By placing the body in extreme situations (death, mutilation, sacrifice, bondage), Piñera, with a deadpan candidness, speaks of domination, the formation of gender, socialization, and the forging (and foibles) of consciousness. Piñera's language, pared-down, even colloquial, is laced with wit and irony. His *Cuentos fríos* (1956; *Cold Tales*, 1988) are gems of the genre as they expose social conformity, human perfidy, poverty, and political rigidity with stark, uncompromising humor. His major novel, *La carne de René* (1952; *René's Flesh*, 1989), lays bare all the structures of domination in society: school, family, church, political movements, magnified and distorted through the prism of flesh. *Pequeñas maniobras* (Small Maneuvers), from 1963, is the story of Sebastián, told as a picaresque novel in reverse, with the protagonist descending the social scale, displaying an ever-increasing ability to humiliate himself. *Presiones y diamantes* (1967; Pressures and Diamonds), his last novel, is a kind of science fiction novel, a cross between Camus's *The Plague* and Godard's *Alphaville*.

Some of his other significant plays are *Aire Frío* (1958), a family satire; *La boda* (1957), a savage look at marriage; *El no* (1965); and a pas-de-deux about fear and death, *Dos viejos pánicos* (1968), winner of the Casa de las Américas Award. The latter, despite the award, was not performed in Cuba until 1990.

Piñera spent the better part of twelve years in Argentina (1946–58), with trips backs to Cuba either to collaborate on the staging of his plays or for personal reasons. Though he published in *Orígenes* magazine, he was never considered part of the group's inner circle like José Lezama Lima, Cintio Vitier, Eliseo Diego, Fina García Marruz, Julián Orbón, and Angel Gaztelu. He was a close friend of José Rodríguez Feo, the magazine's financial backer, who eventually broke with them to form his own magazine, *Ciclón*. Piñera was one of the chief editors and contributors to *Ciclón*, whose tone was more belligerent and willing to take on issues (Sade, homosexuality, political commitment) than *Orígenes*, which its Catholicism (even if unorthodox) was less reluctant to deal with.

Piñera returned to Cuba shortly before the revolution and stayed on afterwards. He was put in charge of Ediciones R, a government-created publishing firm, which also brought out his Collected Works of Theater, (*Teatro completo*), featuring seven of his plays. Despite the revolution's recognition of his importance as a literary figure and dramatist, signs of strain were evident early on. In the famous meeting held with Cuban intellectuals in June 1961, in which Fidel Castro took part, Piñera stood up at one point and said, "I'm scared. I don't know why, but I'm scared." His fears were confirmed a few months later when he was jailed for one night in a government crackdown on prostitution and homosexuality. Nonetheless, Piñera stayed in his job and continued to be published during the 1960s.

The hardening cultural atmosphere around the Padilla affair adversely affected Piñera, as it did Lezama, and for the last ten years of his life (1969–79) he was not published on the island. Younger writers, gay or not, were told to avoid him, as he was viewed as "ideologically suspect." By 1987 a kind of "rehabilitation" had taken place, and several books of his works (stories, plays, and poems) have been published posthumously.

Piñera was unswerving in his view of the world as well as in his literary style. His absurdism, dark humor, and scathing criticism of hypocrisy and grandiosity were applied to all: young and old, conservative and radical, low lifes and aristocrats, believers and atheists. Many writers after the revolution (some with the best of intentions and voluntarily, others out of fear or opportunism) tried to write more popular literature, making it accessible to the masses. Not Piñera. Perhaps that is why currently he (and Lezama) are viewed by the young generations of Cuban artists and writers as inspirational not only as extraordinary artists, but as human beings of unparalleled dignity, honesty, and integrity. Piñera was unique in Cuban letters: his outrageous imagination was at the same time vicious, funny, and implacable. But out of the ashes of desolation, there is an ethical core to his writing that deeply examines Cuban society with ruthless insight.

History and Its Doubles: The Master–Slave Dialectic, or What Happens When Hegel Meets the Keystone Cops

History is haunted by its doubles, by specters that assail the identity of the social, questioning the illusory ideals of collective (or individual) happiness. These phantoms would turn history as epic or tragedy into opera buffa, letting us know that outside the polis we become gods or beasts. These spectres are memory, whose figurative energy erodes oblivion; the body, marked by persecution disrupting the placid narrative of ideology; and flesh-and-blood specters like servants and slaves who threaten to become masters. And there is always the specter of the Other, always poised to steal our enjoyment (*jouissance*), always beyond pleasure, haunting our gratification: apparition, dream, shadows, imitations, a source of dread and horror. For Epicureans, specters were images or semblances that emanated from the corporeal. Virgilio Piñera, in a kind of Epicurean fury, showed us how the body and its specters were the sight, the spectacle of history in all its foldings and unfoldings. Few writers took on these doubles with such ferocious irony as he did. Piñera was one of the most scathing political satirists the island of Cuba has ever had, and the human and social calamities his art depicted were beyond anything being written at the time (1940s and 1950s). Remarkably, his work has acquired a prophetic tone in being able to anticipate many of the political trends or phenomena that would later become so evident or obvious: the fabrications of image-obsessed, sound-bite politics, the brittle absurdity of Soviet Communism, the element of desire and enjoyment (*jouissance*) that underlies different ideologies, the visibility-invisibility of power relationships, the packaging and marketing distortions of commodity politics.

"El Muñeco" ("The Dummy") is one of the author's longer stories and is a bizarre, if not hilarious, mix of political satire, science fiction, slapstick, cloak-and-dagger comedy of errors, and fantasy. It was written over a period of ten years (1944–54) and was included in his *Cuentos fríos* (Editorial Losada, Buenos Aires) of 1956. This short story collection was translated into English as *Cold Tales* (hereafter *CT*) in 1988. This ten-year period, in which the author lived in Buenos Aires, was marked by important, sometimes unspeakable, events: the Holocaust, an enormous Jewish and Nazi Central European immigration to Argentina, the atomic bomb, the first stages of the cold war, the hydrogen bomb, the Perón regime in Argentina (1946–55), the Arbenz government in Guatemala overthrown by a CIA coup in 1954, the Slansky trials in Czechoslovakia, the first accounts of the Gulags. In Cuba, the Batista coup (1952) was followed by the July 26th Movement's attack on the Moncada barracks a year later. This backdrop of bewildering and unsettling events might have made the story seem tentative to its author. Its long gestation period was well worth the wait.

"The Dummy" begins with the narrator stating: "One clarification before I begin: I am nothing more than an inventor of mechanical devices" (*CT*, p. 79). This inventor of mechanical devices, Jonatán Fernández, is concerned with the fate of the president of the country. Why? He notices the president's gestures are becoming robotic, the skin rubbery, the look in his eye turning to a fixed, glassy stare. The brain is beginning to soften. Because he takes part in so many public functions and ceremonies, his authenticity has been drained by another force, what the narrator calls dummification.

How to solve this intractable problem? Jonatán first considers an old literary trick—the creation of an alter ego. He rejects this on several grounds, partly due to the fact that such a creation could take a life of its own and usurp power from the "real" president, so to speak. (More on this later.) Finally, the solution would consist of having the president not appear in public but have in his place someone identical to him. At this point in the narrative Jonatán (the narrator) does not offer details as to how this will happen. But he resolves to meet the president in person so as to confide his plan to him. This is no easy task, however.

Luckily, the narrator meets up with Juan, a Communist Party member whose group has regular, if ceremonial, access to the president. The arrangements are made so that he will accompany a party delegation having a meeting with the president. On his own he arranges an intricate plan to meet with the president alone. When he shakes the president's hand, the latter is able to see that the narrator's smile is the mirror image of his own. This disturbs him momentarily. Jonatán will use the official meeting as a cover to slip away and change into a butler's uniform and sneak unnoticed into the president's secret chamber. Upon entering the dark room he hears a woman's voice ask, "Is that you, Perucho?" At first he pretends to be the cat, but the woman, a call girl, catches on. She complains about the lack of service (they don't feed her, just supply her with martinis) and the long waits; finally, fed up, she departs. Jonatán is relieved, but before he can completely change into the butler's uniform, the president barges in. Smelling the perfume of the departed demi-mondaine, he gets excited and starts chasing after Jonatán, who as a last resort turns on the light.

Jonatán explains his presence and then puts forth the president's problem. After some initial skepticism, the president warms up to Jonatán's ideas. It is mid-October and if nothing is done, the president will turn into a dummy by December. It shows in the pigmentation of his skin and in the eyes, where the "dummy's gaze" leaves him staring at something endlessly without even blinking. To stop the dummification process, Jonatán claims that one must "extract the dummy with the dummy." The president is displeased, claiming that doubles are dangerous because they begin as servants and end up as masters (*CT*, p. 103).

Jonatán insists that he will work by analogy, by building a doll (or dummy) which will become extinguished instead of the president. It will be made of rubber, will execute the president's famous smile, have a clockwork mechanism for the eyes which will stare for one minute and then move on for the next minute, plus certain devices for speaking and body movements. To ensure accuracy of representation, even a twitching left shoulder will be included, since the president behaves that way while attending church functions.

Convinced, the president gives the order to begin working on the project right away, since he wants the dummy to be ready in nine days for the celebration of his third accession to power. Despite his excitement, the president also issues a warning: if the plan is successful, Jonatán will be a national hero; if not, the president himself will kill him with his own bare hands (*CT*, p. 106).

After several days there is a final test which Piñera describes as follows: "The likeness was so astonishing that the President, thinking the dummy was the President, began to give orders that he himself be expelled from the makeshift workshop. The rubber dummy worked so effectively that it caused a dangerous confusion: the President insulted and slapped himself, foamed at the mouth, called himself an impostor, a bad patriot, a traitor, and may other things" (*CT*, pp. 108–9). The president has been seduced by the striking authenticity of the dummy, a further reminder of how dummi-fied he has become. The narrator fears the worst, but fortunately the incident is forgotten and they proceed to the mechanical test. It is a success, but again it almost ends in failure.

Finally, the day arrives for the dummy to make its true appearance. The government explains to the people that the dummy will be part of the anniversary celebration. The dummy appears at a balcony that overlooks an enormous plaza, but the throngs are remarkably silent. They think it is the president and demand that the dummy be brought out. The president comes out and the masses hail him by saying, "There's the dummy! There's the dummy!" (*CT*, p. 111).

After this incident, cabinet ministers, advisors, and top military brass also insist on having their own dummies. Soon the practice is extended to all members of the government and eventually to teachers. Piñera closes with the following: "In the end, the people whose dummies were multiply-ing rapidly over the face of the earth retreated to those mysterious places, the toy stores. There, registered and classified by competent employees, wrapped in cellophane and set out on multicolored cardboard boxes, they stupidly waited to be chosen by a child and torn limb from limb at the hands of innocence" (*CT*, p. 112).

Piñera's story is a complex portrait of technology out of control, and as such echoes Mary Shelley's great work *Frankenstein* (1818). This theme runs through many works of fiction since that of Shelley, not to mention its importance in the genre of science fiction. Aside from Shelley in the nineteenth century, there is Poe's "The Chess Player," E.T.A. Hoffman's "The Sand Man" and "Automata," Hawthorne's "The Artist of the Beautiful," Samuel Butler's novel *Erewhon*, and the early work of H. G. Wells. In the twentieth century, the examples are too numerous to list—from E. M. Forster to Aldous Huxley, from Alfred Jarry to Sam Shepard, from Theodor Sturgeon and Isaac Asimov to Stanislaw Lem. However, the Piñera story's parodic, slapstick quality distances it from Shelley's masterpiece, being more a mix of Dr. Caligari and Buster Keaton.

Jonatán's double of the president has some of the qualities of a robot in being a mechanical device, but its similarity to the original would put it closer to an android. (The fact that it is a rubber dummy gives it a fantastic, almost buffoonish air.) The robot or android partakes of two worlds, the mechanical and the human. As Jean Baudrillard says, it is a perfect synthesis of functionality and anthropomorphism (Baudrillard, 1981, p. 137). It is at the same time symbolic of both and substitutive of both. As machine, an android is expected to work with great efficiency and productivity and, of course, not tire out or need food and sleep like humans do. In Piñera's story this technical competence takes on a political dimension. This is not new. For centuries political thinkers have been trying to develop a *techné* for the organizing and functioning of society. Piñera's story is more concerned with the manipulation of signs and symbols of power as a means to perpetuate rule.

The state and/or society have been likened to a machine for centuries, from Hobbes to Marx. This metaphor is intimately linked, in Western discourse, with certain views concerning nature and technology, most notably with the need to have autonomy from and mastery over nature. As Langdon Winner has pointed out:

> Our thinking about technology, however, seems inextricably bound to a single conception of the manner in which power is used—the style of absolute mastery, the despotic, one-way control of the master over the slave. Other notions central to the historical discussion of political power—membership, participation and authority founded on consent—seem to have no relevance in this sphere. In our traditional ways of thinking, the concept of mastery and the master-slave metaphor are the dominant ways of describing man's relationship to nature, as well as to the implements of technology. (Winner, 1979, p. 20)

The equivalence of slave and machine was underlined by Aristotle in the *Politics*. More than two centuries later, Norbert Wiener, one of the pioneers of cybernetics, would say: "Let us remember that the automatic machine, whatever we think of any feelings it may have or may not have, is the precise economic equivalent of slave labor" (Wolfe, 1979, p. 152). Jonatán's efforts are clearly within the domain of political authority and domination. After all, the goal of the dummy is to continue the president's rule without annihilating him as a human being, since the problem with offering yourself as a fake is that you become precisely that. The outcome of his experiment is a mixed success, to be sure.

Piñera's "The Dummy" touches on crucial elements of the master-slave relationship, not only in terms of technology and politics, but also in a Hegelian sense. In discussing Hegel's *Phenomenology of Spirit*, I will rely on Alexandre Kojeve's lectures (Kojeve, 1991), followed by a psychoanalytic updating of the Hegelian paradigm by Jessica Benjamin (Benjamin, 1988).

For Hegel, his search began with the quest for Absolute Knowledge, something that is possible through Universal Self-Consciousness. How do human beings acquire self-consciousness? It begins with desire. Hegel distinguishes two kinds of desire, however. One is animal desire, directed at satisfying biological needs, and this produces a natural being. What makes a desire truly human and social is the fact that the desire be the object of another's desire toward the same object. This object does not necessarily have to be food. It can be biologically useless, as in the case of a medal, a flag, a coveted symbol. For human history to exist, then, there must be a multiplicity of desires, which will eventually lead to recognition of human subjects by other human subjects. What does recognition entail for Hegel?

In an initial dyad we have two individuals struggling to be acknowledged, and it is a fight to the death in order to establish a situation of independence and mastery. In a desire they both share, each person wants to impose their desire, so that they will be recognized.

> In other words, man's humanity "comes to light" only if he risks his (animal) life for the sake of his human Desire. It is in and by this risk that it "comes to light," i.e., is shown, demonstrated, verified, and gives proofs of being essentially different from the animal, natural reality. And that is why to speak of the origin of Self-Consciousness is necessarily to speak of the risk of life (for an essentially nonvital end). (Kojeve, 1991, p. 7)

The extremity of this situation poses a problem: the struggle for recognition will result in the death of one of the protagonists of the dyad. You cannot be recognized unless your adversary survives. This means that two fundamentally different human behaviors are at work, that of the master and that of the slave. During the fight for recognition, the adversary who becomes the slave fears the other and death enough to sacrifice his or her desire and satisfy the desire of the other (master). S/he must recognize the other without being recognized in return. Therefore, human beings, even in their nascent state, are never just "humans" but masters or slaves. They are constituted by autonomous and independent existences. So, "to speak of the origin of Self-Consciousness is necessarily to speak of the 'autonomy and dependence of Self-Consciousness, of Mastery and Slavery' " (Kojeve, 1991, p. 9).

History for Hegel consists in the dialectical overcoming of both master and slave. The master has achieved recognition and thereby elevates him or herself above nature by having the slave work for him/her. But this is a trap. The recognition is one-sided, since the master is being recognized by an "animal" or a "thing." This is not true recognition, since the master wants to be recognized by another human, a historical subject. If satisfaction is to be measured in recognition by other humans, then the master is never satisfied. To be truly recognized, then, the slave must cease to be a slave. The slave, on the other hand, is also unsatisfied and wants to become an autonomous and free person, meaning that s/he will struggle toward achieving recognition by a free historical subject.

The movement of history will never come from the master. As Kojeve has pointed out: "The Master is fixed in his Mastery. He cannot go beyond himself, change, progress. He must conquer—and become Master or preserve himself as such—or die. He can be killed; he cannot be transformed, educated. He has risked his life to be Master. Therefore, Mastery is the supreme value for him, beyond which he cannot go" (Kojeve, 1991, p. 9). The slave, however, is change, transformation, education, because s/he wants to overcome the slave condition and be free. How does the slave achieve this, if the master wants to continue exercising his/her mastery? Hegel says that it is through work that the slave becomes master of nature, that s/he transcends the merely biological. The slave represses his instinct (for mastery and recognition) in relation to an idea or a concept, and by doing so engages in a specifically human activity, or work. Work negates both nature and the slave's nature by transforming both, and "to be able to transform the natural given in relation to a nonnatural ideal is to possess a *technique*. And the idea that engenders a technique is a *scientific* idea, a scientific concept. Finally, to possess scientific concepts is to be endowed with Understanding, *Verstand*, the faculty of *abstract* notions. Understanding, abstract thought, science, technique, the arts—all these have their origin in the enforced work of the Slave" (Kojeve, 1991, p. 48).

Up to now, our exposition deals with what Hegel referred to as the pagan state and its relationships. Before refining these notions further and discussing Jessica Benjamin's analysis of domination, it might be pertinent to turn to a play Piñera wrote around the time he finished "The Dummy." It is called *Los siervos* (The Serfs) and was published only in *Ciclón* magazine (Piñera, 1955b). The play is a tongue-in-cheek glance at Hegel's master-slave paradigm, but applied to the communist world. It takes place in Russia at some point in the future when the entire planet has gone communist. Nikita Smirnov, the philosopher of the Party, has openly declared himself to be a serf and has published this statement in the Party newspaper, *Pravda*.

Orloff, the prime minister, is baffled and states, "Dialectically, such a thing is impossible . . . and yet" (Piñera, 1955b, p. 9).

Kirianin, an army general, wants to have him disappear; Orloff wisely says he is against creating martyrs. Instead he wants Nikita's plea to go unnoticed. Piñera plays with Hegel's notion of recognition in a triple sense. The first is the most obvious, the recognition factor in setting up the master-slave dialectic. The second is a parody of the first, in that Nikita wants to be recognized as a slave, or serf. That recognition is, pardon the expression, a red herring, since being a slave in the Hegelian sense is not being recognized, it is to be considered an animal or a thing. This contradiction becomes clearer within the wider context of the play. Since the action takes place in a future communist society, there are no masters and slaves, but that precisely is Nikita's point. He sees serfs and masters everywhere, but no one will admit it. His agenda is to denounce the deception of concealed exploitation and servitude under the masquerade of equality.

Kirianin, Orloff, and Fiodor (the Party secretary) agree to ignore Nikita's manifesto and stick to matters of form, but are unsuccessful. When finally confronted with his new cause, Nikita falls to his knees and begins kissing their feet. Orloff reacts quickly. He orders Kirianin and Fiodor to kneel down and offer their rears to be kicked by Nikita. Orloff's prescription to force Nikita to become a master is pure slapstick—the Keystone Cops (or maybe the Commissar Cops) meet Hegel in trying to bend the dialectic into an unrecognizable shape. Orloff's scheme fails, ending the first act.

In Act Two, Piñera begins with Stepachenko, a spy, arriving at Nikita's house. He has read Nikita's piece in *Pravda* and wants to become his master. Nikita agrees, but lays down three conditions: (1) he won't serve a White Russian disguised as a Red Russian; (2) he has to be kicked in the rear; and (3) he must be turned over to the executioner if he rebels. And yet Nikita cautions that a serf who rebels is no longer a serf, but instead becomes a rebel. Again, we can see Hegel's vision of history being sardonically outlined. Work and finally rebellion are the motors of history. Rebellion would be the case of the slave attaining true self-consciousness through an act of liberation (recognition by the Other).

In the following scene, the plot becomes more complicated with the arrival of Adamov, a master from the Ural Mountains. He is deeply troubled, since he lords over four hundred serfs and is concerned that Nikita's audacity will blow his cover. He wants to buy Nikita from Stepachenko in order to punish him and intimidate his serfs into not going public. Reluctant at first, Stepachenko gives in, since this will ultimately signify Nikita's beheading. He and Nikita have an important dialogue in which the dialectic of history is laid out. The master-slave condition is established with the fear of death as the cornerstone of that dynamic. The second phase, according to Nikita, is the serf in rebellion. It is followed by the third, which is the serf decapitated. The fourth phase is that of the master decapitated. The dialogue ends as follows:

Stepachenko: "Do you mean that the serf can triumph?"

Nikita: "The serf can become a lord, and the lord can become a serf."

Stepachenko: "That's most amusing."

Nikita: "Yes, my lord, it's most amusing. It's the eternal return."

Stepachenko (putting on his hat): "You get lost in high-sounding phrases, Nikita. Be careful that those great words don't make you lose your head." (Exits)

Nikita (touching his head): "Your time's up, head." (Touches his rear end). "Dear rear, your time's up." (Piñera, 1955b, pp. 24–25)

Piñera deftly satirizes Hegel continuously, and through his wordplay of head and body not only makes references to Christian theology but humorously and incisively brings to light the important link that Hegel made between death and self-consciousness. Nikita's rebellion is both an acknowledgment of this fact (he will achieve recognition or even become a master) and its dismissal: only the roles will be reversed in a false movement of history. Perhaps death being our ultimate master is what he is rebelling against, knowing well that his actions will lead him to his own demise. Nikita choosing death (through sacrifice) is his way of defeating death and ceasing to be a serf, because thousands of others follow his example in declaring themselves serfs, allowing the truth to be declared openly. Hans-Georg Gadamer has eloquently pointed out the analogy of death as master:

> Unquestionably, the experience of death is the experience of an ultimate dependency in our existence, which the latter in its being-for-self immediately resists. This alien master, who is master over everything, thus stands for everything alien on which our own self-consciousness is dependent. In this sense every cancellation of such an alien reality—and even if it be only a skilled cancellation of the existent form of things—is a liberation of our own self-consciousness. (Gadamer, 1976, p. 71)

But the heroism displayed is shot through with irony, and it anticipates a later story, "The One Who Came to Save Me" (1967), where the main character also tries to defeat death by choosing death. Before his execution Nikita is questioned as to why he has risen against the state, and he replies, "So as to fall." When asked why he wants to fall, he responds, "So as to rise up." Subsequent questions come up with the same answers, as if he were aping with his words some metaphysical yoyo of history. The eternal return is history as "a narrative of misery" (Samuel Johnson), the class struggle as a pie fight.

Returning to "The Dummy," we find Piñera recurring to Hegelian concepts, but more subtly. The narrator, Jonatán Fernández, is in a constant struggle for recognition by the president. After viewing the president during several newsreels, he resolves to rescue him. He imagines being on a first-name basis with the first executive, to the legitimizing importance of the president's smile, described as both an approval and the "equivalent to an order of imprisonment, to exile, to a death sentence" (*CT*, p. 82). All the elements of the Hegelian schema are there: to be able to call the president by his first name, the will to serve the master, and the knowledge of death hanging over his mission should it fail.

This ability or propensity to risk his life is manifested shortly afterwards. Jonatán recalls that it is the president's duty to visit citizens injured by a car in which the president was riding. Sure enough, Jonatán is run over by the presidential vehicle and taken to the hospital with a double fracture. With his legs in casts placed upwards, hanging by weights, he demands to see the president. After repeated efforts to no avail, a presidential aide informs Jonatán that more than a thousand people a year are run over by the presidential limo and tells him to be patient since he will spend over a month in the hospital. Jonatán's search for recognition becomes a labyrinthine tale of identity (his own, the president's), one that is almost an allegory of the construction of political personas.

This identity is structured in an "empire of the gaze," to borrow a term from Michel Foucault. Let us recall that the president's visibility is a ubiquitous yet inaccessible reminder of his power. Jonatán sees him in the newsreels, and later in the street he spots a poster. Many other scenes in the story are structured around looking or being looked at. This is the opportunity, however, to distinguish between the look and the gaze. Freud gave great importance to the active (voyeurism) and passive (exhibitionism) forms of scopophilia, or the drive to look. For him it was part of a human being's development with direct links to the desire for mastery (physical activity) and knowledge (mental activity).

The eye sees from one point, focusing on a person or an object. This is the look, and its association with voyeurism was powerfully articulated by Sartre in *Being and Nothingness*. "For Sartre, the look is fundamentally objectifying: by means of the look the subject is capable of being transformed into an object, reduced from a self-conscious subject, a being-for-itself, to a being-in-itself and for-others. The look can induce in the subject a sense of unmitigated shame at his/her being" (Lacan, 1981, p. 84). Sartre does allow for the look to be reciprocal, so that the person being looked at becomes a subject by looking at the first subject. The gaze, on the other hand, is said to be the "presence of others," although it is not reducible to a single viewer or even an assemblage of viewers. According to Lacan, it triumphs over the look (Silverman, 1992, p. 130). "What this crucial passage from [Lacan's] *Four Fundamental Concepts* suggests is that if the gaze always exceeds the look, the look might also be said to exceed the gaze—to carry a libidinal supplement which relegates it, in turn, to a scopic subordination.

The gaze, in other words, remains outside desire, the look stubbornly within" (ibid.). Lacan defines the gaze in terms of lack: "You grasp the ambiguity of what is at issue when we speak of the scopic drive. The gaze is the object lost and suddenly refound in the conflagration of shame, by the introduction of the other. . . . What one looks at is what cannot be seen" (Lacan, 1981, p. 182).

Jonatán oscillates between the look and the gaze. When he first sees the president in the movie theater, he is somewhat the voyeur. He seems to be within the look, in the world of desire: desire for recognition, desire for power, and desire that borders on erotic ecstasy. But in fact several things indicate that his viewing of the president is not quite so simple. His identification with the president is so intense that he describes certain things that bother him as being "torture." When Jonatán saw the poster he burst into tears. Piñera states the paradox with precision: Jonatán's looking is his empathetic recognition (not a Sartrean objectifying look) of the president's dilemma as a public figure. This emotional recognition is contradicted by the impersonality of the situation encouraged by the medium—we think we know our celebrities. Further on, when he meets the president in person, his smile replicates that of the chief executive. Jonatán's astonishment is his perception of a lack within the president. His authority, his aura, is being usurped by the dummy. His own lack is the desire-as-recognition, to be acknowledged by the president. Jonatán wants to create an intimacy of mutual recognition, rather than the false exploitative intimacy of the movie star image.

These lacks are ensnared by the gaze, more specifically the gaze of power, and here we follow Foucault, who gives the concept of the gaze a historical dimension. In his *Discipline and Punish*, he describes the gaze in terms of a visibility of the power relationship in society. More traditionally power was exhibited as spectacle, where the powerless passively watched; as they looked they inserted themselves into the realm of the gaze. Since the nineteenth century, there has been a shift, where the subject/citizen is brought out into the open, scrutinized, analyzed.

> Traditionally, power was what was seen, what was shown and what was manifested and, paradoxically, found the principle of its force in the movement by which it deployed that force. *Those on whom it was exercised could remain in the shade*; they received light only from that portion of power that was conceded to them, or from the reflection of it that for a moment they carried. Disciplinary power, on the other hand, is exercised through its invisibility; at the same time it imposes on those whom it subjects a principle of compulsory visibility. In discipline, it is the subjects who have to be seen. Their visibility assures the hold of the power that is exercised over them. (Foucault, 1977, p. 187; emphasis added)

If we take a historical example like Nazism, it clearly employed both methods with enormous verve and cruelty. The use of the media, the staging of rallies with dazzling light effects, the careful manipulation of political ritual through the use of symbols, uniforms, mass mobilizations, and the Führer's speeches, would be examples of the traditional approach, albeit within more modern methods. The Third Reich's mania for documenting, recording, testing, examining, and making its citizenry visible to the point of paranoia would exemplify the disciplinary approach outlined by Foucault.

In "The Dummy" we are not dealing with a fascist regime. Given Piñera's Buenos Aires years, the society depicted in the story is probably a mix of Perón's Argentina and prerevolutionary Cuba. It is not entirely undemocratic (there is a communist opposition), but at the same time the society has a charismatic leader as its president. The evocative power of the story makes its analysis of power hold for Latin American dictatorships (charismatic *caudillos*), as well for the modern personality cults under totalitarian regimes. Either or both readings make it relevant to recent Cuban history. The communist opposition, however, has been diminished, by virtue of its recognition and legitimacy. As in the story, it is just another harmless dignitary delegation. They are no longer rebels. Keeping this in mind, it is important to examine at length Piñera's depiction of communists in "The Dummy."

Piñera, seeing the Marxist-Leninist path taken by the Cuban Revolution by 1961, decided not to provoke the authorities again. (He had been jailed briefly [one night] in 1961 for being a homosexual.) In his 1964 edition of the *Cuentos completos* (Complete Stories), forty-four stories were included, but not "The Dummy." Obviously, a play as mordant as *Los siervos* (The Serfs) did not stand a chance of being republished after 1959. "The Dummy" has some barbed criticism of communists voiced through the character Juan, a Party member. He is not a major protagonist in the story (although he has influence in making crucial things happen), nor can the narrative be construed to be exclusively anti-communist. From the previous commentary, one sees that the story is quite critical of the political world in general, and specifically in how politics is constructed as spectacle (theater, ritual, lurid drama).

Jonatán approaches Juan because he needs to talk in person to the president of the country. Through the Party, Juan can facilitate at least meeting the president as a part of a delegation. To make the offer "binding," Jonatán offers Juan a bribe of $2,000, a hefty sum forty years ago. Upon hearing the offer, he "became so flexible, turned so relative, orthodoxy receded from him, that for a moment I was afraid that Juan would end up losing all consistency whatsoever. The mental stretch was so extreme that his feet were touching his head" (*CT*, p. 88). This merely culminates what Piñera had written a few pages earlier when the narrator (Jonatán) declares that he wants to become a Party member, although Juan can detect that it is not out of principle: "If he hadn't been a perfect communist, he would have thought the plan I was sketching out *in mente* during his brief conversation was the most impractical thing imaginable. I say this because I saw in his eyes the typical psychology characteristic of all communists. That is, I saw relativity and orthodoxy" (*CT*, pp. 86–87). Piñera ends the passage with a viciously sardonic reference to Juan's expression going from a smile to a grimace. It is not difficult to find in the two passages quoted here, and in other references made in the story, that Piñera had some of the history of the prerevolutionary Cuban communists in mind.

Founded in August 1925, the Cuban Communist Party (CP) has had some extraordinary figures among its members: Julio Antonio Mella, Rubén Martínez Villena, Nicolás Guillén, Juan Marinello, Manuel Navarro Luna, and Carlos Rafael Rodríguez, to name only a few. During its first decade or so, it functioned illegally or semi-clandestinely. Its newspaper, *Hoy*, began publishing legally in May 1938. In exchange for its support of Batista (who was not in office at the time but still a major power broker), the Cuban CP was legalized on September 13, 1938, and was allowed to have a major influence in the trade union movement. Batista publicly stated his praise: "The Communist Party, as in Mexico, the United States, and France, is officially recognized, and Communism, as a legal force and not as a source of disorder, has become a factor in promoting democratic formulas" (Thomas, 1973, p. 928). Communists were members of the legislature, and some held government positions in certain ministries, usually the Ministry of Labor. During Grau San Martín's administration (1944–48), communists continued to be members of the loyal opposition, with perhaps more emphasis on the adjective rather than the noun.

When Batista engineered his coup in 1952, the Cuban CP did not immediately denounce it, due in part to its relationship with the colonel and ex-president (1940–44) and because of the apathy, corruption, and political gangsterism under Grau (1944–48) and Prío Socarrás, president from 1948 to 1952. Batista was equally tactful and did not dismiss communists working in the Ministry of Labor or close down *Hoy*. A year later, however, things changed, and by November 10, 1953, the Party was outlawed. Even then, communists were not persecuted as mercilessly as members of the nascent July 26th Movement headed by a young lawyer by the name of Fidel Castro.

The Cuban CP's initial reaction to the attack on the Moncada Barracks on July 26, 1953, is well known: it thought it to be an act of foolish adventurism and "putschist" in nature. Fidel's view was equally dismissive, though as the July 26th Movement grew stronger and more popular, the two forces began to discuss points in common.

Many Latin American communist parties were criticized in the 1960s for attitudes and practices similar to their Cuban counterparts: they had become "reformist," "revisionist," too legalistic, pragmatic, and bourgeois. In short, they had lost their revolutionary and utopian edge. It is these aspects that Piñera dwells on in "The Dummy."

If in "The Dummy" Piñera sees the CP as ineffectual, later world events will make him more alarmed. In 1953, a then little-known Polish writer published a book called *The Captive Mind*. It was a searing indictment of Stalinist rule in postwar Poland, written by Czeslaw Milosz, who was later to win the Nobel Prize in 1980. It is possible that Piñera read the book in English; what is certain is that he did review the Spanish-language edition of the book and it was published in the July 1956 issue of *Ciclón*. Piñera's review is incisive and balanced. He does not side with Milosz against the communists or vice versa: he claims all that to be a sideshow. What disturbs him the most is that the book deals with human beings in terms of death instead of life. Piñera lashes out against ideological imperatives:

> What does it matter that the ultimate explanation of these cruel acts be the birth of a better world, or that the Russians justify their acts with their famous motto: "Those who are not with us are against us"? None of that has the slightest importance faced with the proven fact of a "will to slaughter"; it seems that for humankind it is more profitable to kill rather than live with one's neighbor, and it also seems that as humankind progresses through history, that will to kill becomes more imperious and—more horrible still!— more mechanical. (Piñera, 1956, p. 65)

Piñera is quick to point out that the Russians and/or communists have no patent on that "will to slaughter." He steers the reader to another article, in the same issue of *Ciclón*, in which Miguel Angel Asturias speaks of similar atrocities being committed in Guatemala, under the guise of freedom and the defense of private property. Piñera cautions that it is not only in the East where humans are conceived in terms of death. The article ends as follows: "Undoubtedly, East and West are in agreement on one essential point; despite their differences and terrible antagonisms, in short, when it comes to their concept of life, East and West shake hands and march arm in arm in their concept of death" (ibid., p. 66). This should make it clear that to try and paint Piñera as a knee-jerk anti-communist is a misleading and unfruitful endeavor. Piñera was someone with a visceral dislike of all cant, rhetoric, and ideological posturing. He saw these features present in most societies and was equally critical of them, regardless of whether they represented capitalist or communist values.

Returning to the representation of power in the narrative, we see how the story depicts both kinds of power manifestations as defined by Foucault, the traditional and the disciplinary. Indeed, it is crammed with incidents that point to the visibility of meaning and power. Aside from the previously mentioned beginning in the movie theater ("those on whom it [power] was exercised could remain in the shade") and seeing the poster of the president in the street, there are other crucial moments. Toward the beginning, and while he weighs options to solve the president's dilemma, the narrator sees himself in the mirror and lets out a strangled cry, thinking he has saved the president. Quickly, however, he realizes he has succumbed to the notion of the double and the alter ego, which he finds too gimmicky or ineffectual. He then goes on to lay out seven reasons why he rejected the idea, some very logical, some hilarious. All of them have to do with strategies of representation that would affect either the visibility or legitimacy of the president's power. In addition, there is an implicit critique of the double in literature, especially when it is used as a gimmick.

Following Lacan's definition of "the imaginary," we can see the mirror stage informing many aspects of the story (Lacan, 1977, pp. 1–7). The imaginary is where the self recognizes itself as other in the mirror. The self sees a specular image of its body as a totality, represented as a stable, unitary, coherent *corpus*. It leads to a formation of the ego seen as an illusory representation, as a source and focus of alienation. The relationship is a dyadic one, and it works through the mechanism of projection and identification, not unlike the experience of watching films. But, as Lacan points out, this image in the mirror is a misrecognition (*méconaissance*), because the self is not a unitary construct but is sundered by desire and lack.

We see this misrecognition in the narrator not only in the literal sense (when he looks at himself in the mirror) but throughout the story. He joins the Communist Party, even though he is not a communist. From being a communist he becomes a servant. When surprised by the demi-mondaine, he meows like a cat, and when she leaves and the president comes in, he is mistaken for a woman. Finally, he becomes "himself" when he confronts the president and convinces him to go along with his de-dummification plan. But even there his fate and identity are ambiguous: if he, as an inventor and scientist of sorts, succeeds, he will be a hero. If not, the president will strangle him with his own hands. Part of this is Jonatán's picaresque cleverness in trying on different masks as he ascends the sociopolitical ladder to reach the president. But it is also consistent with a kind of empty self buffeted by the "gaze of power" and nonrecognition which subject him. Remember his opening statement: "I am nothing more than an inventor of mechanical devices."

One of the key moments in the story involves a "mirroring effect." When Jonatán, as part of the delegation, meets the president, he smiles to him in exactly the same fashion. Piñera describes a game of dueling smiles with a dizzying mirrorlike effect that both seduces and terrifies the narrator. He realizes the president knows that he is not a communist and feels a current of tension; for the first time someone has been able to duplicate the president's smile.

Piñera's description of the scene beautifully (and buffoonishly) depicts an identification-projection mechanism that is highly revelatory about identity and power. Jonatán has offered a simulacrum of the president's own identity to shock him into recognition. Curiously, the president's recognition of himself in the Other (Jonatán) also produces the insight that Jonatán is not who he appears to be, that is, a Party member. However, he stubbornly repeats what he assumes is an essential part of his identity: his smile. His anger at someone appropriating and using "his" smile is subsumed under repetition, making the smile contiguous with gestures of protocol. A person's smile is a defining, unique aspect of his or her personality. But even that has become overcome by "dummification," as Jonatán tells him later on, when they have their face-to-face conversation. Piñera's merciless critique of political identity is unambiguous. To create a public persona is to fashion an image of oneself for others, again echoing the Lacanian imaginary. This illusory construct is not an intrapsychic phenomenon only, but a political one as well. It is telling that others have used the concept of the Lacanian imaginary as a way of discussing ideology and how it works on the human subject, since it can be likened to misrecognitions about class, gender, race, and nation. The smile constitutes part of the political ego. This political ego is also the embodiment (literally, as well) of power. In his narrative, Piñera shows what happens when the political ego is submitted to the "empire of the gaze": complete self-alienation, or, in the story's language, dummification. Politics and authenticity are incompatible.

This inauthenticity at the service of power always conceals (partially, or more completely) a potential for violence and dismay. Later on, when a first version of the dummy is created, the president slaps and insults himself, accuses himself of being an impostor, a traitor. What greater example of the confusion and misrecognition produced by the imaginary, or of the inauthenticity of the political ego? Of course, the solution (creating a rubber dummy) only compounds the problem. In his *The System of Objects*, Jean Baudrillard tells a story from the eighteenth century about an illusionist who built a human automaton, an exact replica of its creator. The automaton's gestures were fluid, natural, to the point where it was impossible to tell them apart. This caused great consternation among the public. To compensate, the illusionist began to gesture mechanically and appear disheveled. So, in order not to cause anguish, it was preferable to have a man behave like a machine and vice versa (Baudrillard, 1981, p. 62).

This poignant, if not alarming, example of the ominous consequences of technology and society is a crucial concern in the story. Machines are constructed to reproduce human labor; an automaton pushes that mimetic function to an extreme, by imitating movement, gesture, and expression (?). The implacable progress of technology can eventually be a substitute for a more organic, natural world, replacing it with an entirely fabricated one. If the simulacrum is so precise as well as *productive* and *capable of organizing reality*, then it is humans who become abstract. In Lewis Mumford's words:

"The machine leads towards an elimination of functions that ends in paralysis" (in Baudrillard, 1981, p. 63).

Its insidious effects produce discontinuities, fragmentation, a kind of generalized disorientation, similar to what the eighteenth-century illusionist had to do to keep his act going. *"Humans have to yield to incoherence because of the coherence of their structural projection.* Faced with the functional object, humans become dysfunctional, irrational and subjective, an empty form open to all kinds of functionalist myths, to the phantasmagoric projections linked to that astonishing efficiency of the world" (ibid., p. 63). What does Baudrillard mean by a functionalist myth? By giving in to this technological splendor, by investing so much energy (psychic as well) in its signs, they (objects, gadgets, machines) take on the power that magic had in archaic societies. Progress, then, is the myth of modernity, a functionalist myth.

Myth, as a psychic map of society, in its capacity to offer a bridge between reality (social and individual) and the needs of the system, can be exploited for social manipulation as easily as ideology. One of ideology's roles is to make dysfunctions of the social order seem natural (class antagonisms, certain forms of political power, gender inequalities, and so on), which it achieves through persuasion, explanation, distortion, or by omission. In bourgeois society, ideological discourse tries to eliminate any reference to class domination, and equally deny that it connives with power; therefore, since the state exists for the benefit of all society, it is not an oppressive mechanism. Part of its discourse, then, is its constant definition of itself as scientific, or what proponents of Critical Theory would call "instrumental reason."

> In bourgeois ideology Poulantzas holds, this dissembling power takes a specific form: the concealment of political interests behind the mask of science. The end-of-ideology thinkers, who applauded the supposed transition from a "metaphysical" to a "technological" rationality, are thus simply endorsing what was endemic in bourgeois ideology all along. Such ideologies, so Poulantzas argues, are notable for their lack of appeal to the sacred or transcendental; instead they ask to be accepted as a body of scientific techniques. (Eagleton, 1991, p. 154)

Piñera, ever conscious of these dangers, plays out this structure of domination to the fullest. The dummies begin to take over and are increasingly in demand: they become more "real" than the real thing. The president begins to sleep in a cardboard box, and eventually the humans all wind up in boxes in toy stores. What began as a liberating gesture (to free the president from official duties, to cure his dummification, to make more free time for him) turns into its grotesque reversal. The dummy, as political plaything in order to substitute and distract the masses, becomes the embodiment of power. The president, who was supposed to have more time to play (enjoy life, recover his "true" self), winds up as a *thing-of-play*. Piñera has skillfully offered his critique of the "functionalist myth," humorously depicting the "elimination of functions that end in paralysis." Ministers and functionaries become toys.

Returning to the issue of inauthenticity and power in the passage from the story previously cited, we see how this functions at a symbolic level, in a duel of smiles ("It is evident he can't admit such a thing; the fight is on"), which is reminiscent of the Hegelian battle for recognition (truly a life-and-death struggle). The president's smile (it is more like a grimace) is not only a reaffirmation of his identity, albeit one based on a misrecognition but equally a signature of his political ego by also being a visual reminder of his power as ruler.

As societies evolve, the master-slave relationship changes, is transformed. In the bourgeois society in which Hegel lived, there were members of the bourgeoisie (who are no longer masters), proletarians, peasants, merchants, civil servants (who are no longer slaves), and intellectuals (who are neither). But that does not mean that relations of domination had disappeared; on the contrary. Historically speaking, for example, feudalism constructs relationships closer to the purer master-slave paradigm. In precapitalist societies it is the relationship between people that is fetishized. This is what happens between the king and his subjects: he is given royal treatment because the king, in himself, outside of the social relationship with his subjects, is a king. Being a king becomes a "natural" property of the man and is buttressed, of course, by the notion of divine right. Domination is legitimized, then, by the fetishization of human relationships. Capitalist societies create a market in which free people exchange labor, ideas, commodities. They are not bound by a contract of servitude. What is fetishized is the commodity, where, as Marx said, "a relation between men assumes the form of a relationship between things" (*Capital*, vol. 1). Domination is disguised by commodity culture: everyone is free and equal before the law to buy and sell goods, to purchase or sell their labor. But "with the establishment of bourgeois society, the relations of domination and servitude are repressed: formally, we are apparently concerned with free subjects whose interpersonal relations are discharged of all fetishism; the repressed truth—that of the persistence of domination and servitude—emerges in a symptom which subverts the ideological appearance of equality, freedom and so on" (Zizek, 1989, p. 26). Hegel was aware of those shifting patterns of domination, and what "The Dummy" illuminates here is the more subtle areas of his thoughts on intersubjectivity.

For intersubjective relations to take place, or what Hegel called Universal Self-Consciousness, three steps have to be taken: (1) desire, (2) recognition, and (3) reason (universal self-consciousness). There is an important moment in the process of being dominated which has an educational, formative dimension and is instrumental in creating the conditions for freedom: the ability to master, delay, or not satisfy desire. "What matters about the education of servitude is not the breaking of self-will, but the dawning conviction that what is important for self-worth is not the gratification of desire but the dignity of formally free agency. Thus being recognized consists not in the domination of another self-consciousness, but in the mutual relation of different self-consciousnesses who identify their dignity with the freedom they have in common" (Hegel in Wood, 1990, pp. 88–89). For Hegel, then, this universal self-consciousness is the key ingredient in establishing an ethical life, it is " 'the form of consciousness of the substance of every essential spirituality, whether of family, fatherland, state, or all virtues—love, friendship, courage, honor, fame' " (ibid., p. 89). Still, there are persons who insist on dominating others. According to Hegel, that should be viewed as a failure, because that person misrecognizes himself or has constructed an inauthentic self and a misguided sense of self-certainty. What causes that inadequate self to develop?

Jessica Benjamin, in her insightful analysis of domination, sums it up as follows: "Briefly stated, domination and submission result from a breakdown of the necessary tension between self-assertion and mutual recognition that allows self and other to meet as sovereign equals" (Benjamin, 1988, p. 12). She stresses the mutuality that is involved in the recognition process as the child is raised. A parent who gives in to a child increases feelings of omnipotence that only the child exists. "The child who feels that others are extensions of himself must constantly fear the emptiness and loss of connection that result from this fearful power" (ibid., p. 35). This kind of person will flee that emptiness by wanting to dominate others.

Conversely, if a parent is too strict, a child will feel that independence has a high psychic price. Freedom will imply a rejection by the parent, thereby becoming synonymous with loneliness. If a child wants approval, the child will have to abandon its will and submit to the parent, who looms omnipotent in the child's mind. This kind of person will seek to be dominated in order not to feel empty.

"The decisive problem remains *recognizing the other*," argues Benjamin, and that means discovering the other (ibid., p. 40). Here she relies on the work of D. K. Winnicott, who believed "that one of the most important elements in feeling authentic was the recognition of an outside reality that is not one's own projection, the experience of contacting other minds" (ibid., p. 37). Winnicott, in his essay "The Use of an Object and Relating through Identifications," paradoxically states that in order to "use" an object, it must first be "destroyed" (Winnicott, 1971). Some clarifications are in order: first, when the word *object* is used, it refers to humans; second, use does not mean to instrumentalize, take advantage of, or exploit. In Winnicott's terminology, it means a shared reality with another person, to benefit creatively from that person, and thus implies recognizing the Other (object) as an independent self-consciousness.

How does "using" an object imply, then, that it must be destroyed? For that to happen, a subject must view the object (person, the Other) as external and not a projection of one's own subjectivity, therefore, this would not be someone going through the Lacanian imaginary phase. But somehow that externality must be assimilated, but not consumed or annihilated.

> Winnicott explains that the recognition of the other involves the paradoxical process in which the object is in fantasy always being destroyed. The idea that to place the other outside, in reality, always involves destruction, has often been a source of puzzlement. Intuitively, though, one senses that it is quite simple. Winnicott is saying that the object must be destroyed *inside* in order that we know it to have survived *outside*; thus we can recognize it as not subject to our mental control. This relation of destruction and survival is a reformulation of and solution to Hegel's paradox: in the struggle for recognition each subject must stake his life, must struggle to negate the other—and woe if he succeeds. For if I completely negate the other, he does not exist; and if he does not survive, he is *not there* to recognize me. But to find this out, I must try to exert this control, try to negate his independence. To find out that he exists, I must wish myself absolute and all alone—then, as it were, upon opening my eyes, I may discover that the other is still there. (Benjamin, 1988, p. 38)

Recognition, then, following Benjamin and Winnicott (through or in the shadow of Hegel), is a dialectic of the construction of the self that has profound implications ontologically, psychically, socially, and intersubjectively. Indeed, Benjamin speaks of a kind of pleasure in being with the other, which has been insufficiently acknowledged in Freudian theory (with an emphasis on drives) and ego psychology (with its focus on autonomy as the goal of the individuation process). Even with all the fakery that goes on in the story, there is recognition between Jonatán and the president, and the possibility of an ethical situation, if only the president's dummification were not so advanced.

It is not hard to see in Winnicott's idea of "destruction" the Hegelian term *Aufheben*, which in English translates as *sublation*. In German, the term has three simultaneous meanings: (1) to raise, hold up, elevate; (2) to annul, abolish, destroy, cancel, suspend; and (3) to keep, serve, preserve (Inwood, 1992, pp. 283–85). Hegel's concept of negation in the dialectic does not mean a complete canceling or destruction of an object (human or otherwise), but a movement that incorporates *and preserves* the negated object or being. The new level achieved (the elevation) is not one of total harmony (Hegel's dialectic is not a blender which obliterates difference) but one where contradiction is maintained in a tense mutuality.

This dialectic is ironically enacted in Jonatán's effort to be hit by the presidential car so as to make himself visible in the "empire of the gaze." We have already seen how this fits into a Hegelian recognition schema.

What was left unsaid was that he pushed the negative so far so as to have it go all the way through to the positive. He has reenacted the original moment of the master-slave in order to serve the state. By declaring his servitude, he is setting up the possibility to be recognized, not unlike Party philosopher Nikita Smirnov in *The Serfs*. Even though his effort fails, it gives us a glimpse of the internal complexity of Piñera's characters, how they are divided against themselves, that is, how the master-slave dialectic works as internal, intrapsychic phenomenon as well.

Piñera accentuates this with the use of the double, thereby reinterpreting (as well as inverting, parodying) certain concerns of the Enlightenment and Cartesian traditions that deal with mastery and reason. That the master-slave dichotomy was not only visible in society (between different agents or players) but also within the individual ego can be glossed from some of the following thinkers.

Montesquieu: "Man is composed of the two substances, each of which, in its flux and reflux, imposes and suffers domination."

Hume: "Reason is the slave of the passions."

Kant: "Man needs a master."

Rousseau: "He who is a master cannot be free." (Kelly in MacIntyre, 1972, pp. 205–7)

Kant's statement should be understood in a personal as well as a public sense, and for an individual, the master would be reason. It was Descartes, however, with his radical dualism (mind-body) and fetishization of thought, who helped to give ideological shape to the mechanistic world-view in the area of politics. He ardently preached that science and philosophy would enable humans to become "the lords and possessors of nature" (Descartes in Mumford, 1970, p. 78). His detached, "thinking reed," the philosopher, had its counterpart in the autocratic baroque prince, who, breaking tradition and custom, would command obedience and lay down the law. The *cogito* of philosophy had an ally in political absolutism, with its most eloquent expression being Thomas Hobbes's *Leviathan* (1651).

If the monarch was to be the head of society, then the masses were literally the body. Since they both viewed the human body as a machine or a "statue made of earth" (Descartes), the art of government was a mechanics, a technics of how to make the machine run smoothly. It is not surprising, therefore, that Hobbes and Descartes had a fascination with automata. The parallels between these seventeenth-century thinkers and Piñera's president are striking: his insistence on protecting the embodiment of power, the use of a single will to direct society, the belief in technocratic solutions. Piñera shows, however, that Descartes's radical dualism and its political corollary are false. It is the construction of a political ego (inauthenticity) that creates symptoms in the president's body, and, of course, trying to "extract the dummy with the dummy" only compounds the nature of the problem.

There is an ethical dimension to this problem, which Foucault pointed out in "On the Genealogy of Ethics: An Overview of Work in Progress." Toward the end of the interview he speaks of Descartes and his significance in terms of the search for truth, the ethics of selfhood, and the nature of science.

> Descartes, I think, broke with this when he said "To accede to truth, it suffices that I be any subject which can see what is evident.". . . The relationship to the self no longer needs to be ascetic to get into relation to the truth. It suffices that the relationship to the self reveals to me the obvious truth of what I see for me to apprehend that truth definitively. *Thus, I can be immoral and know the truth.* I believe that is an idea which, more or less explicitly, was rejected by all previous culture. Before Descartes, one could not be impure, immoral, and know the truth. With Descartes, direct evidence is enough. After Descartes, we have a nonascetic subject of knowledge. This change makes possible the institutionalization of modern science. (Foucault, 1984, pp. 371–72; emphasis added)

For Piñera, as was true for Foucault, the body of power and the body of knowledge are identical. The disinterested pursuit of truth is a fiction.

Piñera is aware of certain historical precedents in dealing with the body of power and its representation in the ruler. When the president's secret advisor suggests that the dummy could be a wax figure, Jonatán dismisses him by saying, "Wax is *post mortem* material; wax captures an historic moment of the hero and immobilizes him there in history; the wax dummy . . . is a funereal dummy: it has nothing to do with the terrible vitality of the rubber dummies" (*CT*, pp. 107–108). Piñera is referring to the practice carried out with Roman emperors, who had two bodies: a human one and a divine one. In fact, two burials/cremations were enacted: one with the *ossa* (bones) culminating in the creation of a *sepulcrum,* and the second with the *imago,* which resulted in the *templum* (Dupont, 1989, p. 403). The *imago* was a wax mask of the deceased, and this wax dummy was laid out for a week and given a yellow pallor to symbolize the sickness. Doctors came every day and pronounced the dummy sicker and sicker as the week wore on. Slaves were beside the figure to swat away flies, since the *imago* was supposed to stink (ibid., p. 404). While the *ossa* went into the earth, the *imago* went up to the sky, in order to consecrate the emperor as a god, since the Romans did not believe in the immortality of the soul.

Piñera, drawing on this tradition, has Jonatán seem to avoid it by creating a rubber dummy, but in reality he has tried to create a sublime body (one that will not deteriorate or lose value), an *imago,* one that will not be destroyed and "incarnate" the power of the president. But as Dupont reminds us, the *imago* is not a reproduction, an image of the deceased; *it is a part of the body of the deceased.* It stands in a metonymic relation to the emperor, whereas Jonatán has created a replica of the actual, living president. Except that the "living" president has become so "dummified" that his dummy is more real than he is. Jonatán has created a *simulacrum*, or copy, not an *imago*. Only the copy is left since the original has become an effigy. Piñera drives this point home by having the cardinal mention that the Inquisition had pioneered all these techniques. He is referring to the practice of burning heretics in effigy when they could not be apprehended (Hroch and Skybova, 1990, pp. 149–50). In his crucial confrontation with the president, Jonatán makes this process clear to the first executive. He tells him that his case is different from that of a film star because a movie actor allegedly never represents him/herself, but other personae. So, in contracting a dummy, it is always of someone else and not of oneself. Jonatán compares this dummification to icing on a cake. He continues: "You are no longer President of our country, but dummy President of our country. I think the difference is profound, not in degree but in substance. And the consequences: always fatal" (*CT*, p. 100)

Pinera's fascination with doubles was not limited to "The Dummy." It is a central theme in *La carne de René (René's Flesh)*, his vivid and horrifying account of the political body and one of the most unforgettable treatments of desire and power in Latin American literature. In *Un fogonazo* (hereafter *UF*), there is a story titled "El Otro Yo" (The Other Me), written in 1976. A Mr. X, who has just turned fifty, decides to make a replica of himself. Unlike the "The Dummy," the narrative takes place in the future where the technology is available, and X has the financial resources to create another self. No sooner done, they both go out on the street "identical as two drops of water" (Piñera, 1987, p. 57). A rivalry begins between the human X and the mechanical X, since the latter has no signs on his skin of having aged. Mr. X realizes that the mechanical X will outlive him. This point is made in a more uncomfortable manner at a party, when the theme of death arises in conversation. After the hostess, Elena, makes a flippant remark, the mechanical X says: "I feel sorry for him. He doesn't have much time left" (*UF*, p. 60).

Mr. X resolves to destroy the mechanical X. Not with his own hands, but by pulling out the technological plug. When he presents his request to the technologists, they reply as follows: "We never destroy what we create. Our creations are indestructible. You will die; he will remain, and with him, in a certain fashion, you will. When several generations have gone by, no one will remember that he is mechanical, and, therefore, no one will remember you. He will remain in the infinite succession of time, always the same, and always representing you with an overwhelmingly superhuman dignity and beauty" (*UF*, p. 60). Mr. X, furious, feels trapped. He is aware that death awaits him, like all humans, but he is particularly enraged at the fact that he can not inflict death "on the only thing he hated, the mechanical X, the immortal, insufferable, and infallible alter ego" (*UF*, p. 60).

On his deathbed Mr. X tries to convince the mechanical X to switch places long enough so people will think it is the mechanical X who has died (then they will switch back). The mechanical X realizes the futility of this flimsy gesture and tells Mr. X that dying is bad enough; why invite ridicule as well? By then, however, Mr. X has died.

Days later, the mechanical X has an accident in which a radioactive substance stains his skin, so that he now looks like the deceased X. Rumors fly that it was the mechanical X who had died. Although the scientists were chuckling in private, it was public opinion that won out. Piñera then ends the story with: "For the mechanical X, there was no other choice than to admit defeat: it was Mr. X who was immortal in the eyes of all. We could surmise Mr. X's joy in thinking that radioactivity had become his ally" (*UF*, p. 62).

While Mr. X never gives a reason for wanting to construct a double, the progression of the story gives us important clues. In short, there is a desire for immortality (and a fear of aging) reminiscent of Oscar Wilde's *The Picture of Dorian Gray*. Having children is perhaps too indirect a method, and, besides, they too must die. An automaton is, of course, a device that would defy both entropy and decay and death as well. In this sense it embodies the great paradox of all technology: while we constantly build and create things that are faster, stronger, smarter, more efficient, and that make life easier, technology cannot escape that most singular and contingent of events in our lives, death. The scientists in the story do not even want to face the issue of death, insisting that what is created will go on forever. As in "The Dummy," Piñera sees the fragility in technological solutions. Radioactivity has become a source of revenge for Mr. X. He has outwitted death, but like the climbers in "The Fall," the narrator in "The Face," and many other of his characters, it is a pyhrric victory. It is interesting that the victory of immortality in "El Otro Yo" is won through a recognition of a community of people: his friends and neighbors. Similarly, it is the masses in "The Dummy" who do not have dummies made of themselves. Humans are the ones who confer immortality, not technology, nor the imperatives of any kind of system.

When Piñera has the real dummies retire to the toy stores at the end of the story, he seems to be echoing some of the concerns that Heinrich Kleist had in his essay "On the Marionette Theatre" (Kleist, 1989). Marionettes, according to Kleist, have a grace or perfection in their movements because they have only one center of gravity. Symbolically, they represent beings with a purity and innocence that allow them to respond naturally to divine guidance. They are almost weightless and barely touch the floor. Men, however, are rooted in the earth and are clumsy. Their self-consciousness means they are divided souls, that they belong to two worlds, and man's intellectual faculties are incapable of restoring wholeness to the human soul. The only way to achieve that, Kleist suggests, is to pass through the infinite and link up again with the divine: "grace likewise reappears when knowledge has passed through the infinite, so that it appears purest simultaneously in the human body that has either none at all or else inifinite consciousness—that is, in the puppet or in the god" (ibid., p. 420). The children going to the stores to buy toys (i.e., of people who have succumbed to dummification) is both a bit of poetic justice and frightening, signifying an end to innocence. It brings to mind the little girl with the dolls of Nazi leaders who wanders through the set of Hans-Jürgen Syberberg's film *Hitler: A Film from Germany*. In Piñera's universe, the characters are often puppets, but without a center of gravity, without divine guidance. Their passage through infinity is more like a Petrouchka wobbling through the debris and fragments of history.

There is a gender aspect to Piñera's authenticity which will make our view of his treatment of power, truth, ethics, and domination a little more complete. In an autobiographical text, Piñera openly admits his homosexuality: "By the time I had the required age so that thought wasn't merely a translation of spouting nonsense and agitating one's arms, I became aware of three things sufficiently unclean that I would never be able to cleanse myself of ever. I learned that I was poor, a homosexual, and that I liked Art. . . . Of course, I couldn't know at that age what would be the upshot of these three Gorgons: misery, homosexuality, and art, was a frightening nothingness" (Piñera, 1990, pp. 23, 25). Piñera's art was a showdown with these three Gorgons, with his deadpan wit and total dedication to literature. As we shall see, he built his own ethical response to inauthenticity and domination from the depths of these Gorgons.

It might be germane to turn to Jonathan Dollimore's study on homosexuality, which attempts to answer why it is socially marginal but symbolically central in Western culture. The issue of authenticity is paramount for homosexual writers, he says. In that struggle for authenticity (and recognition), he distinguishes between two approaches that writers have taken, which he calls *transgressive aesthetics* and *transgressive ethics*. The former he attributes to Oscar Wilde, the latter to André Gide. Wilde's critique of society is what he calls anti-essentialist in privileging difference, artifice, and insincerity as being more important than essence, authenticity, and depth (Gide). Here is Dollimore's chart (1991, p. 15):

Wilde (transgressive aesthetics)	Gide (transgressive ethics)
surface	depth
lying	truth
change	stasis
difference	essence
persona/role	essential self
abnormal	normal
insincerity	sincerity
style/artifice	authenticity
facetious	serious
narcissism	maturity

Now, Piñera, unlike Wilde or Gide, does not openly address the fact of his homosexuality in his own fiction. He does openly speak of it (but not about himself) in an article on Emilio Ballagas in *Ciclón* (Piñera, 1955a). First, he criticizes those who would avoid the issue of Ballagas's sexuality: "If the French write about Gide taking his homosexuality into account; if the British do the same with Wilde, I don't see why we Cubans can't speak of Ballagas as a homosexual. Or do the French and British have exclusive rights on the subject?" (ibid., p. 42). But then Piñera criticizes those who tried to make Ballagas's homosexuality a rallying banner and who later chastised him for having married and fathered a child. He defends the individuality of the gay writer to interpret his homosexuality as he sees fit. Some will see it as a sport, others as a necessary evil, or as psychological disorder and seek psychiatric help. (Ballagas, according to Piñera, likened it to original sin.)

With Piñera, it will not be a case of finding veiled references to his homosexuality in his fiction, as if his work were merely a sexual *roman à clef*, but more of understanding the homosexual as an outlaw in the area of gender as someone who has the creative freedom to question more radically what it means to be a man. This questioning takes place within strategies of domination and submission; and the homosexual writer puts into place a "transgressive reinscription" (Dollimore) that contests these mechanisms of domination, exclusion, discrimination. Piñera's ethical stance has the transgressive features that characterized both Gide and Wilde, although his humor, his probing of personas, his embracing of the abnormal would seem to put him closer to Wilde. A pair of quotations from each author helps underline these similarities. Compare Wilde's "What was paradox to me in the sphere of thought, perversity became to me in the sphere of passion" to Jonatán's comment in "The Dummy": "I confess that the slightest abnormality excites me so much." Piñera, like both Gide and Wilde, was made more aware of different kinds of oppression (class, race, gender) by his specific oppression as a homosexual in Cuba. Through his writing, he will turn that oppression around by offering "perverse" solutions.

These solutions are part of what I have referred to elsewhere as an "ethics of redemptive failure" (West, 1994). In understanding Piñera's ethics of redemptive failure, like Levinas, we start from the vulnerability of the body: its hunger, pain, fears. The body as biological entity can become the symptom of power relationships; the docile body wanted for social control becomes a springboard for the imagination (doubles, becoming-animal); the social roles within the family become inverted, questioning ethics at large, or the social body. Or the body as psychosexual construct becomes an arena of transgression and sacrifice. These constant transformations, overlappings, disruptions are where Piñera puts into relief the Hegelian blind spot of ultimate mastery, of wanting to incorporate into the movement of the Spirit every manifestation of negativity. But even this mastery is contaminated by slave logic and is ultimately a failure. Piñera's redemptive failure (in rejecting the failure of lordship-type mastery) is his willingness for sacrifice, his daring in going to the extreme, touching the limits of sovereignty, where he can exercise his *dominio propio*, his authenticity.

But authenticity and *dominio propio* have a price. Listen to the words of André Gide: "The borrowed truths are the ones to which one clings most, and all the more so since they remain foreign to our intimate self. It takes much more precaution to deliver one's own message, much more boldness and prudence, than to sign up with and add one's voice to an already existing party" (Gide in Dollimore, 1991, p. 39). Being a homosexual structures your identity so that it wages a constant battle against exclusion, silence, or outright hostility. In his book, Dollimore traces the long history of Christian theology that associates homosexuality with perversion, and perversion with error. And error, of course, is a type of failure. Again, from the depths of "failure," Piñera is fierce in showing that gender and desire are socially constructed. This implies, though, that they can be changed, and it is from this authenticity of sexual difference that Piñera's ethics, starting from the body, go to the social and come back to the body. It is not a matter of making the body a symbol, a privileged signifier, or the site of origin. But by recognizing its vulnerability, the fact that it can be constructed, its role in the definition of self, and the body's stubborn historicity, Piñera's critique takes on a positive role.

Piñera's ethics of redemptive failure is a piercing and disturbing meditation on domination, power, sexuality, and gender. Anguishing and bereft of comfort as his universe may be, it does not lapse into a facile despair. Beneath the calamity, Piñera resounds with a "No!" like his characters, which is not mere negativity or denial: in a world so thoroughly marked by coldness, lunacy, and perfidy, it becomes a stark affirmation of dignity and sanity.

In works like "The Dummy," *The Serfs*, or *René's Flesh*, the author deflates the egocrats and lofty pretenses of those who proclaim freedom while enslaving millions. Cuban political discourse and its utopian impulses have often slipped into hyperbole and grandiosity, offering fertile ground for megalomaniacs. Piñera, from within the "empire of the gaze," the realm of power, be it social and/or familial, questions all the patterns of power we take for granted: parents over children, state or ruler over the nation/people, men over women, heterosexuality over homosexuality, commerce over art, obedience over rebellion, God over man. In a world still fascinated by the erotics of power and domination, Virgilio Piñera reminds us that it is from the body that the ethical is possible, even though it must be sought and made to flourish in a landscape of specters and disaster.

FOUR

Dulce María Loynaz: Cuba's Living History

Dulce María Loynaz has been called "la grande dame" of Cuban letters. It is a label that conjures up someone sipping tea in a palatial residence, surrounded by statues of nymphs and big mahogany furniture. To a degree, that image is accurate, but it does not tell the whole story. Born in 1902, Loynaz's life and literary career span almost the entire twentieth century: her work is one of quiet but enduring revelations, written in a finely chiseled, transparent poetry or prose. Loynaz comes from the Independence aristocracy: her great uncle was Ignacio Agramonte (1842–73), her father was Enrique Loynaz y Castillo (1871–1963), who fought in the Spanish-Cuban-American War (1895–98) and was made a general. His comrades in arms included Antonio Maceo, José Martí and Máximo Gómez, three national heroes.

Loynaz's upbringing was unusual. She did not receive formal educational training until she went to law school; she passed the bar exam in 1927. She and her brothers and sisters were tutored in a variety of subjects, and her mother, María de las Mercedes Muñoz Sañudo, was a solid pianist and singer who taught them much about music. The exposure to an artistic upbringing was significant not only for Dulce María, but also for her brother Enrique, a notable poet, her sister Flor, a poet and visual artist, and her other brother, Carlos Manuel, also a poet. Enrique Loynaz did publish work during his lifetime; Flor and Carlos Manuel's verses remain unpublished to date.

Despite her admirable prose production, Loynaz is known as a poet. Her literary career began early: at the age of ten she published a poem in the newspaper *La Nación*. She later wrote journalistic pieces for the same publication. Her first book of poems, *Versos, 1920–1938*, was published in Havana in 1938. It was followed by *Juegos de agua* (1947; Play of Water), *Poemas sin nombre* (1953; Poems with No Name), *Carta de amor al Rey Tut-Ank-Amen* (1953; Love Letter to King Tutankhamen), and *Ultimos días de una casa* (1958; Last Days of a House). *Obra lírica*, which contains her collected poetry up to the mid-1950s, was published in 1955. All of these books of poems were published in Spain. In 1984, *Poesías escogidas* (Selected Poetry) was published in Cuba, as was *Poemas naúfragos* (1991; Shipwrecked Poems) and *Bestiarium* (1991; Bestiary). The latter two books contain mostly poetry not included in other books or older works. *Bestiarium*, for example, was written in the early 1920s. Finally, in 1993, *Poesías completas* (Complete Poetry), her entire poetic oeuvre, was published in Cuba.

Loynaz's prose consists of three books: *Jardín* (1951), called by the author a lyrical novel; *Un verano en Tenerife* (1958; A Summer in Tenerife), a travel book written about her long visits to the Canary Islands; and *Ensayos literarios* (1993; Literary Essays), a collection of essays and talks. Among the literary topics covered in this book are the poetry of Julián del Casal; the Cuban influences in Latin American *modernismo*, Félix Varela, García Lorca, Gabriela Mistral, Delmira Agustini; and the work of her brother, poet Enrique Loynaz. It also contains an important essay called "Mi poesía: autocrítica" (My Poetry: A Self-Critical Appraisal), from 1950, which is an excellent overview of her artistic views, a definition of her poetics.

The Loynaz home was a true cultural hub, and many distinguished foreign writers including Federico García Lorca, Juan Ramón Jiménez, and Gabriela Mistral would stay at their home when visiting Cuba. Despite this, Loynaz is a loner, and her work does not fall into a school or a movement. In an interview she said that for a writer there's "nothing more dangerous than to establish a school." Clearly, there are influences she readily admits to: Tagore (in her early verses), St. John of the Cross, St. Augustine, Martí, Quevedo, Azorín, the French Symbolists and Parnassians, and Gabriela Mistral. Cuban writers that have shaped her work are Zenea, Avellaneda, Martí, and Julián del Casal, whom she read at the age of nine. I would add four Spanish poets: Antonio Machado, Juan Ramón Jiménez, and, to a lesser extent, Jorge Guillén and Miguel de Unamuno. Though she shared the *Orígenes* group's Catholicism, her poetry was published in their magazine only once (no. 33, 1953).

Over the years she has slowly been recognized, beginning with the Orden Carlos Manuel de Céspedes (1947, Cuba) and the Orden Alfonso X El Sabio (1947, Spain) to the more recent National Prize in Literature (1987), the Orden Félix Varela (1987), and the Alejo Carpentier Medal in 1983. But it was the Cervantes Prize in 1992, the most prestigious in the Spanish-speaking literary world, that brought her international renown and has led to re-editions of her poetry and prose, as well as considerably more critical attention.

In 1959 she became more of a loner, withdrawing from all literary life, and stopped writing poetry. She continued to give talks, write essays, and journalistic pieces, however. The Royal Academy of the Spanish Language, Cuban Affiliate, meets at her house and she is the president. The changes brought about by the Cuban Revolution signified an end to the world she grew up in and wrote about. She remained at the margin of political debates in Cuba and was basically ignored for two decades. In the 1980s, as the Cuban literary climate opened up and began to respond to less ideologically charged criteria, her work began to be revalued and appreciated. Then came awards, editions of her work, more attention, and finally the Cervantes Prize. She has won practically every major literary and cultural award given by the Cuban state and yet remains aloof from "the revolutionary project," as Cubans call it. Loynaz has received her due recognition without having to make a Faustian deal with the state and its cultural institutions. Without making a fuss, in a quiet, but grittily determined way, she has carved out her own independent space. Despite her lofty social background, she is, by virtue of her family, a living part of Cuban history and its family of rebels. Because of this she is virtually untouchable. When queried about why she bothered to remain in Cuba, when the revolution meant the destruction of her life as she knew it, Loynaz replied: "The daughter of an Independence War general does not abandon her country." Her presence—exacting, honest, delicately lyrical, fiercely personal and visionary— has been an important contribution to Cuban culture.

That Dulce María Loynaz was awarded the Cervantes Prize in 1992 surprised many. Thankfully, it gave the Spanish-speaking world (one hopes that translations will follow) an opportunity to rediscover an underappreciated, rare talent. Eugenio Montale's Nobel Prize of 1975 falls into a similar category. Loynaz is an institution in Cuba, in part due to her longevity (she recently died at age 94), but also because her work has a quality that has stood the test of time. The work's deceptive simplicity has a beguiling effect on the reader. You need to reread her constantly and go past what seems like plain literal-mindedness, a trait she also shares with Montale. In a literary world obsessed with writing and publishing as much as you can, where the sheer output seems to be the barometer, replacing talent and depth, Dulce María Loynaz is a refreshing change of pace. In a writing career that spans eight decades, her complete oeuvre consists of one novel, one "travel" book, a collection of essays, and several books of poetry that fit into one not very large volume. With considerable concentration and energy, her work could be read in a week, which does not mean that it should, because going hastily through her exquisitely crafted poetry will not yield its truest pleasures.

Loynaz began writing poetry early, as is evident from the title of her first book, *Versos, 1920–1938*, which brings together about ninety poems written over almost two decades. Not all of them have the same brilliance and depth as "Eternidad" (Eternity), "La mujer de humo" (The Woman of Smoke), "Certeza" (Certainty), or "Tiempo" (Time); but even the early poems show a remarkable maturity in handling image, sound, and feeling. *Versos* already contains the constants of her later work: the nature of love, the love of nature, solitude, and a religious consciousness that at times borders on the mystical, but is equally indebted to Unamuno and Kierkegaard.

Loynaz admirably captures the age-old tussle in philosophy between worldly and otherworldly thinkers. The latter—from Plato to St. Augustine, from Plotinus to Pascal—have made the familiar argument that the chaos and flux of the world, the endless and infinite parade of sensations and passions, will not allow us to see the good and the true to attain lasting knowledge. At the same time Loynaz seems to latch onto any number of things—a shell, a look, a flower, the sea—and find in their contours, radiance, color and shape, an eternity of feelings and insight.

One of her early poems, "Eternidad" ("Eternity"), deals precisely with the issue of the eternal as opposed to earthbound finitude.

> In my garden roses unfold
> but I will give you none:
> no roses, for tomorrow . . .
> tomorrow they will be gone.

In my garden there are birds
singing crystal lays.
I will not give them to you,
they have wings to fly away.

In my garden labor bees
in their fine beehive.
the sweetness of a moment . . .
to you I will not give!

For you, the infinite
or nothing; the immortal
or this mute sadness that
you will never understand. . . .
This sadness without name
of having naught to give
to one who wears upon the brow
signs of eternity . . .

Leave, then, leave my garden . . .
Do not touch the rose:
the things that are to die
should not be touched by you.
(Trans. David Frye)

Loynaz touches on many key topics of literature that stretch back to the
Middle Ages and beyond. But principally she deals with the impermanence
of the physical world, a familiar theme in medieval and especially baroque
literature. At first, it is not clear to whom the poetic voice is addressing itself,
all the more intriguing in that the first three stanzas are punctuated by three
negations: the "I will not gives" (roses, birds, bees). In the fourth stanza,
with the use of words like "infinite" and "immortal," it becomes a little
clearer, and in the next (fifth) stanza, the poet establishes unequivocally that
the "dialogue" is with God. Though Loynaz treats the deity with respect, it
is not mere servitude; her resolute tone establishes her own moral autonomy. In fact, she issues a warning: if s/he touches things in the garden,
somehow God will be tainted by the temporal and disastrously fall under
the corrupting influences of the mortal and the finite.

Slyly, Loynaz is reworking the Edenic myth of the fall, which she but-
tresses with many images of Christian iconography: the rose, the garden, the
bee, and the bird. The rose, of course, is a highly charged and rich symbol in
our culture, being at the same time something that represents heavenly
perfection and earthly passion. In Loynaz's poem the roses unfold as mystery, beauty, and grace, but are equally tinged with a short-lived voluptuous-
ness and sensuality. The rose is associated with fertility, beauty, and creation
as well as virginity. White roses, which evoke innocence and purity, are
linked to the Virgin Mary. Their thorns signify pain, blood, and martyrdom.

The bird and its lovely song is equally steeped in Christian mythology, referring to transcendence, the soul, the spirit, the ability to soar into the heavens, and the imagination. Loynaz does not specify what kind of birds are in her garden. Interestingly, though, she uses their flight to connote transience and impermanence, as well as their traditional meaning (soul, spirit). Their song is part of all the delights of the senses that the poet enumerates in the poem: sight (rose, birds), smell (rose), touch or taste (bees), and sound (the birds).

The bees are also highly charged with meaning in Christian theology and art: they are immortality, rebirth, purity, industriousness, and order. Messengers to the world of the spirits, their honey is an offering to the gods. Bees are equated with Christian vigilance and zeal since it is believed they never sleep. Like birds they can symbolize the soul entering heaven as they fly. Again Loynaz stresses their temporal dimension: "the sweetness of the moment."

One of the most oft-repeated words in the poem is *garden*. In both Western and Eastern traditions the garden has been linked with Paradise, the Garden of Eden being a prime example. Enclosed gardens have long been the symbol of the Virgin Mary (feminine protective principle and virginity). More important, the garden is also the symbol of the soul, where nature, tamed and ordered, is analogous to the spirit or the soul bringing passions and chaotic emotions under control. Gardens are a refuge from the world, both in terms of a spiritual haven and, conversely, as sources of delight and pleasure. Let us not forget the *Roman de la rose*, which is a vast eulogy of these pleasures of feasting, love, and communal bathing, using the garden as focal point.

Loynaz, however, takes the Garden of Eden story and, instead of the downfall of man and woman, fashions it into a kind of warning to God. The Garden of Delights is so seductive that even God, despite his (her) omnipotence, can fall prey to its enchantments. God's corruption would be to become finite and mortal, to submit to the ravages of time. This passage of time will cause much anguish and be the subject of many of her poems. Here it is cause for sadness, and one cannot help but think of the Renaissance and baroque fascination with melancholy, which Loynaz's early verses seem to share.

In a poem such as "Eternity," Loynaz's use of the garden synthesizes certain concerns, expressed in a religious language that is rooted in Christian traditions. The garden will reappear in other poems and later become the subject and title of her only novel, *Jardín* (Garden), which will be discussed further on in terms of her idea of nationhood and which will provide the opportunity to discuss issues of race, gender, and class. But it also lets us see how Loynaz constructs her own authorial voice, its dialogical structure, that often shares similarities with mystic writers such as St. Teresa and St. John of the Cross. Despite those affinities, Loynaz's poetry is not mystical in the sense that it is exclusively concerned with the ineffable union with a transcendent being or deity. In fact, she draws on the mystical tradition, but often within the context of earthly love and sensuality, bringing out the tensions that mystical poetry insinuates.

This should not be surprising since mystical literature borrowed heavily from traditions of courtly love and chivalry (de Rougemont, 1983). This mystical exaltation of love derives from two major sources: (1) eros and *agape*, and (2) the two different strands in mysticism: unitive and autonomous or "bridal." We understand eros as a kind of infinite desire, a divine delirium, which not only encompasses the corporeal, but also a greater striving, a transcendence into heavenly bliss. Plato described this yearning as a kind of enthusiasm (which literally means to be possessed by a deity). This divine indwelling, which leads to the light and union with the divine, means being free of the body. Platonism's dark view of the body (tomb of the soul) comes from Gnostic, Orphic, and Zoroastrian sources, a perspective that will be further developed and refined by Christian thought. Loynaz's early poetry clearly draws on Platonic precedents, but encompasses the multiple dimensions involved: eros as sexual passion, friendship, filial duty, love of beauty, and love of wisdom. Loynaz is drawn to that more mystical eros in a poem called "Siempre, amor" (Always, Love).

> Always, love . . . beyond all flight,
> all bile, all thought;
> beyond men
> distance and time.
> Always, love:
> At the hour in which the body
> frees itself from its shadow . . . And at the hour
> in which the shadow goes imbibing the body . . .
> Always, love . . . (And these two words shipwrecked
> between soul and flesh hammered against the wind!)
>
> (Trans. Alan West)

The poem plays on several ambiguities, one being the "Siempre, amor" of the title, which is repeated four times during the poem. On the one hand, the author might be addressing a specific lover or loved one, although "mi amor" would be more accurate in that context (hence the ambiguity). The other possibility is that Loynaz is talking to love (eros) itself, somewhat echoing the Tristan and Iseult myth of being in love with love. The *siempre* (always) can also mean forever, a kind of eternity which much of the imagery of the poem undercuts with images of putrefaction, death, and temporality. But the love being addressed is one that transcends this finiteness, the eros of divine love and wisdom. And maybe Loynaz's use of shadows is an indirect reference to Gabriela Mistral's "Decalogue of the Artist." Number 1 says "You shall love beauty, which is the shadow of God over the universe" (Mistral, 1971, p. 37).

Loynaz is equally indebted to the notion of *agape,* or Christian love, as originally expressed in the Ten Commandments. *Agape* is concerned with neighborliness, with the ethical dilemmas posed by others. Despite its association with divine matters, it is concerned with this world. It shows a reverence and loyalty to other humans for being who and what they are. Poems like "Profesión de fe," "Amor es . . . ," and "El amor de la leprosa" show this ethical love of *agape.* Here again, Mistral's number 7 from her decalogue synthesizes this type of love and how it relates to art: "The beauty you create shall be known as compassion and shall console the hearts of men" (Mistral, 1971, p. 37).

Both eros and *agape* have a place within mystical thought. Denis de Rougemont sees two main currents within mysticism: one he calls the unitive, "which aims at a complete *fusion* of the soul with the divine. The second stream may be called *epithalamian mysticism,* which aims at the *marriage* of a soul to God, and which therefore implicitly maintains an essential distinction between creature and Creator" (de Rougemont, 1983, p. 153). I prefer the term *autonomous* or *bridal* for the second current. Loynaz uses both currents to express the sometimes violent movements of her soul. Unitive mysticism builds on passion, a "sweet cauterizing" that sears the desiring subject. De Rougemont says that unitive mysticism, which entertains the possibility of divine love (the felicitous union between God and soul) implies that human love, being a pale reflection of its divine counterpart, will lead to unhappiness. Conversely, bridal mysticism assumes a divine unhappiness—because the fusion is not possible or complete—but a certain happiness within the limits of human love. Loynaz's poetry dwells considerably on states of unhappiness, and words like *sadness* recur in her poetic imagery.

Juegos de agua (1947) could be translated literally as "Water Play," but I prefer "Play of Water" for two reasons. First, it captures the spirit of the playfulness as something spontaneous, not controllable or given to chance. But more important is the meaning of action, motion causing an effect, as in the play of light on water. This second definition evokes texture and nuance, and Loynaz's play of water seems to be written on (or in) water as well. She divides the book into three main categories: "Agua de mar" (Sea Water), "Agua de río" (River Water), and "Agua perdida" (Lost Water).

Once again Loynaz takes on images with powerful universal meanings. She draws on most of them: water as the source of existence, fertility, as liquid light, as renewal (baptism), flux of the world, and of time. She also draws on the darker, more somber aspect of water, as in the poem "Isla" (Island).

> Surrounded by sea everywhere,
> I'm an island rooted to the stalk of the winds . . .
> No one listens to my voice if I pray or scream:
> I could fly or sink . . . I could, at times,
> bite my own tail as a sign of the Infinite.
> I'm earth sundered in pieces . . . There are moments

in which the water blinds me, makes me cowardly,
in which water is death where I float . . .
But open to the tides and cyclones
I weld into the sea a root of shattered breast.

I grow from the sea and from it die . . . I rise up
to entwine myself in knots unbound . . . !
I'm devoured by a sea beaten by archangels's
wings without heaven, shipwrecked!
(Trans. Alan West)

There is a kind of Promethean battle going on here, often repeated in her verses, echoed in many poems where she struggles with the unhappiness of love, the devastations of solitude, the anguish of yearning for eternity and unperishable beauty in a world that decays. In one of her early poems, "Geography," she says, "An island is / an absence of water surrounded /by water: An absence of /love surrounded by /love." In "Island," she builds on that earlier poem, making the absence total. Love, however, seems to have disappeared from this poem, except in the diminished form of shipwrecked angels without sky or heaven. *Cielo* in Spanish has the double meaning of sky and heaven. Loynaz, in this poem and throughout the book, will fashion her own geography, her own sea, her own cosmology in her play of water.

In the second section, "River Water," Loynaz compares herself to the river in a short poem which is closer to an autobiographical aphorism. The entire poem reads as follows: "I will be like the river, plunging headlong, and crashing, and leaping and writhing (contorting) . . . But it gets to the sea!" Here and in other poems of this section one can detect echoes of José Martí's *Versos sencillos*, where he speaks of brooks, streams, and rivers in the mountains. In another poem, "Embrace," the river becomes a lover, but Loynaz's erotic imagery is again tinged with a kind of Wagnerian gloom.

Today I've felt the
whole river in my arms . . . I've felt it
in my arms, trembling and alive
like the body of a green man . . .

This morning the river has been
mine: I lifted it out of its ancient
river bed . . . And I took it to heart!
The river weighed greatly . . . The river,
pained, palpitated from being
wrenched apart . . .—Cold fever
of the water . . . : It left a bitter taste
in my mouth, of love and death . . .
(Trans. Alan West in Agosín, 1994, p. 43)

Given its length, perhaps its liquid dolefulness should be likened to a Schubert *lieder*, but what is striking about the poem is the startling image of her lifting a river out of its river bed, wrenching it from its "body." And in the imagery of the poem there is an undercurrent of possessiveness made all the more futile by its own strength, since that strength proves to be destructive.

Even when describing a more tranquil scene, Loynaz seems to be observing a lurking threat. "El remanso" (The Calm/Pool) starts off in a kind of peaceful and pastoral mode, with water imagery providing a soothing repose.

> The tired river took shelter in the shade
> of sweet trees, of the serene
> trees that do not need to run . . .
> And it stayed there in a bend.
>
> The calm, already there. A bit of root
> ties it to the shore of its soul:
> As it reflects light and shadows
> it sleeps, having a dream without distances . . .
>
> It's noon: A dove drifts
> by the blue sky . . .
> The river is so still
> that the hawk, hidden in the branches
> momentarily doesn't know
> where it will sink its claw:
> into the fine bird of the air
> or into the bird, finer still, of the water . . .
> (Trans. Alan West in Agosín, 1994, p. 44)

Loynaz uses the stillness of water as a mirror, emphatically shown by the hawk's confusion. Her references to light and shadows and the soul, as well as the illusory aspect of a reflection, almost read like a reworking of the Platonic myth of the cave; the hawk's preying instinct, if we want to take our allegorical pitch further up the scale, could be interpreted as an image of desire.

The water images are multiple: at the beginning of the poem the river is tired and looks for shade under the trees. It is a simple but effective image: the river has been working too hard, with a barely concealed reference to time. Then the river becomes quiet, an invitation to meditation in the newly found silence, since its music has been temporarily stopped. And finally, as mentioned before, there is the image of the river as mirror. In a mere sixteen verses, Loynaz has taken a seemingly innocuous midday scene where water comes to a rest, with a hawk in the trees, and has turned it into a moving, meditative piece that reflects on time, nature, and desire.

In "Almendares" her tone turns a little more elegiac. It is graceful, full of musical allusions, and sensual. She describes the river's color as "pallid and dark /—Color of tropical women." She compares it to the Amazon and the Nile, and while it has neither the horizons of the former, nor the mysteries of the latter, its beauty still compares favorably to both. The poem ends with "I wouldn't say it's the most beautiful river . . . But it is my river, my country, my blood!" Consistent with the general theme of her book, Loynaz seems to evoke pre-Columbian as well as Egyptian-Babylonian river cultures of the past. The latter apparently influenced Thales of Miletus's thinking: water as *arche*, as primary substance, which Loynaz, in her book, echoes through her use of aquatic imagery. Water as primary, universal substance is overlaid by Loynaz's pantheism, which here takes on a patriotic flavor, but it is an intimate patriotism, far from the bristling of swords and shouts on the battlefield.

More typical of the book are some of her shorter poems, such as "La fuga inútil" (Futile Flight), "El espejo" (The Mirror), "La nieve" (Snow), and "La nube" (The Cloud). Three of them are so short they can be quoted in their entirety.

Futile Flight, Futile Fugue

The water of the river goes fleeing from itself:
it is afraid of its eternity.

Snow

Snow is water
tired of running . . .
Snow is water
detained an instant—water at a point
Water emptied of time and distance.

The Cloud

Cloud, journey of water through the sky
Cloud, cradle for child-water,
rocking itself in the air pierced
by birds . . .
Cloud, heavenly infancy of rain.
(Trans. Alan West in Agosín, 1994, pp. 46–47)

Loynaz is without a doubt a poet who can take the infinite textures of nature—in this case water in its different incarnations—and make them into insightful meditations on time, creation, and memory. In "Futile Flight, Futile Fugue," the title in Spanish is "La Fuga inútil." *Fuga* means to flee, but it is also the word for the musical term *fugue*. In that play of meanings, echoing the play of water of the whole book, Loynaz has set up her own counterpoint: movement (time, melody) versus eternity (stasis, silence). The fugue not only answers (echoing the subject in a different key) but also presents countersubjects that comment on or contest the original "melody."

This is achieved with a kind of reverence which Mistral's decalogue, number 10, registers pointedly: "Each act of creation shall leave you humble, for it is never as great as your dream and always inferior to that most marvelous dream of God which is Nature" (Mistral, 1971, p. 37). Each one of these brief poems is not only a "marvelous dream" but a self-appraisal (of the poet) in the act of creation.

Loynaz's next book, *Poemas sin nombre* (1953), is quite different from *Juegos de agua* (1947). The language is rendered in a poetic prose, often a sentence long. The poems, 124 in all, are numbered with roman numerals. Their aphoristic and sometimes philosophical nature remind one of Tagore's *Lover's Gift*, *Crossing*, and *Stray Birds*, but the voice is unmistakably that of Loynaz. The poems have a more desolate feeling than her previous work, as, for example, poem XIII: "You have wings and I don't: with your butterfly wings you play in the air, while I learn the sadness of all the roads of the earth." There are moments of great loneliness, but somehow Loynaz's solitude seems a haven, perhaps even the sacred space where she can create. (Emerson considered solitude a stern friend, a place where inspiration could thrive.) Still, poem VII seems unsettling: "Many things were given to me in this world: only pure solitude is entirely mine." A few pages later, in poem XXX, we read the following: "Solitude, solitude, so sought after, dreamed of . . . I love you so much, that I'm sometimes afraid that God will punish me some day by filling my life with you." If loneliness can be interpreted as a homesickness for God, then poem XXX expresses the fear of a really cruel God. Poem XCVI might give us a better clue to understanding her solitude. In it she says: "I won't exchange my solitude for a little bit of love. For a lot of love, yes. But a great deal of love is also solitude . . . Let it be spoken by the olive trees of Gethsemane!!" Given Loynaz's Franciscan spirit, however, maybe her solitude is closer to Nietzsche when he said, "[Solitude] makes us tougher toward ourselves and tender toward others: in both ways it improves our character."

Three poems deal directly with poetry, all within the last fifteen of the collection. In poem CXI, she speaks about distilling her poetic voice, reducing it to the essentials. But maybe she went too far: "I've been stripping the bark of my poetry so much, that I got to the seed without savoring the pulp." This harks back to a talk she gave three years before, in 1950, called "My Poetry: A Self-Critical Appraisal," in which she argues for a poetry that should not be too adorned, too obscure: on the contrary, it must be direct, precise, agile. Loynaz is not arguing for a simplistic type of verse or one stripped of ambiguity, neither of which are evident in her own work. She adds two other important points about how she conceives her poetics: one, poetry is a kind of movement, a passage from one reality to another. It is not a goal, which is always unknown, but the arrow spiraling from the visible to the invisible, from the world around us to that which transcends our normal senses. The second is poetry's need for a vertical expansion, as if it were a tree: "Poetry must equally have an instinct for heights. . . . Having its roots in the soil doesn't impede a tree's growth; on the contrary, it nourishes that effort, it sustains it in its impulse, it creates the base for projecting upwards. Poetry, like trees, is born from the earth, and draws sustenance from the earth, but once born, it doesn't seem appropriate that it go about like pigs, plunged in mud" (Loynaz, 1993, p. 139). From there she goes on to speak of the poetry tree growing upwards as requiring a clear, direct expression and language.

From the above it should be clear that Loynaz is not calling for a "pure poetry" or an "ivory tower" approach to art, even though the nature of her poetic language seems close to that of "pure poetry." Her directness, intimate tone, and use of everyday words indicate that she is far from obscure. Her poetic universe speaks of love, solitude, and nature with a disarming simplicity. But this simplicity is not to be confused with simple-mindedness, bucolic affectation, or sentimentality.

In poem CXXI, Loynaz's definition of poetry is more unruly than usual. In a frank, hungering voice she says: "Poetry, divine and savage beast . . . When will I be able to mark your flanks with my branding iron!" It is difficult to reconcile this image with the previously mentioned tree image going upwards into the sublime. Maybe nourishing the verticality of the tree implies the "taming of the beast," be it horse, pig, or whatever. It is consistent with what Loynaz says about poetry being "that passage toward an unknown goal." The divinity and savagery she mentions is to a certain extent beyond human control, and her poetry has exemplified the not always gentle wrestling with subhuman and suprahuman forces.

All of these forces are evoked in the last poem, CXXIV, one of the most heartfelt homages to the island of Cuba ever written. It is a paradisical poem from beginning to end. It extols the ocean, the birds, all of the natural wonders of the island, in a language that borders on the rapturous and mystical. Were it not for the fact that the poem was written by an accomplished poet, skilled in handling metaphor and image, it would almost be an embarrassment. It borders dangerously on the sentimental, but it bears mentioning because the utopian dimension of the island has been a recurrent topic in Cuban literature, expressed in varying voices by the likes of José Martí, Heredia, Guillén, and Lezama Lima, and as a counterutopia or dystopia by Virgilio Piñera and Reinaldo Arenas. Interestingly, though, this idyllic ending of *Poemas sin nombre* will be followed by a much more somber portrait in *Ultimos días de una casa* (1958; Last Days of a House).

The entire book is just one poem, her longest, some 521 verses long, and was originally published as a thirty-one–page volume in Madrid, including a preface by Antonio Oliver Belmás. In this last book of poems, published months before the triumph of the Cuban Revolution (1959), Loynaz takes stock of her life. It is a harsh poem with an ominous beginning: "I don't know why it formed—it's been days now—/this strange silence: / a silence without profile, without thorns, / penetrating me like muted water. / Like a tide up in the air by the moon / the silence covers me slowly." Some critics and commentators see *Ultimos días de una casa* as a prophetic work that was able to foresee how Loynaz's genteel world was going to be shattered by a violent revolution. She has not written another book of poems since 1958, although previously unpublished work has come out in book form in 1990 and 1991. And, of course, she has continued to write and publish essays and journalistic work—but no poetry. She claimed that she was too old to keep writing the kind of poetry she had been creating all her life and that the total change that took over Cuba would make her work seem dated. No doubt her poetic sensibility was not the stuff for guerrilla poetry and Marxist-Leninist aestheticians, so she quietly shut the doors of her house and kept working and living quietly.

Ultimos días de una casa begins with that "strange silence" already mentioned. Why strange? Several stanzas later the author gives us a partial answer. She compares the current silence to that of the past: "But the silence was different then: / it was silence with a human flavor." Somehow the silence that engulfs her is impersonal and is tied to the loss of her house. The author undoubtedly sees the forces of history in the widest sense of the word: mechanization of work, a massification of architectural structures, and a bureaucratization of social life. (Perhaps this explains the image she uses later in the poem, saying that "life is a treadmill of illusions.") This lack of union between the house and the person who lives in it is likened to a kind of death, both of the house and of its inhabitants. For Loynaz the house is her *axis mundi*, a sacred space, if you will. A house is imbued with a cosmological purpose. Mircea Eliade has written convincingly about this: "Habitations are not lightly changed, for it is not easy to abandon one's world. The house is not an object, a 'machine to live in'; *it is the universe that man constructs for himself by imitating the paradigmatic creation of the gods, the cosmogony*. Every construction and every inauguration of a new building are in some measure equivalent to a new beginning, a new life" (Eliade, 1976, p. 27).

In this poem Loynaz describes the details of that small cosmogony: the furniture, the light and shadow in the different rooms, the people who lived in it. She even compares the imprints and marks left by pieces of furniture to wounds on a body. Even before this description she has already equated herself with the house: "soy ya una casa vieja" "(I am already an old house"). Later she will say, "I feel myself already a sick house / a leprous house." The decaying metaphors are barely held back by reminiscences of a *Nochebuena* (Christmas Eve) when she was eight years old.

Bachelard has spoken of the importance houses have in terms of memory: "We comfort ourselves by reliving memories of protection. Something closed must retain our memories, while leaving them their original value as images. Memories of the outside world will never have the same tonality as those of home and, by recalling these memories, we add to our store of dreams; we are never real historians, but always near poets, and our emotion is perhaps nothing but an expression of poetry that was lost" (Bachelard, 1970, p. 6). Loynaz's poem is indeed the kind of memory that has the "protective tonality" of which Bachelard speaks, but not enough to shelter her from the hard reality of her dispossession: "Life is always / a door stubbornly closed / in the face of our anguish."

In speaking of the anchoring nature of the house, Bachelard says that it also serves or protects the daydreamer, that it allows the dreamer "to dream in peace." The structure of Loynaz's poem is like a daydream: it focuses on some detail, then drifts away, latching onto something else, and so on. Suddenly the author gains "consciousness" again and begins another memory, exploring another corner of the house. "Memories of dreams, however, which only poetic meditation can help us recapture, are more confused, less clearly drawn. The great function of poetry is to give us back the situations of our dreams. The house we were born in is more than the embodiment of a home, it is also an embodiment of dreams. Each one of its nooks and corners was a resting place for daydreaming. And often this resting place particularized the daydream. Our habits of a particular daydream were acquired there" (Bachelard, 1970, p. 15). As the poem progresses the reveries keep coming up against the dark foreboding and silence that began the poem. Toward the end, it almost seems as if the whole poem has been a dream. This theme of being asleep and waking up from dreaming is not unusual in Loynaz's work. In *Jardín*, her only published novel, the protagonist, Bárbara, is compared to Sleeping Beauty, and the author also borrows from Calderón's *La vida es sueño* (Life Is a Dream). Here is the final part of Loynaz's "Last Days of a House":

> I have slept and I awaken . . . Or I haven't awakened
> and it's still the lacerating dream,
> the shoreless anguish and death in pieces.
>
> I have slept and I woke up inside out,
> on the other side of the nightmare,
> where the nightmare is unmoveable,
> unyielding reality.
>
> I have slept and I awaken. Who awakens?
> I feel severed from myself,
> sucked in by a
> monstrous concave mirror.
> I feel without feeling and knowing myself,
> scattered entrails, unhinged skeleton,
> and the other dream I was dreaming, thrashed.
> Something swarms over me,

something hurts terribly
and I don't know where.
What buzzards bite into my head?
From what beast is the fang that tears my flesh?
What moonfish buries into my side?

Now I swallow the truth whole!
It is men, men who
harm me with their weapons.
men I mothered
without birthing, wife without
fulfillment of the flesh, sister without brothers,
daughter without rebelliousness.
It is the men and only them,
made of better clay than mine,
whose greed was greater
than the need to hold on to me.

I was sold at last,
because I became so worthy in their accounts,
that I was of no worth for their tenderness.
And if for tenderness I'm unworthy, then I'm worth nothing . . .
And it's time to die.
(Trans. Alan West in Agosín, 1994, pp. 42–43)

The ending of this extraordinary poem is replete with images of persecution and alienation. Some of them border on the gothic, with a vampiristic touch: "sucked in by a monstrous concave mirror," buzzards biting away, fangs tearing flesh. This devouring is counteracted by another ingesting image: "Now I swallow the truth whole!" But all these images are consistent with the equation established between herself and the house. She gives it a narrative boosting when she says: "what I am telling is not a story; /it is an upright history, /which is my history /it is an honest life that I've lived, / a certain style the world is losing." The poet directly takes on history with a capital "H" and her own history, which is, of course, part of Cuban history. Another kind of history, perhaps, but still important, the kind that never makes it into the history books. If she were writing in English, she would probably say it is "her/story," which actually plays on the meaning in Spanish as well: *historia* can mean history as well as story, narration, tale.

Few poets have captured the beauty and importance of the home as emotional center, sacred space, cosmological model that holds chaos at bay, as the locus for memory and dream as in this poem. The house, the home, is the privileged space of the imagination. But the imagination is always turned toward the future, not toward the past. Loynaz's poem, despite its rather dire ending, is not a literal death but a crucial moment of renewal or resurrection. In *Ultimos días de una casa*, it is the power of the imagination that can reconcile memory and history, dream and wakefulness, sacred and profane space. Again, Bachelard: "Imagination has the integrating powers of the tree. It is root and branch. It lives between earth and sky. Imagination lives in the earth and in the wind. The imaginative tree is imperceptibly the cosmological tree, the tree which summarizes a universe, which makes a universe" (Bachelard as quoted in Kearney, 1991, p. 94). For Dulce María Loynaz, the imaginative tree is the tree of poetry. Its root is the living history of Cuba as seen through her heart, its branch and leaves, the turbulent formation of Cuban nationalism that often goes back to the resting corners of its past to revive its dreams of independence.

Loynaz began writing the novel *Jardín* (Garden) in 1928 when she was twenty-six. Typical of her patient and careful writing methods, it took her seven years to complete. It took another sixteen years for her to publish the novel, at the end of 1951, in Madrid. Reviews were extremely positive (see Simón, 1991). As opposed to her book of poems, *Poemas sin nombre* (1953), which she called an ascetic book, Loynaz classified her novel as "sensuous, baroque, languorous." It is an unusual novel that lingers on details with exquisite poetic insight, but is remarkably slight on psychological information, except for the main character Bárbara. Some critics have pointed out the affinities with the work of Marcel Proust, but just about any work of fiction that dwells on the past or is imbued with the intricacies of memory is inevitably called Proustian. Perhaps opera is closer to home, particularly the way it stops the "action" and suddenly a soprano sings an enchanting aria. And *Jardín* specifically recalls Wagner, who, more than anyone, was able to dilate a detail languorously into an entire scene or a whole act. There is a further similarity to Wagner: the ability to turn the plot of a fairy tale into high art.

Loynaz addresses the very nature of her novel in her "Prelude," written in 1935. Here are the first few sentences: "This is the monotonous and incoherent story of a woman and a garden. There is no time or space, as in the theories of Einstein. The garden and the woman are in any longitude of the planet—of great curvature or of more tension, and placed at any latitude—higher or lower—of the circumference of time. There are lots of roses. It isn't, thank God, a human novel. It might not even be a novel" (Loynaz, 1993d, p. 7). Despite some of the disclaimers, *Jardín* is a novel, even if an unorthodox one. But perhaps that is of less interest since the novel's definition in our century has become increasingly more elastic. Several critics have pointed out the cinematographic techniques of the novel, particularly the use of flashbacks, which Loynaz has admitted to in interviews (Simón, 1991, pp. 55–56). This cinematic quality led Luis Buñuel to express interest in filming it, but the project never came to fruition.

The other point that might need explaining is Loynaz's comment that "It isn't a human novel." The author does not imply with this statement that the novel describes a world devoid of human virtue or that the narrator is some reptilian incarnation of evil, but that the characters are closer to archetypes than the norms of nineteenth-century realism. In the "Prelude," Loynaz says she could have called the main character Psyche instead of Bárbara, that the "Symbol [is] the only school, only manifestation that still excites me, and, perhaps the only one I could aspire to" (Loynaz, 1993d, p. 8). Loynaz's understanding of symbol is not a crude one-to-one relationship between certain people, objects, or natural phenomena and a given trait, but more the exploration of psychic states that are common to all souls.

The novel can be divided into two parts, roughly speaking. In the first, the main character, Bárbara, reminisces about her family's past by looking at certain portraits and photos. One of the most intriguing family members is her great grandmother, also called Bárbara, who, it was rumored, died by being poisoned or by committing suicide. Bárbara lives alone in the house; the only other person is a black servant named Laura. In this first part (chap. 5), Loynaz also has a gloss of the Sleeping Beauty legend. Eventually, Bárbara discovers a small pavilion in the overrun garden that contains letters of her great grandmother. Vicariously, she relives her dead relative's love affair by reading the intense and romantic letters. The letters, however, end, albeit with a dark and ominous tone that suggest an unhappy conclusion to this nineteenth-century love tale.

The second part of the novel is shorter than the first and begins with a seaman she meets on the beach who enchants her sufficiently for her to abandon her garden. They sail away on his boat to Europe, where they live, get married, and have children. They live through the war, and, though no countries are named, it is clear that World War I is being described. Soon after the war, yearning for her garden, Bárbara decides to go back to the island. Since she arrives at night, a fisherman helps her find her way. There is both a sense of relief and foreboding as she makes her way back to the garden. Unfortunately, one of the walls crumbles and kills her.

From this simplified plot overview, there are some evident parallels to her later poem *Ultimos días de una casa*, not least of which is the linkage of house, garden, and nation. For critic Ileana Rodríguez, the novel "draws a transparent picture of national deterioration" (Rodríguez, 1994, p. 103). Loynaz has frequently employed garden metaphors in her poetry, as in "Eternidad" (discussed at the beginning of this chapter) and in poem CXXIV of *Poemas sin nombre*. In most of these circumstances, the garden had positive connotations, but in *Jardín* it is more ambiguous, if not downright negative. The author and critics have pointed out that the garden is often opposed to the sea in the novel, as evidenced in the quotation from Jules Michelet that begins Part 4: "There, face to face, the eternal enemies: Man and Nature, Earth and Sea." I concur with this analysis, but would point out that the sea is often associated with images of death, particularly in the beginning.

Despite the tantalizing descriptions, and the sensuality of the natural surroundings, Bárbara is in a kind of prison, albeit densely foliated. In her book *Un verano en Tenerife* (1958), Loynaz has a truly suggestive passage that applies equally to *Jardín*: "I read somewhere, I don't remember exactly, that the worse prisons are those raised next to the sea. Because the sea, similar to Tantalus, offers the prisoner the broadest of horizons, and because of the indominable nature of the waves, is continually reminding one of the idea of freedom" (Roberto Friol quoting Loynaz in Simón, 1991, p. 530). Though we should not lose sight of the fact that Loynaz is here speaking of another island, the Canary Islands, the quote is applicable to her novel, as critic Roberto Friol has suggested. The garden is an island within an island, and it is a prison. In this regard, the allusion to Sleeping Beauty is appropriate, but so is the protagonist's name. St. Barbara was a Christian martyr locked up in a tower by her father, a prisoner of male rage. The garden is gender defined. Bárbara is the garden, a theme that is constant throughout the novel.

Fina García Marruz has keenly observed that Loynaz has striven to give a new spatial metaphor in her fiction: "One speaks of the *selva* [jungle] by José Eustasio Rivera, of the pampa in *Don Segundo Sombra*, of the plains in *Doña Bárbara*, of the Great Savannah in Alejo Carpentier, but none of it is related to *Jardín* from our Dulce María Loynaz. And could it not be stated, from the very beginning, there is a common link of centering space, of nature—our American nature—and the subsequent histories, not like a background scenario, but like a rooting theme?" (Simón, 1991, p. 549; trans. in Rodríguez, 1994, p. 103). Of course, these other works have been written by male writers and the *selva*, the pampa, the plains, and the Great Savannah are all outdoors, in the great wilderness, where a different kind of history takes place. Loynaz seems to point toward an alternative historical space that is not part of the four B's of male narrative history: the barracks, the battlefield, the bar, and the brothel. But Loynaz does it by turning intimate biography into myth and, ultimately, into history.

Despite the mythical quality of the narrative, the garden itself has a history. It stores part of the family history that Bárbara discovers in the pavilion, the love letters that she will breathlessly pore over. By going to the past and reading those letters, Bárbara is already marking a certain distance, from both that very past and its stifling gender roles, with its rapacious rhetoric of love. The letters she reads are written by a man roughly a hundred years earlier than the action of the novel: her (and the reader's) reading of these letters introduces a critical dimension to the plot and to its central character.

The letters are important because they will mark the passage between the Edenic part of the novel, where Bárbara is restricted to the garden, protected from the outside, and the moment where she goes out into the world, or "the fall." She sails off with her newfound love, and they go to the United States and Europe, though mostly the latter. Loynaz is unequivocal in how important this is in terms of Bárbara's freedom. It is a significant gain for her, but not enough. She finds life in Europe cold and indifferent, and long way before Milan Kundera, Loynaz has a marvelous chapter called "Prisa" (Being in a Hurry), which is really about the virtues of slower-paced living. Curiously, though, the novel has some Futurist moments when Loynaz describes the beauty of machines in terms that could only be described as ecstatic. The war, however, drives her back to the garden, but it is not exactly a triumphant return.

The novel begins with Bárbara looking through the iron bars of the garden watching automobiles go by. She walks through the garden and sees the moon peeking over the top of the house. Then the moon begins descending and crashes at Bárbara's feet, its splinters flying by her face. She picks up its pieces, wraps it in a shawl, and then buries it in the ground and plants the branch of an almond tree over it. It is a perfect symbolic portrait of Bárbara at the beginning, with powerful religious connotations. Aside from the obvious garden, there is the almond and the moon. The almond is symbolic of virginity, the self-productive principle and also sweetness, charm, and delicacy. It also represents divine favor and approval, as well as the purity of the Virgin. Many portraits of the Virgin are enclosed in almond-shaped figures (the *vesica piscis*, or *mandorla*). It hardly needs reminding that the moon represents feminine power, but also the rhythm of cyclic time, the universal becoming; its different phases signify perpetual renewal and enlightenment.

The end of the novel has Bárbara in the dark accompanied by a fisherman who shows her the way back to the garden. Here, however, Loynaz begins to transform the Christian symbolism or iconography (including that of the fisherman). The moon is out, of course, but unlike St. Barbara, the protagonist ironically dies from precisely what the saint is supposed to protect us from: sudden death and falling objects (and lightning). Bárbara's death is sad, but it is not tragic. The wall of the garden helped separate her intimate, sacred space from the outer, profane space of the world. The fact that it crumbles could mean that their mutual exclusivity was not a healthy thing, perhaps symbolized by the protagonist's "sacrifice." Speaking of *Tristan und Isolde* (Wagner's opera), Joseph Kerman said it was not a tragedy but a religious drama. By this he means that the work's "fundamental sense is of a progress towards a state of illumination which transcends yearning and pain" (Kerman, 1956, p. 195). He further adds that three other factors should be present: "that the nature of the experience be properly religious; that this experience is the main matter of the [work]; and the religious experience is projected in a dramatic form" (Kerman, ibid.) *Jardín* meets these criteria admirably. The novel's rhythm has an inexorable pace that leads to Bárbara's death, but her death has a certain ascent that makes it an ironic religious drama in the form of a novel.

Why ironic? Aside from the previously mentioned reversal of the St. Barbara legend, there is the final page of the novel. After her death, workers from the Iron Workers Union are digging through the debris of the garden and find a concave, but round metal disc. It is the moon that Bárbara interred at the beginning. The worker picks it up, thinking that if he cleans it up he can use it as a plate, but decides against it and throws it away. It is as if at the end of *Tristan und Isolde*, with the lovers still embracing, the stagehands began walking on the set to clean up for the next performance. And yet . . . the last line of the novel reads: "Bárbara, from behind, from above, from below, everywhere, always . . . , places her pallid face against the iron bars . . ." Loynaz, 1993d, p. 247).

None of this necessarily invalidates seeing *Jardín* as a "transparent picture of national deterioration," but more important is how Loynaz has remained true to her tropes. Despite the garden crumbling and killing her protagonist, the garden's iconic importance remains, not just as a Garden of Eden image, but as alternative historical space that values the garden/women's lives as historically important and necessary. But even beyond that is the steadfastness of her character to return to the garden (home/nation) and stick it out, no matter what. In this the name of the character is well chosen: St. Barbara's faith was so great that she risked her life. It was her father who beheaded her, but he was subsequently struck by lightning, which is why St. Barbara is eventually syncretized with Changó in Santería. This steadfastness is seen in Dulce María Loynaz's life (she never left her home in Cuba, even though there were plenty of reasons for her to do so) and her work. Each word stakes out a plant, flower, or tree in the battered and unforgotten garden of Cuba's history. Like quiet warriors, they preserve the garden with the sturdiest of roots. This garden houses the secrets and treasures of the country: its yearnings for independence, its strivings to establish a unique culture, its hopes for overcoming the violence of class warfare. It is the house where the nation dreams.

FIVE

José Lezama Lima: The Re-Enchantment of the Wor(l)d

"He is the only one among us that can organize discourse as if it were a medieval hunt." These words of Cintio Vitier on the writing of José Lezama Lima evoke rich, densely figured tapestries, with animals, unicorns, lush vegetation, vivid colors: such was the verbal wizardry of this extraordinary poet. José Lezama Lima (1910–76) was one of the key figures of Cuban literary life in this century. Starting with the publication of one of the most startling poems published in the Spanish language, "La muerte de Narciso" (1937), Lezama was a constant presence in Cuban letters for almost the next forty years, as well as an unusual kind of compass for current writers and artists. Whether in the form of essays, poems, articles, or narrative fiction, everything he wrote had an unmistakable poetic enchantment to it.

Lezama founded several magazines, but it was *Orígenes* (1944–56) that was the most influential of all, and not only in Cuba. Octavio Paz called it "the best magazine in the Spanish language." It published forty issues and sponsored the publication of twenty-three books; it opened its pages to the finest of local and international talent. Among the Cubans were Cintio Vitier, Eliseo Diego, Fina García Marruz, Gastón Baquero, Lorenzo García Vega, Lydia Cabrera, Virgilio Piñera, and Angel Gaztelu. With excellent translations, they published Valéry, Joyce, Eliot, Wallace Stevens, Spender, Virginia Woolf, Camus, Heidegger, and others. Its covers were designed by distinguished artists such as Wifredo Lam, René Portocarrero, Mariano Rodríguez, Rufino Tamayo, and José Clemente Orozco.

Long-deserved recognition came with Lezama's novel *Paradiso* (1966; trans. 1974), which caused considerable controversy when it first

came out because of the homoerotic scenes in chapter 8. Allegedly, it
was the intervention of Fidel Castro himself that allowed the book to
be distributed. *Paradiso* is a family saga rich in symbolism, and also a
parable of creation and salvation. According to Lezama, this is possible
through the poetic image, for he believed that poetry was a form of
knowledge, a way to arrive at truth—human, cosmic, or divine. This
was anchored in his Catholicism, which drew on St. Augustine, Pascal,
St. Anselm, Nicholas of Cusa, St. Paul, the Gnostics, as well as the Cuban
revolutionary José Martí. Lezama was equally versed in pre-Socratic
philosophy, Taoism, pre-Columbian mythologies, and the Egyptian
Book of the Dead. Curiously, Lezama's roaming intellectual passions
were reigned in by his physical immobility. He left his native Cuba only
twice. In part this was due to his inordinate fear of travel, brought about
by his father's death abroad when Lezama was just a boy.

After the revolution, Lezama held important positions in the Cuban
cultural bureaucracy, but after the controversy around *Paradiso*, things
changed. Due to the more restrictive cultural policy implemented after
poet Heberto Padilla was imprisoned (1971), Lezama was marginalized
and not published for six years, from 1970 to 1976, the year he died.
Letters published after his death by his sister Eloísa indicate that he was
often invited abroad but denied visas by the Cuban goverment, which
believed he would defect. But soon after his death, in 1977, his posthumous work was published in Cuba, notably the book of poems *Fragmentos a su imán* (1977) and the novel *Oppiano Licario* (1977). It was
followed by a collection of prose pieces and essays under the title of
Imagen y posibilidad (1981) and *Fascinación de la memoria* (1993), which
includes talks, short essays, letters, and other unpublished materials.
His work continues to spawn a generation of critics and interpreters
that is beginning to rival the Joyce "industry."

Interest in Lezama takes on an urgency in Cuba since the collapse of
Communism in Eastern Europe and the Soviet Union: Cubans are
avidly reviewing their own past. Whereas Marx and Lenin were the
authors to quote, now it is Cuban writers and thinkers from the nineteenth and twentieth centuries: Martí, Luz, Fernando Ortiz, Levi Marrero, Moreno Fraginals, Lezama, Carpentier, and others. Lezama and
Orígenes offer several things to Cubans looking for alternatives: a look
at a plurality of philosophical traditions (from St. Augustine to Heidegger, conversing with Afro-Cuban traditions) and political thought
(from Plato to Habermas); a more nuanced look at the relationships
between state power and intellectuals; and the ethical stance of the
person who creates within a concrete historical reality. In a recent and
popular film, *Fresa y chocolate* (Strawberry and Chocolate), Lezama's
ethical resilience and integrity was a subtle but constant presence.
Perhaps the generosity and joy of his vision is captured in these words
about Goethe, equally applicable to Lezama: "As Nietzsche said: 'He
does not negate anymore.' His attitude was basically affirmative without entirely becoming serene, let alone saintly." To Max Weber's "dis-
enchantment of the world," Lezama responds with a re-enchantment,

so poignantly expressed in a poem: "The violet sea longs for the birth of the gods/since to be born here is an ineffable celebration." Lezama combines in these few words the importance of nature in establishing a cosmic and mythological presence that seems to equate Cubanness with the continuous birth of something miraculous. The medieval hunt has become a creation myth, a numinous sign, the world opening in our hands.

DRAGONS AND THEURGY: LEZAMA'S IMAGES OF HISTORY

"I am ravished by being able to see words like fish in a waterfall." There is a confluence of grace, magic, nature, and time in this brief sentence that aptly summarizes José Lezama Lima's concerns as a writer. But more than a writer, Lezama was an entire tradition, a realm of literature unto himself. I echo with these words what Borges said of Quevedo, but it is even truer of Lezama. Despite his reputation as a "difficult writer," he has, through his poetry, his two novels, and his dense, serpentine essays, had a profound effect on Latin American literature. The ripple effect, the generative power of his words and thinking, has proved an ample ground from which other writers can draw sustenance, if not inspiration. In the case of Cuba, writers like Severo Sarduy and Reinaldo Arenas owe a huge debt to Lezama. So do novelists like Carlos Fuentes, Mario Vargas Llosa and Edgardo Rodríguez Juliá, short story writer Julio Cortázar, poets like David Huerta, and many young Cuban verse makers of the 1980s and 1990s.

Lezama's reputation derives mainly from two sources: his poetry and *Paradiso* (1966; Eng. trans. 1974 by Gregory Rabassa), one of the most extraordinary Latin American novels of the last half century. However, much less attention has been paid to his essays, none of which has ever been translated into English. One of his seminal books of essays is *La expresión americana* (1957), a verbal and conceptually rich brew that meditates on the nature of what is truly American, culturally speaking.[1] Most take Lezama to mean Latin America when he uses the term *American*, but in fact he mentions Melville, Whitman, and Emerson, which gives his definition an inclusiveness that was rare in the 1950s on either side of the border. The book originated in five talks he gave at the Centro de Altos Estudios del Instituto Nacional de la Cultura (Center for Advanced Studies of the National Institute of Culture) in January 1957.

In these talks, Lezama speaks to a theory of Latin American culture, in his inimitable poetic voice, establishing analogies across vast amounts of time and place. In one segment of three pages, for example, he goes from the *Popol Vuh* and pre-Columbian Mexican chants to the hunting of unicorns, to asides on maps and gardens, Columbus, Marco Polo, and Kubla Khan (featuring a marvelous story about music before doing battle), to William Henry Hudson and a dig at Hegel's anti-Catholicism. Lezama looks at history through metaphor, or even better, tries to conjure up different metaphors of history, what he called "las eras imaginarias" (imaginary eras). In this he was close to the ideas of Giambattista Vico, which will be discussed further on.

Lezama was not traveling on new terrain: there were many precedents for these types of reflections, such as Pedro Henríquez Ureña's *Seis ensayos en busca de nuestra expresión* (1928); Alfonso Reyes in *Visión de Anáhuac* (1917), *La Ultima Tule* (1942), or *Letras de la Nueva España* (1946); Mariano Picón-Salas in his *De la conquista a la independencia* (1944); and *Radiografía de la pampa* (1933) by Ezequiel Martínez Estrada. In Cuba the most significant precedent would have been Fernando Ortiz's work, especially his *Contrapunteo cubano del tabaco y el azúcar* (1940; *Cuban Counterpoint*, 1947/1995). Lezama's originality lies in the way he interprets myth and history, the particular weight and ethos of his baroque aesthetic, and the ethical dimensions of the historical figures he highlights such as Fray Servando Teresa de Mier, Simón Rodríguez, and José Martí. In his search for "la expresión americana," Lezama topologically describes it as "an open gnostic space" ("un espacio gnóstico abierto"). But before we turn to "imaginary eras" and "open gnostic spaces," we need to examine some of the terms Lezama uses to speak about the cultural hybridity of Latin America.

When Lezama refers to "la expresión americana," he is not trying to derive an "essence" of the American, an ontological grounding that would lend itself to a kind of nationalist or even continental expression of either spirit or character. Lezama, despite his poetic and mythological bent, is very much a historicist who did not believe in the static nature of *lo americano*. For Lezama it means trying to configure a historical narrative of the American imagination. Narrative is used in a free and playful sense, since the way Lezama fashions his historical narratives, as we shall see, is a heady mix of commentary on paintings, philosophical musings, florid poetic descriptions, careful textual commentary, and suggestive metaphor. They are closer to fiction than what would normally be acceptable for standard historiographical prose. For Lezama the imagination has not only an aesthetic weight, but a philosophical, religious, and ethical dimension with deep resonance for the understanding of history. Central to this understanding of history is the ability to produce and recollect images, which implies that the imagination is an ideal instrument in the creation of knowledge. Lezama would understand la *expresión americana,"* then, to be a speculative journey of becoming that seeks to understand poetically and reenact Latin American cultural production as immersed in a still living historical imagination. (I use words with Hegelian and Platonic resonances to set the stage for their elaboration further on.)

Julio Ortega, among others, has pointed out that Lezama uses a "fictional treatment of the tradition, its free use as a form of language. Tradition is seen as a changing present and the critical perspective as instrument which reorders that dialogue" (Ortega, 1991, p. 245). Lezama treats the Western tradition as another culture, not *the* culture, and by doing so he clearly is in the spirit of Borges. It is important to keep this in mind as we examine the beginning of Lezama's essay, since its discussion of European painting and the I Ching seem to place its concerns at a great remove from Latin American history. But in these first few pages Lezama offers us a glimpse of his approach to history, which he describes as an "animistic counterpoint." Like Hegel's dialectic, it is a method that is not a method, "but a name for ingenuity, for ingenious activity itself, which takes a continually varying shape depending on the content before it . . . struggling [with] the limitation of the image, the production of the unseen" (Verene, 1985, p. 11).

Lezama begins by speaking of the difficulty of historical sense and vision precisely because the meaning of history consists in "the production of the unseen." Cleverly, and with great dialogical skill, Lezama brings together examples of visual representation: five paintings from the Middle Ages and early Renaissance. It is as if Lezama were saying let us travel to the heart of the visible to make the invisible shine forth. The five works of art are: *September* by the Limbourg brothers (finished by Jean Colombe), a manuscript illumination from the early fifteenth century; *The Corn Harvest* by Brueghel (1565); *The Last Judgment* (in which Chancellor Rolin is depicted; 1443–51) by Rogier Van der Weyden; *The Madonna with Chancellor Rolin* by Jan van Eyck (1435/37); and *Guidoriccio da Fogliano on Horseback* by Simone Martini (1328).

First Lezama compares *September* with the Brueghel painting, principally because of what they depict: peasants working in the fields. But in drawing the two together there is a historical distance that must be accounted for. In the illuminated manuscript there is still a strong hierarchical relationship manifested by the castle and its dominance over the lives of those working in the fields. The height of the castle piercing into the heavens only reinforces the importance of the bond between lord and serf. But in its use of color and disposition of form, there is a certain magic to the scene, undergirded by the links between the human, the natural, the social, and the divine. The Brueghel painting, *The Corn Harvest*, already indicates a world not governed by feudal lords but of nascent capitalism. The town is far in the distance; a church is closer, partially obstructed by a tree and other vegetation. It is August: among the heat and intense labor, some peasants are having refreshments or reposing; others are still working. The sustenance provided by the harvest underlines the rich depiction of nature. As Lezama points out, the former (*September*) is marked by a kind of magic spell, the latter by "the cantabile of its own joy" (p. 50). Without skipping a beat, Lezama moves on to two different portraits of Chancellor Rolin. The Van Eyck (with the Virgin) is the earlier of the two and an extraordinary work that handles space with consummate skill. The Van der Weyden is a more austere portrait, with dark colors, and Rolin looks more like a monk, not like the powerful and wealthy man he was. In contrast, the Van Eyck painting is sumptuous with lush color and is a vivid portrayal of the temporal power of the earthbound recognizing the infinite power of the divine. For Lezama, the key element is the baby Jesus, which gives the painting a kind of joyful luminescence, with a light that penetrates the chancellor, even if there are no outward manifestations of this "piercing." This light, says Lezama, "modifies him and gives him a new life" (p. 51).

Finally, Lezama eases in to the Martini painting. A rider on horseback (Guidoriccio da Fogliano) dominates the painting, flanked on either side by castles in the background. The rider and his horse tower in comparison in a weird but believable display of perspective, accentuating the play between history and myth. Lezama links up the castle of *September* to the similar structures in the Martini painting, claiming that the latter is the opening up of the doors of the medieval castle, compared shortly after to the soul leaving the body, drawn from one of the images of the I Ching.

Even a cursory glance at these paintings calls up a series of associations and raises questions about what Lezama chose to emphasize in them. Lezama has a strong hellenizing streak in his outlook. Are the two paintings that feature peasants an indirect nod to Werner Jaeger's *Paideia?*

> Homer's poetry brings out one fundamental fact: that all culture starts with the creation of an aristocratic ideal, shaped by deliberate cultivation of the qualities appropriate to a nobleman and a hero. Hesiod shows us the second basis of civilization—work. The later Greeks recognized this when they gave his didactic poem the title of *Works and Days.* Heroism is shown, and virtues of lasting value are developed, not only in the knight's duel with the enemy, but in the quiet, incessant battle of the worker against the elements and the hard earth. It is not for nothing that Greece was the cradle of a civilization which places work high among the virtues. (Jaeger, 1945, p. 57)

Whatever the motivation, these themes will come up during the rest of the essay, whether Lezama is discussing the *Popol Vuh*, the *gauchos* in Argentina, the *corridos* in México, or the importance of rural life and nature as part of Latin American culture.

Other questions persist: *why* did Lezama make no reference to the historical circumstances of the Martini painting? It was commissioned to celebrate a series of castles captured (and previously lost) by Siena and has an undeniably civic and political purpose—the "heraldic pose" of the horse reinforces this civic message by the juxtaposition of animal and landscape. Or why didn't he choose Van der Weyden's *St. Luke Drawing the Virgin*, visually almost a mirror image of the Van Eyck, and which it obviously has paid hommage to? Or, sticking to the figure of the chancellor, why isn't there more about Rolin as historical figure or icon? Lezama's analysis (and omissions) reveal much about his historical "method." His approach to history shows a remarkable indifference to the facts and, like Spengler, is more attuned to metaphor or to a startling image which can capture both commonality and difference, sometimes stretched over what looks like a temporal abyss. Even the most obvious is up for grabs, and Wilde's challenge undergirds his comments: "The mystery of the world is the visible, not the invisible."

More than a baroque fascination with painting and *écriture*, Lezama is providing both a model and critique of representation and how it embodies the historical. Later we will discuss the role of images in recollection (Hegel), but for the moment let us explore the ontology of painting. Before photography, visual documentation of the historical centered on painting (or sculpture). Painting's ability to capture the likeness of the human figure (or objects) is legendary: thus we have paintings of battles, famous scenes, coronations, funerals, portraits of kings, nobility, thinkers, and other artists, as well as still lifes, landscapes, and the like. Religious painting has often been able to capture the relationship between the human and the divine, as in Van Eyck's *The Madonna with Chancellor Rolin*. Lezama is astute in his choice of the five paintings because they exhibit a wide range in the sense of depicting nature, peasants at work, worldly power and politics, the supernatural, humans, animals, vegetation, and even angels. There are moments which gather the cosmic rhythms of the earth, flashes of the divine, the flow of time, and the humble movements of humans at work.

And yet this great power of resemblance makes Lezama want to tease out the age-old distinction between seeing and knowing, not only a gradual unveiling of the invisible, but a radical examination of what is *in* the visible. In this sense Lezama agrees more with the philosopher Maurice Merleau-Ponty, who thought that painting expresses what exists, than with Sartre (who said that painting expresses what does not exist). Given Lezama's Catholicism, one cannot help thinking of the ancient polemic with the Iconoclasts, arguing over the import of divine, natural, and artificial images. Lezama obviously would not side with the Iconoclasts, but would instead agree that archetypal images are a product of the mind, images of the mind which brought them forth. And "for this reason Philo calls the Logos, which is the pleroma of Forms, the Image of God, which in turn is the archetype of all else: as God is the Father of the Image, the Image is the pattern of other beings" (Sheldon-Williams in Armstrong, 1970, pp. 506-7). Lezama would agree with Philo's statement, since it pertains to the truth-fulness of representation. Vico's statement about the truth was probably not far from his mind: "Divine truth is a solid image like a statue; human truth is a monogram or a surface image like a painting" (Vico, 1988, p. 46). Lezama's poetic exploration of history is a conversation between the statue and the painting in the spirit of Plotinus, who said: "The wisdom of the gods and of the blessed immortals cannot be expressed in words, but only by beautiful images" (as quoted in Huyghe, 1962, p. 4).

Painting as representation bears on representation in history. Lezama is not a realist in matters painterly or historic. His understanding of history comes by way of poetry and the ability to generate images and metaphors. It is the *imago's* participation in history, he argues, that can bring about an *era imaginaria*, an imaginary era. Although he makes brief reference to it in *La expresión americana*, he returns to it several times in his writings of the late 1950s and 1960s. What exactly did Lezama mean by the term? Unlike Toynbee or Spengler, an *imaginary era* is not synonymous with a civilization or society, nor is Lezama interested in explaining them in terms of biological metaphors (beginning, growth, maturity, decline, disintegration) of why they arise or disappear. Obviously, if an imaginary era coincides with a civilization, or if its adherents have state power to be able to shape a society, the imaginary era stands a greater chance of surviving, as was the case with ancient Egypt. But Lezama also refers to the term as being a subculture within a dominant society, like the Orphics or Pythagoreans. An imaginary era usually takes a long time to coalesce, implying a temporal dimension that is historical if not millenary, and through this expansive process achieves an ability to make certain images and fashion a way of thinking. Both become living metaphors that act *in* and *on* history. Is an imaginary era an archetype? Lezama suggests a relationship between the two, meaning that an archetype, which by definition is not historically bound, becomes an imaginary era when it acquires a historical specificity and is incorporated into the shifting constellation of a concrete historical formation. An imaginary era would need to recreate and disseminate several archetypes and bring them under one or a small number of central metaphors to be able to constitute an imaginary era. For example, many cultures have quest or heroic journey archetypes, but different imaginary eras will imbue them with their own meaning. A Buddhist interpretation will see it in terms of reincarnation, a Catholic one as a symbol of resurrection.

In *La expresión americana*, Lezama claims that we must move away from the so-called modern emphasis on cultures and focus on imaginary eras instead (p. 58). Why the insistence on the imaginary eras? He clearly was dissatisfied with modes of historical explanation that were realistic (Aristotle), rationalist (Hegel), positivistic (Comte), mechanical (Voltaire), and materialist (Marx and others). Their cause-effect methodology is too simplistic, one-dimensional, and insufficiently nuanced. Ramón Xirau has insisted that Lezama, following Plato and Plotinus, was of the tradition that believed lower realms of reality were to be explained by superior forms. This implies that the *imago* (eternal images) cause and give substance to the personal, the poetic, and the historical. For Lezama, there is no history without the presence of the numinous. This sacredness gives imaginary eras a certain continuity for, according to the Cuban poet, an imaginary era never completely dies out. Its hegemony may end, but certain of its elements are picked up by future societies or imaginary eras (e.g., certain images of the Egyptians are retrieved and transformed by Christianity). For Lezama, Christianity is one of the central imaginary eras, suffusing his analysis of other imaginary eras.

How does this relate to (Latin) American history? Lezama mentions three pre-Columbian societies that were imaginary eras: the Incas (Fortresses of Stone/The Flood), the Aztecs (The Cult of Blood), and the Mayas (perhaps a combination of the previous two). He even hints at the formation of possible new imaginary eras in post-Columbian history, centered around his notion of a baroque Counter-Conquest exemplified by Sor Juana Inés de la Cruz, the Andean artist/architect Kondori, and the Afro-Brazilian architect Aleijandinho, or what he calls the era of "infinite possibility" inaugurated by José Martí, only to be continued by the events of the Cuban Revolution in 1959. Lezama was tentative here, suggesting that Cuba's insurrection might lead eventually to the creation of an imaginary era. It is doubtful that Lezama would still entertain that thought if he were alive today.

A step down from the concept of imaginary era is what Lezama called "great choral groups," whose importance or ability to create certain associations and/or images throw a dazzling light on history. Examples abound: the retreat of Napoleon's Army, the Holocaust, the storming of the Winter Palace. They function as "hypostasized metaphors" and again are not limited to a simple-minded causality. To a degree, these "great choral groups" are emblems that might signal the beginning or end of an imaginary era, or of one of its phases. But they are emblems with historical specificity. They do not have the millennial intricacy of an imaginary era, but they do contain a lightning-bolt intensity that makes us profoundly question our most cherished notions. A twentieth-century example will suffice: after the Final Solution, it is no longer possible to look at trains as unalloyed tokens of human and scientific progress. With these definitions in mind, we can return to the paintings and see what more they reveal about Lezama's thinking about history.

Is the opening door (soul-body) the only link between five European paintings and the Chinese I Ching? Lezama gives us the clue in another essay titled "La biblioteca como dragón" (The Library as Dragon), from 1965, published in a book of essays, La cantidad hechizada (1970). In his essay about Chinese culture and Taoism, Lezama recalls a saying by Goethe along the lines of "Whenever a threatening cloud seems to hover over the world, I obstinately seek refuge in that which is most distant (or remote) from us" (Lezama, 1971, p. 219). Goethe's remarks were made in relation to China, and Lezama picks up the cue and adds that for the Chinese distance or remoteness is paralleled by the sacred kings who embody that remoteness. Furthermore, Lezama claims that distance is productive and creative, that it is an image. It is linked to the rule of Fou Hi, who embodied certain fertility traits, with a double identity of earthiness, of being a peasant deity, and a heavenly, more mysterious force. Lezama attributes to the Chinese, three thousand years before Christ, a separation of the earth and the sky, and says that its subsequent history is the attempt to bring the earth back up to the sky by way of an embryonic image (ibid., p. 222). This separation will also be a constant of Egyptian art, another culture that held particular fascination for Lezama.

It is precisely this separation of earth and sky, the divine and the human, which constitute the common theme, so to speak, of the paintings that Lezama has commented on. This bears a resemblance to Heidegger's expression *geviert* (the fourfold convergence of earth and sky; human and divine), as well as his frequent references to proximity and remoteness. As Fred Dallmayr points out: "Heidegger . . . described human *Dasein* as a creature of distance or farness, a distance that alone can nurture a true closeness to things and fellow human beings" (Dallmayr, 1993, p. 200). Lezama's *lejanía* and its Taoist underpinnings are conversant with Heidegger's observations, which are generally subsumed under a wider rubric of journeying and homecoming. Heidegger says that "Homecoming is a transit through otherness" (ibid., p. 161).

Lezama's historical "methodology," his imaginary eras, are prime examples of "homecoming through otherness." Chinese alchemy, Egyptian cosmology, Etruscan society, Mayan myths, medieval theology, and Renaissance magic are all markers of this road to strangeness, to "foreign-ness," not as a way of getting lost or forgetting but as a means of acquiring the depth and texture necessary to create *la expresión americana*. We must return again to Lezama's dragon. In his essay he links the dragon to that which resists being pinned down. The word in Spanish is *inapresable*, with rich associations ranging from elusive, resistant to capture or domination, to slippery or even mysterious. Semiotically we could say that *inapresable* is polysemy, the rich plurality of meaning and interpretation that underlies metaphor. *Presa* is also prey, something you hunt or persecute. Lezama's use corresponds to these meanings of not being trapped or imprisoned, being indomitable.

Of course, the dragon has many possible meanings in Chinese culture: two facing dragons are a symbol of yin-yang and the terrestrial and celestial realms, as well as intelligence, spirituality, the power of change and infinity. But for our purposes, one should especially note its function as a kind of analogical magnet. The dragon is considered a composite of different creatures: "His horns resemble those of a stag, his head that of a camel, his eyes those of a demon, his scales those of a carp, his neck that of a snake, his belly that of a clam, his claws those of an eagle, his soles those of a tiger, his ears those of a cow" (Cooper, 1978, p. 56). These are the nine resemblances that Wang Fu mentions when speaking of the dragon. Lezama calls his dragon, or analogical magnet, "animistic counterpoint."

It is through analogy that Lezama is able to achieve "homecoming through otherness," to bring together often disparate eras or cultures, so that their otherness can dialogue to the point of fashioning a dragon. Gadamer reminds us that the word *symbol* in Greek was literally a token of a house you had been to, an object broken in two that would be rejoined many years hence in act of recognition and homecoming (Gadamer, 1986, p. 31). Analogy can work in different ways: through morphology, content, archetype, function (meaning), or, in Lezama's case, "animistic counterpoint." He rejects a morphological account of analogy, indirectly criticizing Oswald Spengler's approach. He offers the example of comparing the shape of a bull's horn and a Byzantine tiara; one of Spengler's more famous morphologies is the comparison between Rembrandt's browns and Beethoven's string quartets. Lezama was certainly sympathetic to Spengler's poetic side, but felt that his morphologies were limited to the more obvious or overtly visible of analogies. Lezama goes one step further: his "animistic counterpoint" avoids what he calls the barren comparisons of Spengler, whose objects of comparison remain frozen in their respective domains. By animism Lezama seeks to give the relationship between two distant realities (or images) a live and animate "relationship." The relationship is, in effect, metaphorical, for several reasons. Like any analogy, a metaphor sets up a field of identity and difference. Second, it is figurative, in many senses, first by transcending the literal and then having a "prophetic" (Auerbach) quality that "works" in the past, while projecting toward a future point. Third, analogy carries a historical specificity. This is why Lezama says that what avoids the "frozen-ness" of Spengler's approach is the *sujeto metafórico*, the metaphorical subject. Is this subject a person, a *cogito*, a Spinozan substance, or some type of Kantian transcendental ego, a kind of philosophical metasubject? Well, yes and no. At one level, Lezama is referring to himself and his own particular way of writing/interpreting history, but at another he seems to be referring to a method, but it is a methodless method in that it changes according to the content of what it discusses. It is not a device applied externally to the object under consideration. It is a synonym for ingenuity, as Donald Verene says about Hegel's dialectic. And, as will be discussed later, ingenuity is the ability to compare, form analogies and metaphors. Metaphor is central to Lezama's thought and creation, integral to the narrating and comprehension of history. As Aristotle reminds us: "But the greatest thing by far is to be a master of metaphor. It is the one thing that cannot be learnt from others; and it is also a sign of genius, since a good metaphor implies an intuitive perception of the similarity in dissimilars" (*Poetics*, as quoted in Verene, 1981, p. 173). Metaphor is more conceptual than linguistic, which is why it can "tell us something new about reality" (Ricoeur).

The metaphorical subject engenders the animistic counterpoint, and it is by way of counterpoint that we can configure an imaginary era, or more modestly comprehend the slippery dynamics of history. They (the metaphorical subject/animistic counterpoint) bear an uncanny resemblance to what Merleau-Ponty called "the flesh." The French philosopher was fond of quoting Cézanne, who said, "The landscape thinks itself in me and I am its consciousness." He was equally fond of Klee's saying: "In a forest, I have felt many times over that it was not I who looked at the forest. Some days I felt that the trees were looking at me, were speaking to me. . . . I was there listening. . . . I think that the painter must be penetrated by the universe and not want to penetrate it. . . . I expect to be inwardly submerged, buried. Perhaps I paint to break out" (Merleau-Ponty, 1964, p. 167). These quotations, aside from indicating the animism that Lezama referred to, will also be important when we discuss Lezama's views on nature, specifically as it relates to "an open gnostic space."

But they also illustrate Merleau-Ponty's view of flesh as involving a reversibility, a chiasmic intertwining which is central to his aesthetic views. Like Lezama, Merleau-Ponty wanted to steer a course between naturalism (empiricism) and intellectualism (rationalism) and tried to develop a theory of artistic creation that would be "a fusion of self and the world, not imitation of the world as object by the painter as a subject, nor a subjective projection of the world by the artist's imagination" (Johnson, 1993, p. 13). This fusion of the self and the world is not a blurring or total identification of self and world, but an ongoing dialogue between the two that avoids the twin dangers of dualism, objectivist or subjectivist. The lessons for history are clear: to write or think about history cannot seem merely a process whereby the historian is a subject examining history (the object), nor can it be entirely the subjective product of the historian's mind. Otherwise, it becomes autobiography at best, solipsism at worst. Merleau-Ponty's bodily perception, his idea of flesh, can be useful at this point.

Flesh is not just matter, molecules of meat, if you will. In trying to explain its enigmatic comprehensiveness, Merleau-Ponty says the following: "The flesh is not matter, is not mind, is not substance. To designate it, we should need the old term 'element' in the sense it was used to speak of water, earth, air, and fire, that is, in the sense of a *general thing*, midway between the spatio-temporal individual and the idea, a sort of incarnate principle that brings a style of being wherever there is a fragment of being. The flesh is in this sense an 'element' of Being" (Merleau-Ponty, 1968, p. 139). His definition comes in the context of seeing and painting, where the seer is caught up in what is being seen, claiming that the body offers a kind of "natural reflection." Vision implies that the body is both transparent (a window) and reflective (a mirror). Galen Johnson sums up the importance of these traits: "Flesh and reversibility are notions meant to express both envelopment and distance, the paradox of unity at a distance or sameness with difference, finding a new ontological way between monism and dualism" (Johnson, 1993, pp. 47–48). Lezama's ontology, with Christian and Platonic overtones, also carries pre-Socratic themes as well, echoed by Merleau-Ponty's definition of flesh as being an element. Perhaps he had Anaxagoras in mind, who thought the basic elements were made up of an infinite amount of qualitatively different seeds, captured in the suggestive phrase, "I call the world flesh in order to say that it is a pregnancy of possibilities" (Merleau-Ponty, 1968, p. 250). Lezama brings these same sentiments into a Catholic overview: "In resurrection, the *potens* spills forth, exhausting its possibilities. When the *potens* acts upon the visible, its derivations are (and act upon) the realm of *physis* [nature]; when it develops within (or on) the invisible, it bears us the prodigious gift of the image of resurrection" (Lezama, 1971, p. 151).

Merleau-Ponty often said that the body was not a thing but a work of art, and similarly spoke of the work of art as an individual (Merleau-Ponty, 1962, pp. 150–51). Lezama often spoke of poetry, or the poem, as creating a kind of body. Poetry, for Lezama, was the source for human understanding and potentiality. In poetry, he said, were the essences expressed by imaginary eras, and "the history of poetry is none other than the study and expression of imaginary eras" (Lezama, 1971, p. 174).

The quotation from Cézanne and Klee, and the reversibility of Merleau-Ponty's definiton of flesh, indicate a common thread: a nondualistic approach to vision, to perception. This unitive solution is consistent with Lezama's, even though his Catholic-Plotinian-baroque outlook brings a different register to this issue. But there is more: behind these thoughts there is an inherent metaphorical reality. If, following Kenneth Burke, we can agree that metaphor is representational (by creating a similarity from difference) and that it provides a perspective (of A in terms of B, and vice versa), the previous paragraphs have been describing a metaphorical subject in the process of creating meaning.

It is the metaphorical subject, according to Lezama, which becomes the vehicle for ushering forth those new realities, metaphors, as Ricoeur says. This metaphorical capability plays an important role in the task of remembrance, and like Vico and Hegel before him, Lezama would agree that memory is the mother of the muses. Lezama's dialogue with the past reveals a unique sensibility and memory that is worth examining more closely. His historical memory seems to draw on several sources: Heidegger, Plato, Vico, and Hegel. Heidegger's use of the word *andenken* (recollection or remembrance) indicates not just a return to something finished and over with, but a fertile meeting ground which speaks to us in an ever-changing historical existence.

Once we are fully attentive to recollection, he [Heidegger] observes, "we discover that the recollected memory in its return does not stop in the present in order to serve merely as a substitute for the past. Rather, the recollected vaults beyond our present and suddenly faces us from the future. From there it approaches as a still unfulfilled promise, as an unexplored treasure." Seen from this vantage, the poet's greetings are a solicitation for an encounter, more specifically for a dialogue between two modes of historical being. Far from aiming at consensus, this dialogue carefully maintains distance between the partners, *where distance does not equal rigid separation but rather a "letting be" granting open space for self-discovery and indigenous freedom.* (Dallmayr, 1993, p. 153, emphasis added)

While Heidegger's words are addressing a poem written by Holderlin ("Andenken"; "Remembrance"), they have a vivid affinity with Lezama's poetic historiography. The images or imaginary eras that Lezama "recollects" from the past are recreated and reconfigured to speak again in a new way, in an "open space of self-discovery," as "unfulfilled promise" to be realized in the future.

Vico's triple classification of memory would seem to encompass Lezama's use of the term as well. For Vico it consisted of *memoria, fantasia,* and *ingegno.* By these three terms Vico meant the following: *memoria* is remembering, the power of the mind to bring to it something that is not in the mind. This implies a spatial and temporal faculty in making present something which is not, and creating a "now" which "has been." *Fantasia* is the ability to alter, represent, imitate; it is the mind's power to take objects and shape them into a human form or dimension. This mimetic ability is not a naive realism, but the vitality of symbolic forms to take sensations or brute facticity and give them cultural meaning. We will see how this representation is not a repetition or copying, but a bringing forth of something concealed, the creation of a "knowledge of essence" (Gadamer). *Ingegno,* or ingenuity, refers to the capability of taking things and ordering them into new or different relationships; it implies forming comparisons, similes, metaphors, or scientific thinking. All three forms come together to constitute memory, and, as Vico reminds us, memory is the mother of the muses (Verene, 1981, pp. 96–127). Vitally linked to this recollective imagination is the ability to form images, not concepts. Here again Lezama would be at home with Vico, whose use of the image is rooted in historical reality. For Lezama, the image is paramount, particularly to his notion of *las eras imaginarias.* But in terms of the "recollective imagination," here are his own words: "To remember is an act of the spirit, but memory is like a plasma of the soul, it is always creative, spermatic, because we memorialize from the roots of the species" (p. 60).

Remembering from "the roots of our species" clearly has Platonic echoes, particularly his notion of *anamnesis,* or recollection. Most will recall Plato's thoughts on recollection as a predetermined knowledge, which through the Socratic method are remembered by questioning and prodding. One has acquired all the knowledge that is necessary, but we forget, and through *anamnesis* (recollection) we retrieve it. But it is not quite that simple. It is in Plato's *Meno* where anamnesis is most thoroughly discussed. One section in particular is often quoted: "All nature is akin, and the soul has learned everything, so that when a man has recalled a single piece of knowledge—learned it, in ordinary language—there is no reason why he should not find out all the rest, if he keeps a stout heart and does not grow weary of the search, for seeking and learning are in fact nothing but recollection" (*Meno,* 81d). Emilio Lledó has made a brilliant and suggestive analysis of this passage (Lledó, 1990, pp. 119–39). We cannot examine his argument in full detail here but must be limited to what seems germane to Lezama's notion of recollection and how it relates to his historical thinking.

The process of recollection is not merely recapturing a past moment, intact and exactly how it occurred. It is not going back and recognizing that which is already known, but is equally a confrontation or a warm encounter with the unknown. Gadamer, following Plato, observes that in *anamnesis* you grasp the essence of what is recollected, not just the contingent elements, which is why he says: "The joy of recognition is rather the joy of knowing *more* than is already familiar" (Gadamer, 1993, p. 114). This is reminiscent of Heidegger's comments cited earlier. For Plato "considers all knowledge of essence to be recognition." A work of art's recognition also produces this knowledge of essences, which is why Aristotle in his *Poetics* said: "Poetry, therefore, is more philosophical and more significant than history, for poetry is more concerned with the universal, and history more with the individual" (Aristotle, 1968, p. 17). Lezama's memory produces that kind of recognition that Plato spoke about, allowing him to reconstruct imaginary eras, his poetics of history.

Knowledge, then, is not what has passed, but points toward the future. Lledó underlines two essential points: *anamnesis* is linked to learning/understanding (*mathenein*) and searching (*zetein*). What this implies is that the learning-understanding-searching axis is drawn to an unknown. The psyche extends itself toward what it does not know, and often the object of our search is not known. The essence of knowledge comes not so much from the plenitude of an answer but in the possibilities brought about by questioning. It is the Socratic method of questioning and response, its dialectic, that can bring about the speculative nature of consciousness and recollection.

What is the basis for this recollection? According to Lledó (and Gadamer as well), it is the *logos*. It is language which makes dialogue possible, as well as recollection, because *logos* is not only enunciation but also reason or cause (Gadamer, 1991, p. 34). Of course it also means discourse, speech, as well as narrative, argument, a true account (as opposed to *mythos*). But for Lezama, perhaps Heraclitus is closer to the heart, who by definition saw the *logos* as the all-pervasive formula of organization which is divine (*nomos*). Or better still, the *logos* can be seen as an active force in the universe, generative (*logoi spermatikoi*), material, and associated with fire. This rich welter of divine, creative, fiery, and erotic associations is consistent with Lezama's own views, his own logocentric ethos. Aware of the kind of word magic that accompanies mythological consciousness, Lezama skillfully recreates that "magic" when he visits the imaginary eras he is so fond of (Orphics, ancient Egypt, Taoism). But even when he is not directly addressing the issue of imaginary eras, Lezama seems to exemplify George Steiner's image of history: "History, in the human sense, is a language net cast backwards" (cited in Hughes, 1988, p. 1). Following Heidegger above, we might add that the net is also cast forwards.

Casting the language net is immersion into the *logos*, a dialogue with self and others that brings forward utopian dimensions to both the past and the future. What gets caught in the net is what makes Lezama's historical imagination so fruitful: tales of Chinese emperors and Egyptian funerary practices, snippets of pre-Socratic philosophy, memories of nightfall in the Caribbean, images that cascade, producing a never-ending sense of wonder. In a splendid essay on Lezama, Severo Sarduy compares the poet's language as a kind of double of nature that devours reality, or, to put it differently, it is culture performing a reading of nature. Like an incantation, the word deciphers, or perhaps reciphers reality (Sarduy, 1970, pp. 62–65). And with perhaps Picasso in mind, Sarduy says that when Lezama wants something, he pronounces it. This mythic presence of language should not seem surprising, since both Christian and non-Christian symbolic forms are testimony to the power of language, particularly in creation myths. In fact, Lezama's verbal prowess is like those "momentary deities" that Ernst Cassirer speaks about, a flash of the sublime or the sacred that stirs simultaneously a feeling of danger, awe, uniqueness, a condensation of feeling, image, and thought that always, somehow, gets tied in to a larger context.

Lezama's privileged status for poetry would have him in agreement with Johann Hamann, who said that "Poetry is the mother tongue of humanity" (Cassirer, 1953, pp. 34–35). This bears a remarkable resemblance to Vico, but Lezama's keen appreciation of Vico goes further than the latter's notion of *sapienza poetica* (poetic wisdom). One of Vico's great contributions to historical thinking was how important language was to understanding a given society. If we take a familiar Marxist metaphor of base and superstructure, Vico would be neither a materialist (base determines or overdetermines the superstructure) nor an idealist (the contrary). He sees a relationship between laws, types of reasoning, human nature, and even kinds of writing. Moreover, he saw the transition from different kinds of societies (from theocratic to autocratic to democratic) as also revealing transitions in tropological expression (metaphor–metonymy–synechdoche–irony). (See White, 1978, p. 209 for Vico's table.)

Vico's tropological analysis and the use of expressions such as "imaginative universals," his theories on memory (already discussed), his *verum-factum* principal, his belief in Providence coupled with a profound sense of history and culture (Western and non-Western), are important to Lezama's own thinking on history, particularly his *eras imaginarias*. The following words by Verene, which are about Vico, can equally apply to Lezama: "Vico's ideas constitute a philosophy of recollective universals which generates philosophical understanding from the image, not the rational category. . . . This philosophy places the image over the concept, the speech over the argument, and the mythic divination over the fact" (Verene, 1981, pp. 19, 30).

Despite his essays on his poetic system or imaginary eras and his voracious philosophical appetite, Lezama never claimed that he was a systematic philosopher. But his ability to think through combining a series of startling images and metaphors, his skill in exploring certain myths, despite their complexity and heterogeneity, do reveal common themes and concerns in his thinking. But it is a unity that emerges from the sacred, admirably expressed in the following phrase: "Nothing is incoherent since everything has a sense of the marvelous" (quoted in Molinero, 1989, p. 101).

This thinking in images brings us to Hegel's notion of recollection, as developed in his *Phenomenology of Spirit*. We have mentioned in the introduction how the word *Bild* in German (image or picture) is the basis for the words *education, culture, formation, shaping* (*Bildung*). It forms the background of Hegel's writing about recollection (*Erinnerung*). In what follows we rely on Verene and how he interprets pictorial thinking, recollection, and the concept in Hegel (Verene, 1985, pp. 1–13).

Why is *Erinnerung* so important to Hegel? According to Verene, it is the name given by Hegel for the power of consciousness to have speculative knowledge of its own activity. As we will see, speculation has no negative connotations for Hegel; it implies going beyond the merely sensory, and by doing so makes what was initially subjective, objective. It is like the imagination in being able to unite very different thoughts and things, but unlike it, has a conceptual basis. "Here Hegel says that the forms of spirit in their contingency are history and in their conceptual organization are the science of the coming into appearance of knowing, and that both together are conceptual history or recollection" (Verene, 1985, p. 3). Verene shows how important metaphors and images are to understanding the *Phenomenology of Spirit*, for the comprehension of Hegel's subject itself, which is the speculative understanding of history, reality, and spirit. Recollection is a process by which we form images and bring them to our consciousness. It is "the form through which recollection works" (Ibid., p. 4). There are four stages of recollection: a first stage in which the subject, overcoming the mindlessness of nature, remembers a series of self-images. It is followed by a recognition of recollection's systematic power, an internalization which Hegel underlines by hyphenating the word (*Er-innerung*). This ability to internalize the image is what makes recollection give way to the possibility of absolute knowing (third stage). Finally, the fourth stage "is the realization that recollection in both its sides—in its power to call forth images and in its power to know them, to organize them into a totality—is conceptualized history" (ibid., p. 5). Hegel's mapping out of this process is driven by the concept, which is where Lezama would part company with him, though it should be said that concept for Hegel is not some arid intellectual construct, but something that can gather within its realm the amplitude of experience, be it empirical, emotional, religious, or spiritual.

Just as in the *Phenomenology of Spirit*, Lezama does not use metaphors and images as a way of dazzling the reader, as a rhetorical flourish. They are integral to defining self-consciousness, and in the context of *La expresión americana*, we can understand the proliferation of images as that gallery which constitutes the formation of Latin American identity and consciousness. If Hegel saw the image as a stepping stone to the concept, Lezama would already claim that the image contains the conceptual. (To Hegel's credit, we should say that he did not view the image as something false on the way to the "truth" of the concept but as the origin of the concept, which is recollected in the act of knowing.)

The internalization of the image as a basis for shaping or educating is consistent with Lezama's efforts with *Orígenes* (both the group and the magazine), often described as a *paideia*. *La expresión americana* could be seen as one attempt at a Latin American *Bildungsroman* of history. But unlike a novel, or a more traditional straightforward narrative approach, Lezama's poetic and "imaginative universals" are brought out as if marshaling the vast forces of "large choral groupings" in an incessant conversation of East, West, Africa, and Latin America, through his "animistic counterpoint." And despite Lezama's erudition and vast dialogue with many different cultures, he did not equate culture with "high culture." Proof of this are his substantial analyses of *gaucho* poetry, of the Mexican *corridos*, the art of José Guadalupe Posada and other popular artists or poets during different parts of *La expresión americana*.

It would perhaps be stretching it to claim that *La expresión americana* was a kind of Latin American *Phenomenology of Spirit*, if only because of what we said before: Lezama does not claim to be describing an "essence" of the Latin American spirit. But both he and Hegel did see spirit as historically based, not some ethereal substance floating above the world. Spirit and its development constitute what we know as history. In Lezama's case, maybe spirit should be replaced with *sujeto metafórico* (with some affinity to Ortega's vital reason). Unlike his predecessor, Lezama would see the distinctions Hegel made about original, reflexive, and philosophical history as too rigid—better to leap from one to the other, taking from original history its poetic nature, from pragmatic (reflexive) its analogical method, and so on. By doing so Lezama is able to fashion a unique vision of history, drawing on the important insights of Plato, Vico, and Hegel about memory and recollection.

Before discussing Lezama's idea of "open gnostic space," we will examine some more affinities (and differences) between Lezama and Hegel. In discussing *La expresión americana*, usually the antagonisms are drawn with Hegel's *Philosophy of History*. But, as we have seen with the *Phenomenology of Spirit*, there are other writings that reveal these affinities, which also include *Lectures on Aesthetics*, the *Philosophy of Right*, and some of the earlier writings. In what follows I make no claim that Lezama was a Hegelian through and through, even if unconsciously so. The aim is a more modest one: it is hoped that the convergences (confluences, Lezama might say) in their thinking will yield new grounds for understanding Lezama, another twist (or melody?) in the "animistic counterpoint."

In *La expresión americana*, Lezama makes rather pointed references to Hegel and his views on America, engaging Ortega y Gasset on the way. Many critics have used *La expresión americana* as a way of pointing out Lezama as an anti-Hegelian. But as several contemporary thinkers have shown—Derrida, Adorno, and William Desmond, among others—the temptation in thinking we have "surpassed" Hegel is illusory at best and in the case of Lezama, pernicious.

It might seem foolhardy to affirm this, especially when Lezama has soundly taken Hegel to task in his essay. With reason Lezama criticizes Hegel's Eurocentric bias in viewing world history as he does, particularly his understanding of Africa (as not being part of history), or his dismissal of the western hemisphere by including it in his geographical review, thereby defining it as part of nature (but again, not part of history). Lezama says these mistakes "show a scandalous incomprehension," and undoubtedly the Cuban is correct in pointing out these errors. In a more religious vein, he criticizes "the closed pessimism of Hegelian Protestantism," also pointing out Hegel's anti-Catholic prejudices in trying to explain Latin American underdevelopment. Lezama would probably agree with Ortega in claiming that Hegelian thought contained a "certain blindness to the future," expressed with particular vehemence regarding America. According to Ortega y Gasset, the future alarmed Hegel because it represented the irrational (Ortega, 1981, p. 88). Hegel says that America is the land of the future and that at some distant time it will become important. Hegel says the following: "What has taken place in the New World up to the present time is only an echo of the Old World—the expression of a foreign life; and as a Land of the Future, it has no interest for us, here, for as regards History, our concern must be with that which has been and that which is. In regard to Philosophy, on the other hand, we have to do with that which (strictly speaking) is neither past nor future, but that which is, which has eternal existence—with Reason; and that is quite sufficient to occupy us" (Hegel, 1956, p. 87).

Notwithstanding Hegel (and Lezama's) blind spots, it would be fruitful to keep in mind Ortega's metaphor about Hegel: "In his errors, as does the lion with its powerful bite, he always manages to get in his teeth a big chunk of the palpitating truth" (Ortega, 1981, p. 88). Let us examine some of Hegel's and Lezama's bites, so we can see where they come together on issues of history and art.

In his *Philosophy of History*, Hegel says "the History of the World is nothing but the development of the Idea of Freedom." This strikes us as obvious nowadays, but before the Enlightenment this was not necessarily the most important barometer for understanding or evaluating the historical evolution of societies. More important, Hegel saw freedom not just as an individual's ability to do what s/he wanted, but intimately linked to notions of intersubjectivity (recognition of others), justice, the law, and limits set by society and nature. Freedom internalizes rather than supplants necessity. In *La expresión americana*, Lezama deals with several Latin American figures who were key in the independence struggles of the continent: Fray Servando Teresa de Mier, Simón Rodríguez, José Martí, Sor Juana Inés de la Cruz. Even when he speaks of people who did not assume an openly political struggle (as in the cases of Kondori or Aleijandinho), Lezama embeds them within a rebellious spirit analogous to other types of defiance.

Significantly, Lezama gives a radically poetic thrust to this freedom, by underlining the aesthetic and ethical dimensions of the New World baroque. For Lezama, the baroque that grew out of Latin America was not merely a copy of the European baroque, but inevitably marked by its natural surroundings and social context. It became a hybrid baroque, incorporating new words, images, and realities. As Lezama says, it was an art of Counter-Conquest, not of the Counter-Reformation, and ultimately linked to Enlightenment concerns. The Latin American baroque not only remakes the classical as well as European baroque in terms of aesthetics. Through its rebellious search for new forms and hybrid expressions, it makes a statement about its own identity and reality, its autonomy and sovereignty in every realm, from the artistic to the political. The Latin American baroque is one of the signifiers of the continent's freedom.

Curiously, Lezama focuses on figures that one could say were ultimately "failures," in a certain sense, living the ends of their lives poor, unrecognized, killed in battle, or in exile. Even the exception, Fray Servando Teresa de Mier (1763–1827), spent most of his life in jails or running from the authorities. But their thought and actions always have a kind of germinative aspect that is taken up later by other figures or movements. For example, in the case of Fray Servando, Lezama points out that being persecuted by the Church does not necessarily draw the priest away from Catholicism, but in a way makes his religious beliefs more inclusive, that instead of breaking away from all tradition, Fray Servando enlarges it. Lezama sees in this kind of adaptability, pluralism, and syncretic thought a quintessential aspect of American thought and culture.

Both Hegel and Lezama follow Vico in seeing a certain progress to the historical process, going back from theocratic societies to more democratic ones by way of aristocratic-monarchical states, and so on. In Hegelian terms, we could say that the master-slave relationship has become less onerous, but still part of the turbulent dialectic of history. Both, as Christians, saw a sacred dimension to history, a kind of providential design, though they might have differed on how the nature of the divine intervenes in history. As some critics have pointed out, Lezama, despite his fervent belief in resurrection and divine causality, does not reject change, nor does he stray from having a dynamic image of history. For Lezama, history is a reflection of the image through time, somewhat similar to what Plato said about time being a moving image of eternity. There is a large component of the eternal or the absolute in Lezama's definition of the image, which is similar but not identical to Hegel's Absolute Spirit. According to María Zambrano, it was Hegel who "discovered that history was an inexorable vicissitude of the spirit." But spirit changes, evolves, negates, and surpasses itself, its content is highly historical, and in its philosophical journey arrived at some not very Christian outcomes: "Reality cannot be nature as created and made forever, but that other reality which man is the bearer of, of which the individual is the mask which both expresses and contains it [that other reality]; a mask which sacrifices itself reciting its part, only to be later stripped away. His [Hegel's] Christianity had to conclude in an idea which is quite un-Christian, so pagan, that the individual is the mask of the *logos*" (Zambrano, 1993, p. 14). The tragedy of humankind is not being able to live without the gods, and in that vein Zambrano concludes that for Hegel history thus takes the place of the divine.

At the same time, though, both Lezama and Hegel see history as a theodicy, that is, as a justification of the works of God, understood in a way that does not oppose faith and reason. Given the follies and absolute depravities of history, a theodicy tries to explain the nature of evil as meaningful rather than absurd or senseless. This in turn brings up questions about necessity and freedom. In Hegel's words:

> Our intellectual striving aims at realizing the conviction that what was *intended* by eternal wisdom, is actually accomplished in the domain of the existent, active Spirit, as well as in that of mere Nature. Our mode of treating the subject is, in this aspect, a Theodicy—a justification of the ways of God . . . so that the ill that is found in the World may be comprehended, and the thinking Spirit reconciled with the fact of the existence of evil. Indeed, nowhere is such a harmonizing view more pressingly demanded than in Universal History. (Hegel, 1956, p. 15)

For Hegel, harmonizing the divine or providential with the passions of the world requires explaining a disjuncture between what men attempt to do and the ultimate consequences of their actions, a kind of double which manifests itself within and behind those passions. That double, in Hegel's vocabulary, goes by the name of "the cunning of reason," where transindividual elements are expressed. Here universal goals and particular intentions meet. Providence becomes in Hegel the cunning of reason, and the interpretation of Christianity becomes the province of speculative reason. To speculate is not mere contemplation, seeing, or conjecture, but also by way of its mystical side it takes us to a mirror metaphor, so dear to Lezama. In an interview, Lezama linked his faith in resurrection with a specular trope, which by way of the image can recuperate its lost similarity (with the Creator): "Image for me is life. In this I have roots back to St. Paul; we see through mirrors in an image." Nicholas of Cusa, among others, said that God could not be known directly, only by his effects (nature, etc.), which were partial mirrors of the divine. To speculate, then, means to go beyond the sensorial and arrive at the supernatural. In this regard we can speak of Lezama's historical thought (or his poetic system) as being speculative. Hegel sees speculation as a conceptual process, not necessarily linked to a mirror metaphor, even though his thoughts on reflection invite that kind of association. More important is speculation's ability to (re)unite elements, things, and concepts which seem opposed or disparate, and, in contrast to analytic thinking which leads to understanding, speculative thought is closer to the poetic imagination. However, it goes beyond the poetic by being conceptual and presupposes the work of understanding. This is close to the *eros cognoscente* (erotics of knowing) seen in Lezama's poetry and essays. With his baroque theodicy, laced with Platonic echoes, Lezama defines it as such: "Man strives for God, but man enjoys (savors) all things in a banquet whose finality is God."

Speculation as gift of the imagination takes us directly to what Hegel said about historical writing and aesthetic consciousness. For him, historical writing was a verbal art, closely linked to poetic expression. Just like Vico, he characterizes poetry as a form of knowing, with which Lezama would be in complete agreement. This knowledge is tropological, a metaphoric process. Similarly, both would coincide with the ancient Greeks in seeing a close relationship between poetry, history, and philosophy. The first philosophers wrote in verse and called their work histories. It is not surprising, then, that the word "history" in Greek comes from the root of the same word, *eidenai* (to know by seeing) that is also the root for the philosophical terms *form* and *idea* (Gillespie, 1984, pp. 1–4). History is what one had seen or witnessed, a key concept that early Christianity reworked to its advantage. For Christians it was crucial to be a witness of the divine, and it is that witnessing that gave the apostles their subsequent authority as bearers and transmitters of the new doctrine.

Both Hegel and Lezama would agree with Aristotle in seeing poetry as more philosophical than history, by virtue of not being encumbered by the inessentials, allowing it to go to the marrow, to the universal. It draws humans closer to intelligibility, and as a result Hegel assigns art (along with religion and philosophy) a special place in the realm of Absolute Spirit. This does not mean that art is uprooted from history. On the contrary: "Art is not anti-historical or a-historical. It is rather an imaginative appropriation of one of the essential strivings of historical man" (Desmond, 1986, p. 61). Among the characteristics of a work of art relevant to history are, Desmond says, "its concrete uniting of spirit and sensuousness; its dialectical wholeness; its attempts to make present a unification of freedom and necessity and of individuality and universality; and most especially being marked by an intrinsic end" (ibid., p. 61).

Poetry is born of a separation between the consciousness of its object (from which it is separate) and a desire to recreate that lost unity. According to Hegel, this creates two principal classes of poetry—classical and romantic—the first being universal and objective, the latter particular and subjective. The tension between the two generates three types of poetic composition: the epic, the lyric, and the dramatic. The epic is external; it remains wedded to an empiricism of episodes and deeds. The lyric is interiorized, constantly changing, limited by its emotiveness. Only dramatic poetry is capable of synthesizing the two. As Hayden White has pointed out: "[Hegel sees] history as the prose form closest in its immediacy to poetry in general and to the Drama in particular. In fact, Hegel not only historicized poetry and the Drama, he poeticized and dramatized history itself" (White, 1974, p. 88).

Given this aesthetic slant, Hegel situates historical writing between poetry and oratory, although he underlines the fact that historical inscription cannot have the freedom of the former, nor the "interest" of the latter. This intermediate position occupied by history is explained by its having a poetic form but a prosaic content. Since history is not just laying out events and dates but an attempt to understand what has happened with a certain coherence, logic, or meaning, there are two tensions, according to White, that pursue the imagination of the historian: a critical tension and a poetic one. The critical dimension implies a selection: there are certain things that will be suppressed from a narrative, but you cannot invent anything, nor, of course, add anything new to what happened. The poetic factor means describing the vitality and uniqueness of what has happened as if the reader were witnessing them anew, so that their idealness takes shape. From this to Lezama's imaginary eras it is not very far. But we need to go a little further with Hegel before going on with Lezama.

If we ask, "How does Hegel put together the plot of history?" a double answer would be necessary: as tragedy and as comedy. Following White we can say that at a microcosmic level Hegel sees and describes history as tragedy, but at a macrocosmic level it is treated as comedy. In his scheme White associates the former with a mechanistic mode of argument, a radical ideological mode, and a global trope of metonymy (of a reductive nature). For comedy, the mode of argument is organicist, ideologically conservative, and the global trope is the synecdoche (of an integrative nature). To complicate matters further, White says that Hegel's thought begins in irony, since he sees consciousness as a paradox and human existence as contradiction (White, 1974, p. 29). Perhaps we are closer to Old Comedy, where the heroic and the ironic are mixed. Of course, historians can combine modes of emplotment with a different mode of argument, ideological implication, and tropes that are not normally associated with it. (White's examples indicate such noncorrespondence as with Michelet and Burckhardt, as does Hegel's two modes of emplotment, which yield conservative and radical implications to his historical viewpoint.)

Hegel's microcosmic level abounds with examples of tragedy: individuals or civilizations that are faced with war, defeat, or extermination; obstacles that frustrate the will of a person or a nation. The tragic *agon* is not entirely destructive, of course. In the ashes of desolation, there is always a kind of epiphany which illuminates the dilemmas of human existence, its limits. In comedy, of course, there is hope, even triumph (no matter how temporary), where a reconciliation of forces (natural, social, divine) takes place. Harmony is established between opposing forces, not by eliminating one or having one best the other, but by transformation. Hegel's *aufhebung* perhaps captures this tension of opposites that is preserved, taken forth, annulled, and surpassed, and it echoes the *coincidentia oppositorum* of Cusa, a thinker close to Lezama. The tragic perspective is illuminating but specific, partial; it is caught up with a given culture or civilization. The comic perspective incorporates that of tragedy because it globally encompasses the totality of different forces in a dynamic harmony. Comedy is a dialectic of reconciliation. Some have criticized Hegel's notion of reconciliation, alleging that it is conservative, accommodating to the forces that be. But this is not true; reconciliation seeks to harmonize the terrible divisions in human society not by accepting the status quo necessarily, but by reconciling humans with their history as a totality. This happens as the spirit acquires greater self-consciousness (and freedom), a dialectic within history that implies a fierce struggle with nature, custom, and convention.

Macrocosmically, Lezama also had a comic vision that sought reconciliation, unitive solutions through the image, a kind of *aufhebung* where eternity and resurrection are embodied. "The image as an absolute, the image that knows itself as image, the image as the last of all possible histories. . . . The image is the secret cause of history. . . . The image at times abandons itself to the suspension of its first causality, to attain a total illumination, where causality disappears to give us a spell of permanence in its scope, counterpoint or city" (Lezama, 1971, p. 23; 1981, pp. 19 and 104–5).

Both Hegel and Lezama adopt an organicist mode of argument to elucidate history, that is, within a plurality of dispersed events they seek a crystallization, an integration which is more important than the sum of its parts. We saw an example of this integrative conjoining while discussing Lezama's analysis of paintings being linked up to the I Ching. An organicist explanation does not want to establish laws for history, but instead proceeds by principles or ideas. These principles or ideas create an image or prefigure the end of a process or a totality, proceeding metaphorically. Tropologically, the organicist manner recurs to synecdoche, its most notable example being the microcosm-macrocosm relationship. Lezama clearly uses this figure in his essays, especially when he relates an image to philosophical discourse in order to reinforce a point. No doubt the micro/macrocosm continuum is well suited to the comic vision of Lezama since it establishes a well-defined causality between the human and the divine, what has been called "the great chain of being."

Comedy's history goes back to Comus, a Greek fertility god whose cult entailed a ritual springtime procession that represented rebirth, rejuvenation, and resurrection. All three of these R's are close to Lezama's vision of poetry and history. Despite both comedy and tragedy being characterized by "excess," one could say that both also explore an alternative reality, one deeply marked by the imagination. (But not always; often the excess is an obsession, a neurotic tick, or the exaggeration of a normal trait.) This imaginative exploration is often the catalyst for reconciliation, and comedy is the epitome of the reconciliation of social forces, a quiet kind of utopianism. Finally, it is important to remember comedy in terms of how it was used by Dante in his *Divina Commedia*. Lezama's love of Dante was no secret, evidenced by the title of his great novel *Paradiso* (1966). Dante's masterpiece is an image of reconciliation: worldly, cosmic, theological, and divine, through redemption and resurrection. E. R. Curtius, another author much admired by the Cuban, summed up Dante's work this way: "The *Divina Commedia* is at the same time a *Comédie Humaine*, for which nothing human is too high or too low. Dante's poem moves wholly in the transcendent. But it is everywhere penetrated by the breath of history, by the passion of the present. Timelessness and temporality are not only confronted and related, they are also merged and so interwoven that the threads are no longer distinguishable" (Curtius, 1956, p. 366). This could also be said of much of Lezama's work.

More common is Lezama's legendary use of metaphor, whose power of articulation and ingenuity go to the heart of what art or historiographical discourse (re)present. Kenneth Burke defines metaphor in terms of perspective, of understanding one thing by way of another, bearing a striking resemblance to the way Hegel understands the movement of dialectics. More important, though, it shows that metaphor is more conceptual than linguistic, and in Lezama's case much more so, because his essays and poetry proceed in long metaphoric chains in order to elaborate a thought by images. Lezama, in his own *Bildung*, philosophizes using poetic metaphor. In his essay, "Prelude to the Imaginary Eras," the unconditioned and causality form the axis of the text; the images and metaphors are rich, starting with trees and forests, Bacon's *experimenti sortes*, a Buddhist sculpture of Apsara, a small mule in a work by Balzac, the quality of the color blue in paintings by Van Gogh, and a short excursus on a popular saying, "A Chinese girlfriend brings good luck," to name only the first in a long rosary of images.

An example will show how important the figurative is for Lezama, since its connotations are rhetorical, religious, philosophical, and historical. In "A partir de la poesía" (Starting from poetry), Lezama speaks of a last imaginary era, that of infinite possibility, incarnate in the figure of José Martí (1853–95). "Feeling oneself poorer is to penetrate into the unknown, where the advice of certainty became extinguished, where finding a shaft of light or a vacillating intuition is paid in kind by death or a primordial desolation. To be poorer is to be surrounded by the miraculous, to fashion the animism of each form; it is a form of waiting that becomes creative, born of the distance between things" (Lezama, 1971, p. 179). This creativity of absence is like that of death and grief, where restoring the lost plenitude requires creative imaginative leaps. Memory, or recollection, might be the grieving of history, but instead of restoring a lost plenitude (an impossibility), it allows the past to speak (sing?) to us from the vantage point of the future. Perhaps that explains Lezama's phrase "death engenders us all anew."

This description of poorness becoming infinite possibility also reads like a version of Hegel's master-slave dialectic. At first, the slave is nothing, and the master's initial recognition is not true recognition since it recognizes a nothingness, or more accurately a nobody. From that nothingness the slave acquires (self-)consciousness through work and eventually becomes a historical subject. From an initial defeat, there is an eventual defeat of the master and servitude. In this essay, Martí prefigures the historical events of the Cuban Revolution; in *La expresión americana*, Lezama analyzes Martí as a culminating figure of nineteenth-century libertarian struggles. The figurative element of Martí's life and thought (as realization or as portent), central to Lezama's concept of imaginary eras, forms part of the speculative economy of the Hegelian term *aufhebung* (annul, conserve, elevate). And it shows a strong affinity to *figura* as employed by Eric Auerbach, whereby there is a story (literal sense), embodied by a figure which is fulfilled in the future (*veritas*). The *figura* holds the *veritas* within, veiled, and only its future realization unfolds the truth. The *figura* is not a symbol or an allegory; it is fulfilled in history. Its prophetic value is related to historical interpretation, which is why Auerbach says, "Real historical figures are to be interpreted spiritually, but the interpretation points to a carnal, hence, historical fulfillment—for the truth has become history or flesh." (Auerbach, 1959, p. 34). Lezama remolds that figurative interpretation, which received its maximum use in the Middle Ages, and he makes it function within his poetic system, his imaginary eras, as part of an endless wave of analogies that end in the image. He allows us to see history as the flesh of truth, from eternity, which for Lezama was the eyes of faith, for Hegel the eyes of reason, equally eternal.

One of Lezama's most important departures from Hegel is captured in his phrase "an open gnostic space." On several occasions in *La expresión americana* he makes use of the term as a description of America's uniqueness. Central to this "definition" is nature, which for Lezama is a formative part of (Latin) America's culture. Lezama here shows his preference for Schelling's famous saying, "Nature is spirit made visible, and spirit is nature made invisible." Nature (visible spirit), says Lezama, loves to dialogue with humankind, "and that dialogue between the spirit which reveals nature and humans, is landscape. . . . And in America, wherever the possibility of landscape bursts forth, there also exists the possibility of culture" (p. 167). Lezama is generous with details about landscape: corn and pre-Columbian cultures, chocolate and the baroque, the Romantics and their exaltation of landscape (from Heredia to the *gauchos* to Martí and Darío), and the *ombú* and *ceiba* trees, which he calls "historicized trees, with respectable leaves, which in the American landscape take on the value of writing, where a sentence is stated about our destiny" (p. 170). *Hojas* in Spanish can mean both leaves and page or folio, which evokes a well-known concept about the book of nature.

Some critics have pointed out that Lezama drew on the Romantics such as Novalis to portray nature as a text to be deciphered. This is true, but in the Western tradition the image extends as far back as the Bible, Silvestris, St. Bonaventure, Nicholas of Cusa, Montaigne, and Galileo, to name only a few. It is quite possible that Lezama had in mind Fray Luis de Granada's *Introducción del símbolo de la fe*, where in book 2 this metaphor is expressed with great vividness and eloquence. Fray Luis's book, with its rich descriptions of nature, animals, plants, and so forth, written in some of the most exquisite Spanish prose ever, is ultimately Catholic apolegetics. His evocations of nature served a moral, theological purpose; nature is alive by virtue of being "ciphers of transcendence," to borrow a term from Karl Jaspers. De Granada was a Renaissance thinker in that he saw the natural order as an expression of intelligence, but that intelligence was outside of nature, in the mind of a divine creator who ruled over nature. The ancient Greeks would attribute that intelligence to nature itself, as a vast living organism endowed with soul and thought (reason). Lezama is definitely closer to the Greek view of nature, despite his ideological affinity with Fray Luis de Granada. Building on the microcosm-macrocosm/tragic-comic images, as well as Schelling's statement on nature, Lezama's historico-natural views might be summed up in the words of George Santayana: "Everything in nature is lyrical in its ideal essence, tragic in its fate, and comic in its existence."

As Ernst Robert Curtius says, the nature of antiquity is always inhabited, by either men or gods. Lezama builds from that literary tradition, which is perhaps why he was fond of quoting Pascal's saying, "Since true nature is lost, everything can be nature" (Lezama, 1970, p. 145), which is Lezama's way of saying that everything can be culture as well. But in America, "the open gnostic space" is not only a territorial extension, but a spatial metaphor for culture as well, in that it becomes landscape. This does not mean being a *locus amoenis*, but an active presence, a transformative, metaphorical power that significantly defines (and limits) the nature of history and culture. Perhaps this points to the true meaning of the phrase "nature abhors a vacuum," to which could be added, "history abhors disorder or discontinuity." For Lezama, nature, through the power of the word, becomes culture; history, by embracing the numinous, becomes marvelous. Many writers have dedicated their work to embodying this important theme: Carpentier in *The Lost Steps* and *The Kingdom of This World*, García Márquez in *One Hundred Years of Solitude*, Wilson Harris in the *Guiana Quartet*, Neruda in *Las alturas de Macchu Picchu*, or Sor Juana's "Primer Sueño."

Why does Lezama refer to the spatial/cultural configuration of America as an open gnostic space ("un espacio gnóstico abierto")? Why the specific reference to Gnosticism? First is the syncretic nature of Gnosticism itself. Its sources are incredibly complex and intertwined: Hellenic, Babylonian, Egyptian, Iranian, as well as Jewish and Christian. In Fernando Ortiz's terminology, it is transcultured; in Lezama's, it is a kind of "animistic counterpoint." Lezama places high value on cultures or artists that can draw on many different sources and yet still create something unique from that heterogeneity. He begins the fifth section of *La expresión americana* ("Summas crítica de lo Americano") by making reference to three artists he greatly admired: Stravinsky, Picasso, and Joyce. All of them, of course, are known for transforming the most disparate elements, languages, and cultures into extraordinary works of art.

Is there a relationship between Fernando Ortiz's counterpoint and that of Lezama? From a chronological perspective, it is clear that Lezama had read and admired Ortiz's magnum opus, but he never makes a direct reference to it in *La expresión americana*. Like Lezama, Ortiz in his *Cuban Counterpoint: Tobacco and Sugar* uses the two agricultural products as organizing metaphors for Cuban society, culture, and history. Ortiz does have a much stronger empirical basis than does Lezama, even though he can willfully interpret facts in ways that might seem capricious to some historians. Despite this, Ortiz does his homework, drawing on edicts, historical documents, anthropological findings, scientific studies, economic theory, and so on, whereas Lezama's "raw materials" are drawn from literature, mythology, religion, and poetry, as well as history. Antonio Benítez-Rojo, for example, sees this work by Ortiz as postmodernist before its time, with its literary flourishes, its metaphorical logic, and its imaginative use of historical narrative. Even though his counterpoint is formed by tobacco and sugar (often radically opposed), his thinking is not marked by polarity, or by thesis-antithesis types of contradiction. "It's a question of voices that come from different centers of emission, from differing moments and discourses, which coexist beside each other in a complex and critical relationship, one that it is impossible to clarify entirely" (Benítez-Rojo, 1992,

p. 174.) Obviously this plural, decentered way of thinking is dear to Lezama, but he draws on a much broader canvas: his *eras imaginarias* or "great choral groups" are rarely accompanied by the wealth of empirical detail found in the work of Ortiz.

Perhaps because of the syncretic nature of Gnosticism there is no central scripture, issuing forth a plurality of interpretations, even though there are some common themes and images. It was marked by a sense of nonconformism, individualism, creativity, and a fertile imagination (Jonas, 1963, p. 42). Gnostics were eventually accused of being heretics by church authorities, because of their differing interpretations of the Gospels, their hermeneutic freedom. The parallels with other moments in history (from the Inquisition to communist purges) are not lost on Lezama. This pluralism is central to Lezama's thinking, so aptly captured by poet and Lezama scholar César Salgado, who says that "he was a Catholic who didn't believe in heresy." Words that no doubt have a social resonance in contemporary Cuba.

Gnosis, of course, is usually translated as *knowledge*, which is not totally accurate. It pertains to knowledge from sense perception or experience, but not scientific knowledge (*episteme*). For the gnostics, *gnosis* meant self-knowledge, and of the universe, to "be transformed through enlightenment into the actual object of knowledge, overcoming and removing the dichotomy between subject and object" (Filoramo, 1990, p. 41). Lezama is playing on the full range of meanings of *gnosis*, and how it pertains to the American landscape, as an important element in the generation of knowledge and self-knowledge of history and culture. Nature or landscape has a gnostic dimension; the spatial has a spiritual realm, Lezama would say, in agreement with the gnostics. But unlike them, he would not see the origins of the universe as an act of ignorance but would agree with gnostic doctrine in seeing knowledge as an act of redemption. Lezama was not sympathetic to the anti-cosmic radical dualism of gnostic thought.

Cosmologically speaking, the gnostic view of the world is rather bleak: "The universe, the domain of the Archons, is like a vast prison whose innermost dungeon is the earth, the scene of man's life. Around and above it the cosmic spheres are ranged like concentric enclosing shells" (Jonas, 1963, p. 43). The layers of matter in space remove us further and further from God, the gnostics say; and they also compare the experience of the world in terms of alienness and exile. It is no wonder that many have pointed out the links between gnostic thought and existentialism. Clearly, Lezama does not see the earth or nature in these gnostic terms, which is why his expression must inevitably take the course it did: "open gnostic space." Open because opposed to the closed nature of gnostic space, but open also because it is a transcultured and transculturating space, the place where the "metaphorical subject" can make the "animistic counterpoint" happen.

Giovanni Filoramo points out that there is an Orphic antecedent to gnostic myth. Lezama wrote one of three essays on imaginary eras on

Orphism; the other two are on Taoism and Egypt (all in Lezama, 1971). And both are essentially stories of origins of the cosmos, which recall Lezama's paraphrase of Nietzsche: he who goes back to the origins will find new origins. Going to the origins is a germinative act, a new beginning, piecing together the dismembered body of Orpheus. For Francis Bacon, whom Lezama read attentively, Orpheus is the paradigm of a new kind of wisdom or knowledge. With his lyre, he held all of nature in rapt attention. He conquered through harmony, not through strength, like Hercules (Briggs, 1989, pp. 1–3). This relationship between art (music) nature, and knowledge perfectly describes Lezama's phrase about the "open gnostic space." It is a space of desire as well, exemplified not only in nature images, but also in our previous discussion of paintings: "Sight opens all space to desire, but desire is not satisfied with seeing" (Starobinski in Leppert, 1996, p. 101). For Lezama, desire is the shadow cast by seeing when it seeks out history. And what the shadow gathers in the visible, as well as what it un-conceals from the invisible, forms an an "open gnostic space."

This space, as noted, is open to different cultures and voices, but not in a passive way. It is transformative, creative, transculturating, whereby the imagination takes a utopian dimension, but not in a prescriptive way. This act of historical imagination is described by Paul Ricoeur:

> The imagination has a metaphysical function which cannot be reduced to a simple projection of vital, unconscious or repressed desires. The imagination has a prospective and explorative function in regard to the inherent possibilities of man. It is, *par excellence*, the instituting and the constituting of what is humanly possible. In imagining his possibilities, man acts as a prophet of his own existence. We can then begin to understand in what sense we may speak of a *redemption through imagination:* by means of dreams of innocence and reconciliation, hope works to the fullest capacity. In the broad sense of the word, these images of reconciliation are *myths*, not in the positivistic sense of legend or fable, but in the phenomenological sense of religion, in the sense of a meaningful story of the destiny of the whole human race. Mythos means word or speech. The imagination, in so far as it has a mytho-poetic function, is also the seat of profound workings which govern the decisive changes in our visions of the world. Every real conversion is first a revolution at the level of our directive images. By changing his imagination, man alters his existence. (Ricoeur, 1965, pp. 126–127)

Like few writers or thinkers, Lezama truly saw the imagination as an act of faith, as a kind of primary fire that can warm up and light up the universe, or at least the island of Cuba, or perhaps as a dragon that can piece together the sundered elements of its history. Lezama's optimism was legendary, always seeking out a positive interpretation of events. In *La expresión americana* it shows up time and time again, in the figures of Sor Juana, Simón Rodríguez, and Fray Servando. Even a troubled thinker like Pascal becomes a springboard for transformative images. Pascal has been described as "uneasy, burning, greedy for the absolute." How unlike Lezama, who approached the absolute with the innocence of a lamb, lapping at its shores with a tranquil, sensuous joy.

It is this redemptive nature of the imagination which can bring important insights into the historical process. No one reads Lezama for an empirically based understanding of history, but his images and tropes do trigger a series of paths that can be examined. Imaginary era, a baroque of Counter-Conquest, metaphorical subject, animistic counterpoint, great choral groups, open gnostic space, are all expressions that when explored begin to yield a way of approaching history, culture, even politics, with a different perspective, capable of resisting monistic or mechanistic explanations. And should we think that Lezama's poetic understanding of history is naive, we would do well to remember that for Christian thinkers the Book of Daniel exercised an enormous power over their conception of history for more than fifteen hundred years. Unbelievably, Daniel's four stages of history came from the interpretation of a dream.

Let us return to Lezama's opening statement: "I am ravished by being able to see words like fish in a waterfall." The image of fish brings to mind several different associations: Christian, alchemical, gnostic, Yoruba, even Taoist. Fish are linked to fecundity, procreation, the powers of water as origin, with lunar deities. In Christianity fish are inextricably coupled with baptism, immortality, and resurrection. It is also a eucharistic food, and the apostles were called fishers of men, as was Orpheus. For alchemists it is the archane substance; for the ancient Egyptians it is the phallus of Osiris; for the Chinese, abundance, wealth, regeneration and harmony. In Afro-Cuban lore, Yemayá is "the mother whose children are the fish," the life-giving force.

For Lezama, words have that generative capacity, which is one of the meanings of *poiesis*. They are the basic elements of a kind of theurgy, which is the ability to manipulate the gods through their occult tokens, most often in natural objects, statues, and so on, based on the notion of cosmic sympathy. As said before, Lezama's *logos* are like those "momentary gods," especially if we keep in mind what Frye said about Homer, that gods were ready-made metaphors (Frye, 1983, p. 7). In Lezama's discourse the blocks of images shift around, collide, explode, shimmer like gods.

The waters are the amniotic fluid of the imaginary eras. The metaphorical subject is that fisher of men or words, seeking the realm of the image, the secret soul of the *logos*. The waterfall is stopped or transformed by the fish in animistic counterpoint. The desire born of that longing, the shadow of its memory, is the dragon of history colliding with and eluding the net of language.

NOTE

1. References with only a page number apply to Irlemar Chiampi's superb critical edition of Lezama's *La expresión americana* (1993).

SIX

Severo Sarduy: Histories as Desire

Reading the work of Severo Sarduy is like walking into your favorite pastry shop: your whole body inhales the intoxicating, delectable sweetness, then your fingers and tongue take over like hungry serpents. He was not Cuba's first gay writer, nor the first Cuban author to deal with homosexuality. What he managed to do was make his gayness a celebratory, erotic affirmation, a mix of baroque theater, rumba wiggle, postmetaphysical philosophy, religious mysticism, all performed as a kind of writerly "voguing." Sarduy was born in 1937 in Camagüey, Cuba, and as a young writer was linked to the iconoclastic writers around *Ciclón* magazine such as Virgilio Piñera, José Rodríguez Feo, Antón Arrufat, and Fayad Jamís. Sarduy went to Paris in 1960 on an art scholarship and never returned. He was close to the thinkers and writers of *Tel Quel* magazine such as Roland Barthes, Jacques Derrida, Philippe Sollers, and Julia Kristeva and worked for Éditions du Seuil, where he published the works of the Latin American boom writers such as Fuentes, García Márquez, and Cortázar. Sarduy was equally brilliant as novelist, poet, and essayist. His first novel was *Gestos* (1963), but Sarduy's critical success began with *De donde son los cantantes* (1967; *From Cuba with a Song*, 1972, 1994), an unorthodox exploration of Cuban identity. Sarduy's work grew more experimental with *Cobra* (1973; Eng. trans. 1975, 1995) and *Maitreya* (1978; Eng. trans. 1987, 1995). He published three more novels in his lifetime. *Colibrí* (1984) is a parody of jungle novels and of boom writers such as Vargas Llosa, Carpentier, and Fuentes. *Cocuyo* (1990) describes the rite of passage of a picaresque, grotesque child, and *Pájaros de playa* (1993), an island where a group of young people are ravaged by a terrible affliction, is Sarduy's rueful, poetic, and searing meditation on AIDS, which terminated his life in 1993. His books of essays include *Escritos sobre un cuerpo* (1969; Eng. trans. 1989), *Barroco* (1974), and *La simulación* (1982). Sarduy was a gifted poet, publishing *Un testigo fugaz y disfrazado* (1985) and *Epitafios* (1994). His neo-baroque aesthetics were informed by cosmological and scientific models and metaphors. *Big Bang* (1974), a collection of poems, includes texts pertaining to astronomy, a subject he dealt with in *Nueva inestabilidad* (1987), not to mention *Barroco*. Sarduy also wrote plays, collected in *Para la voz* (1977; *For Voice: Four Plays*, 1985). His *Cristo de la Rue Jacob* (1987; *Christ on the Rue Jacob*, 1995) is a series of essays and epiphanies with a strong autobiographical flavor. Sarduy practiced and preached an erotics of reading/writing, and his rich, elegant, sensuous prose prompted García Márquez to say that "he wrote in the most beautiful Spanish of our time."

A rarity in Cuban intellectual circles, Sarduy never made public declarations either in favor of or against the Cuban Revolution. His decision not to return can be interpreted, of course, as expressing an incompatibility with the post–1959 fidelista regime. But his equally discrete position of not engaging in anti-communist name-calling and vituperation like other writers (Cabrera Infante, Arenas, Montaner) was not based on adherence to Marxism-Leninism, but a reluctance to embrace the inevitable polarization that has been (and still is) the Cuban intellectual's staple for decades: either you are a revolutionary (left-wing, progressive, anti-capitalist) or a counterrevolutionary (right-wing, reactionary, bourgeois). Sarduy was consistent in his approach, and it shows in his fiction, where the issues of identity, ideology, and even gender are fluid notions. While keenly aware of the ideological nature of art and culture, Sarduy was inimical to using political labels to define a work of art reductively. He let his art do the talking: a work of witty complexity, poetic flash, spiritual warmth, and plain outrageousness.

"Intercultural dialogue unleashes the demons of history," says Guillermo Gómez-Peña, but in the work of Severo Sarduy the demons sing, cross-dress, and salaciously flirt, breathing the erotic fire of literature. In our anxiety-ridden climate permeated with the politics of identity, reading Severo Sarduy is a refreshing, parodic, and bold romp through all the dis(guises) of our current obsessions with gender, race, multiculturalism, and historical representation. He decribed his work as neo-baroque, and he drew inspiration from the work of José Lezama Lima, poststructuralist thinkers such as Barthes, Derrida, Deleuze, and Bataille, Tantric Buddhism, the paintings of Wifredo Lam, Botero, and the Spanish Golden Age, and Cuban popular culture (Santería and music). In Sarduy, language and image are paramount: his characters change or transform themselves at random, and plot is secondary or nonexistent—the text is always conscious of (and undermining) its author(ity).

Most critics have focused on the "deconstructionist" elements of Sarduy's fiction to the detriment of the profoundly Cuban concerns of his work. Fortunately, three of his novels have been reissued, all exquisitely translated by Suzanne Jill Levine, where we can observe how Sarduy has put the idea of transculturation into overdrive. *From Cuba with a Song* (1967) is an unorthodox exploration of Cuban identity that features Auxilio (Help) and Socorro (Mercy), two transvestite prostitutes that embark on a series of journeys and transformations that raucously examine three ethnicities of Cuban culture: the Chinese, the African, and the Spanish. Sarduy himself embodied these ethnicities, as did his compatriot Wifredo Lam (1902–82), whose art he greatly admired. The novel has four main parts: (1) "Curriculum Cubense"; (2) "By the River of Rose Ashes"; (3) "Dolores Rondón"; and (4) "The Entry of Christ into Havana," followed by an important three-page debunking "Note" at the end.

In "Curriculum Cubense" we meet Auxilio and Socorro (Help and Mercy), who are looking for God in a self-service grocery store. During the novel they will be referred to as the Flower Girls, the Ever Present, the Siamese Twins, the Symmetrical Ones, the Divine Ones, the Thirsty Ones, the Majas, the Fates. From this enumeration alone we can see the variety of sources that Sarduy draws upon: Greek and Oriental mythology, Spanish culture, and Yoruba legend. In Santería, the twins (*ibeyes* or *jimaguas*) are beloved by all the major orishas since they are children (and are the patron saints of children). They are the children of Oshún and Changó, Yemayá being their adoptive mother. Known for their playfulness, the *ibeyes* are the only orishas known to have defeated the Devil. The Devil had set traps in the roads and would subsequently eat all humans who fell into them.

Yemayá gave the twins little magic drums. These they played until the Devil became tired, but as long as they kept drumming, the Devil kept dancing. This continued until the Devil was exhausted and agreed to withdraw the traps. Similarly, Auxilio and Socorro play their metaphoric drums, either by evading the traps of patriarchal and monocultural identity or exhausting through parody traditional and canonical texts.

In part two, "By the River of Rose Ashes," Mortal Pérez, a blond Spaniard who begins the novel as an old general, desperately pursues Lotus Flower, an actress in a Chinese burlesque opera house in Havana. In this section the language is highly metaphorical and figurative, in tune with the constant (un)maskings and carnivallike atmosphere, a saucy parody of Lacan's concept of desire. Pérez's lust turns to murderous rage, as he finally sends Lotus Flower a watch with blades that will cut her wrists. He moves across the street from the theater where she performs . . . and waits.

Lotus Flower is also a transvestite, but Mortal Pérez does not seem to know. Everything he seeks seems to evaporate, an endless procession of signifiers which seem to echo Lacan's views on desire and language. According to Lacan, desire is not biological: "Thus desire is neither appetite nor satisfaction, nor the demand for love, but the difference which arises from the subtraction of the first from the second, the phenomenon of their splitting" (Lacan, 1977, p. 287). Desire, though, is based on a lack that is never satisfied in the physiological sense. It arises from a splitting of the subject, in wanting to recover a lost object, the pre-oedipal mother. More important, this desire cannot be truly spoken. As Judith Butler says: "Desire then appears as a gap, a discrepancy, an absent signifier and thus only appears *as that which cannot appear*. The speaking of desire does not resolve this negation. Hence, desire is never materialized or concretized through language, but is indicated through the *interstices of language*, that is, what language cannot represent" (Butler, 1987, p. 193). Of course, Pérez desires Lotus Flower in the appetite sense, but it is precisely this element that Sarduy parodies, since the Spaniard conflates the two (desire, appetite). And so Mortal Pérez is constantly chasing a phantasm, which Sarduy embodies in a gender difference. When Mortal goes to Lotus Flower's dressing room, a bald Chinaman wearing a *guayabera* and slacks, with a grapefruit on a tray, walks out: the "real" Lotus Flower. Toward the end of the chapter the narrator asks: "Where do all the objects come from, where has the preceding scene unfolded?" (*From Cuba with a Song*, 1994c, p. 55). Sarduy, echoing Lacan, would say from that split in the subject who must constantly try to name his desire and endlessly, metonymically spins out signifiers to cover over that void. This is driven home by Auxilio and Socorro, who say to Mortal Pérez in unison: "Ming [Lotus Flower] is pure absence, she is what she is not. There is no water for your thirst" (ibid., p. 38). This is a perfect expression for desire. If we set up an equation, we could say that Demand minus Need = Desire. It is the irreducible residue between need and demand that also transcends them both. Desire, therefore, can never be satiated "since it always refers to a repressed text" (Ragland-Sullivan, 1987, p. 77). This repressed text is the Other or (M)other, who is the infant's primordial originating figure of unconditonal love, total union of subject and object. Many others will surface in a person's life, but they will be signifiers twirling about the repressed text or void. In *From Cuba with a Song*, we see various efforts at quelling that void: (1) through transcendence (Auxilio and Socorro searching for God); (2) through sexual union (Mortal's attempts with Lotus Flower); or (3) through power and social positioning (Dolores with Mortal). All, of course, ultimately fail.

Sarduy also plays on Eurocentric notions of Oriental eroticism, the exoticism of the Other during this sequence. That this desire is a quaint, outdated notion is belied by David Cronenberg's recent film *M. Butterfly* (1992/93), about a French diplomat who falls in love with a woman from the Chinese opera. When he first hears Song Liling performing an aria from Puccini's famous opera (set in Japan), he is captivated by her mesmerizing voice. But soon he enters a world of mistaken identities, sexual bewilderment, political intrigue, betrayal, spying, and ultimately death. The diplomat, appropriately named Gallimard (also the name of an important publishing firm in France), is unaware that men sing women's roles in traditional Chinese opera. He, like Mortal Pérez, has constructed a fantastical object of desire, as well as a model of femininity based on the exotic other: a docility of character, beautiful, silky clothing, an erotic modesty with a long tradition, and so on. The amazing thing is that Gallimard falls for Song Liling (John Lone) during the time of the Cultural Revolution (1966–76), when the Chinese Communist Party would view all of this behavior as decadent, bourgeois, as a hangover from a humiliating past. The film not only depicts sexual duplicity, but political treachery as well. Gallimard's lover is also spying for the Chinese government. Oblivious to this reality, Gallimard lives for the erotic body or the body of desire: fantasy becomes more real than the "real body." This comes to a head at the end of the film, when Gallimard and Song Liling are in a police wagon on the way to jail. Gallimard has just been tried in court for treason (and Song Liling for spying), with the added shock of finding out that his lover is "really a man." Song strips and offers "himself," his real body, telling Gallimard to touch him since it is the same skin. Gallimard refuses, since, as Slavoj Zizek says, Song Liling is now out of his fantasy frame of desire (Zizek, 1995, p. 107). The real is not only prosaic, but becomes destructive.

This gives rise to guilt, and in Gallimard the guilt becomes so extreme that it produces a psychotic identification with Butterfly, which he reenacts in prison (dressing as Cio-Cio-San), ultimately committing suicide. Zizek's interpretation is compelling (he even claims the suicide is an ethical choice, also echoing the original opera), but not entirely satisfactory. One could equally argue that desire and identification, though related, are not the same. In our traditional, heterosexist gender roles (male-female), what we desire (males who seek females and vice versa) is not what we identify with (males with other males, females with other females). Gallimard has desired Song Liling because she was a "woman." When she no longer is, desire has imploded. As a male he can identify with him/her, but only by becoming a "woman." This, however, reinstitutes the fantasy all over again. His grand finale in the prison is an attempt to make desire and identification coexist in erotic harmony, but in fact it can only lead to death (Dollimore, 1991, p. 305). In Sarduy's work, similar forces are at work about identification-desire and cross-dressing as transculturation, both of which are vitally linked to his notion of writing. These themes will be addressed further when his novel *Cobra* (1972) is discussed.

The following section (part two), "Dolores Rondón," is about a Cuban mulatta of the same name who marries Mortal Pérez, now a senator. He rises to national prominence, but then is disgraced, as is Dolores, who returns to the provinces, dying in poverty. A baroque *décima* is her epitaph, warning others about the futility of worldly pursuits. (A *décima* is a poem composed of ten-verse strophes, octosyllabic or nonosyllabic, that classically rhymes as follows: a–b–b–a–a–c–c–d–d–c, or with other variants.) Sarduy's language is more colloquial, more in tune with the Afro-Cuban dimensions of this chapter, but suffused with conceits about narrative discourse and figurative speech. The *décima* has long peasant roots in the musical folklore of Cuba, Puerto Rico, and the Dominican Republic. They deal with a wealth of subjects: country life, the joys and woes of love, or an exaltation of nature. *Décimas* form part of music composed for Christmas, as is the case with the Puerto Rican *aguinaldo*, or with secular forms of music, as is the *son* from Cuba, or *música jíbara* from Puerto Rico. In a *controversia*, singers will get together and improvise the *décima* as they go along. The title of Sarduy's novel is a *décima* from a *son* composed by Miguel Matamoros, and is probably the best-known song in Cuba after the "Guantanamera." It is these popular roots that Sarduy explores in this section with great humor. He uses the very verses of the *décima* about Dolores's life to structure his narrative, which means that the chronology of the tale is out of sequence.

The story is fairly straightforward. It narrates the life of a Cuban mulatta from Camagüey, Dolores Rondón, who seeks fame and social position through her pursuit of Mortal Pérez, a senator and prominent political figure. She meets him on the campaign trail, seduces him, and they marry. Later on, Pérez attracts the ire of the prime minister when he tries to pass off a Cuban dancer from the provinces as a Hawaiian dancing girl. Accused of "white slavery, drug smuggling, importing liquor illegally, an attempt against public morality, traitor to the party, atheist, etc." (p. 80), Mortal's political career abruptly ends and with it, that of Dolores. In telling the tale, though, Sarduy weaves in the elements of Cuban syncretic religious cul-

ture, that is, Santería, asides on rhetoric and narrative, plus a savage parody
of Cuban political life of the 1940s and 1950s.

Santería has been described as a syncretic blending of European Catholicism and West African Yoruba philosophico-religious beliefs. In fact, it is an
example of Ortiz's transculturation. Earlier we spoke of the *ibeyes* or twins
fatiguing and outwitting the Devil. The term *devil* already implies transculturation, since the Yoruba pantheon has no orishas (deities) that are solely
the incarnation of evil. Orishas can do good as well as evil. The "Dolores
Rondón" section features many references to orishas such as Ochún,
Obatalá, Ogún, Changó, Elegguá, and Yemayá, aside from the already
mentioned twins. In fact, Dolores's downfall is attributed to the fact that
she does not render tribute to the orishas as she ascends in social position
and power.

Let us begin with the twins, or *ibeyes*. As said previously, they are
associated with supernatural forces in many cultures from around the
world. In Central American mythology there are numerous examples of
sacred twins, the best known being Hunaphú and Ixbalanqué from the
Mayan *Popol Vuh*. In Japan, Izanagi and Izanami are a brother/sister pair,
part of a creation myth, as are Osiris and Isis in Egyptian lore. More
importantly:

> Twins are strongly charged with taboo, valencies of interdiction and persua-
> sion. Their baffling power lies in their ambiguity and the generative force of
> their off-balance bonding, taken . . . as a sure mark of the Sacred. In fact,
> nowhere is sacred ambivalence more deeply and vividly embodied than in
> the archetype of the twins. This ambivalence is what allows it to operate,
> alternately, as a wounding and healing influence, as that which generates
> order or disorder as if by caprice. While the modern, rational mind wants to
> resolve this terrible inconsistency of the Sacred in a final closure or an
> all-encompassing aim, both ancient and aboriginal peoples prefer to accept it
> as it is, without looking for a way to bargain ourselves out of the dilemma.
> (Lash, 1993, p. 8)

In Sarduy we will see how the inconsistency, the healing and wounding,
the generative ambiguity relate to issues of identity, culture, and writing.

Some places in Africa attribute evil to twins and at one time would kill
twins if borne by humans. But in Yoruba culture they play a positive role,
and in Cuban Santería, the birth of twins is seen as a mark or sign from
heaven. They are often linked to deities of water, also true in other cultures.
For example, the mother of Romulus and Remus, Rhea, was a river goddess,
and Leda, the mother of Castor and Pollux, was a daughter of an ocean god.
In Santería, their adoptive mother was Yemayá, mother of life and of all the
orishas. She owns the waters and represents the sea, primordial source of
life. In alternative renderings of the story of the twins, they are the offspring
of Oshún, orisha of the rivers, Yemayá's sister. Dolores Rondón at one

moment says, "I am the legitimate daughter of Oshún, queen of the river and the sky." This is not so surprising since like Oshún she is sensual and likes to sing and dance. And it is these traits that draw Mortal under her spell. Oshún was the orisha who convinced Ogún (the orisha of iron and blacksmiths) to come out of the forest when he became fed up with killing and bloodshed. She twirled about with her yellow kerchiefs, smeared honey on his lips, and, dancing as she went along, drew him out of seclusion. In similar fashion, Dolores links up with a modern, political buffo version of Ogún, Mortal Pérez, who was a general in the first part of the novel.

The twins are closely linked to fertility because of their association with water and the connotation of abundance associated with their conception. As such, they are equally linked to rain and thunder, which is also not surprising, since their father is Changó, orisha of thunder (and music). The representation of the *ibeyes* (dolls placed on altars) has them dressed in white with red belts or kerchiefs (red is Changó's color) (López Valdés, 1985, p. 141). Other major orishas, such as Olokún, Obatalá, and Abeyí, have given birth to twins. The emphasis on twins is significant in this chapter because of Auxilio/Socorro, who are mirrored and parodied by two new characters, Narrator One and Narrator Two, semiological twins, if you will. In subsequent works, Sarduy will continue to use doubles and twins: in *Cobra*, Cobra and Pup are identical though not the same size, and in *Maitreya*, La Divina and La Tremenda are also twins.

The two narrators engage in literary talk and gossip, particularly about water and a dog. Narrator One talks about a dog, "which is a word, and throw a pail of boiling water on him, which is the exact sense of the word. What does the dog do? And what does the word do? And so we have a dog-word, water-sense: These are the four parts" (Sarduy, 1994c, p. 58). Narrator Two does not understand, which Narrator One responds to with a riddle, which is unsolvable. As González Echevarría has pointed out, this not only refers to linguistic and literary theory, but to Afro-Cuban beliefs. When a dog shows up at a political rally of Mortal Pérez, everyone shouts "Water!" As we saw before, water is linked to Oshún (Dolores), Yemayá, and the twins. Furthermore, a dog is the guardian of Elegguá, the orisha of the crossroads, who looks over the four cardinal points. Dolores's tombstone, where the *décima* is inscribed, is at a crossroads. (Dogs are also used in sacrifices, particularly to Ogún; they also figure as omens in India as well.) There's more: a child born after twins, called Ideú, is known as a guardian or dog of the twins. In this chapter, Auxilio and Socorro are joined by a third sister Clemencia (Clemency). González is correct in seeing that the two Narrators, using a European method of decoding language and meaning, are unable to capture and understand the Santería code that underlines these passages.

Obatalá is mentioned several times in this chapter. S/he is the creator of the earth, sculptor of human beings, and reigns over all things to do with the head, both thoughts and dreams. White is his color as he is the orisha of purity, harmony, and reconciliation. Since all the orishas respect her, she often mediates in disputes between bickering orishas. Sarduy's inclusion of Obatalá completes the four elements since Changó (fire), Oshún-Yemayá-the twins (water), and Oyá (wind) all figure prominently in this section. Oyá is linked to the dead and inhabits cemeteries. Since Obatalá wears white, and Dolores claims to meet her maker wearing Obatalá's white robes (aside from the references to Oyá), González Echevarría assumes that white is linked to death in Santería. This is too narrow an interpretation. There is nothing in Santería that links Obatalá (or the color white) exclusively with death. If Dolores is wearing white robes, it is for the same reason that *babalaos* (Santería priests) do, because of purity. The twins (or *ibeyes*) also wear white. Santería, as a transcultural phenomenon, is too rich and complex to be so statically viewed, more so within a text by Sarduy, where the transculturation undergoes further metamorphoses, as when Auxilio turns into Ella Fitzgerald to say her last few lines. Sarduy draws on Afro-Cuban beliefs, but does not make it the "master signifier" of the chapter. Instead he plays it off the baroque *décima* used in epitaphs, poststructuralist theory, and political discourse, in order to create a rich, polyphonic, and hilarious buffo representation. Sarduy's textured "staging" has semiotics, politics, and the divine crash together, teasing out all the ramifications and layers of the plot.

Obatalá is also the semi-visible presence behind the last segment of the book, "The Entry of Christ into Havana." Many of his/her *avatares* or *caminos* (avatars, paths) relate to the figure of Christ (Olofi is also syncretized as Christ, being the mediator for Oluddumare, the All or godhead figure). Obatalá is also from the mountains, and the stones placed in tureens to make offerings to him/her are called *oké* (*de la loma*: from the mountains). This plays nicely into the "Son de la loma" by Matamoros, the guiding metaphor of much of the novel. In his Igbá-Ibó path, Obatalá is linked to the all-seeing eye of Providence. This derives from Assyrian-Babylonian mythology, and by the Middle Ages in Europe it was represented by the Eye within a triangle. There are many direct and indirect references to eyes and seeing in this last part embedded within a mystical-baroque visual culture. Obatalá's powers are supposed to come from male and female attributes, which is not unusual in Santería, where many orishas are women and where avatars of an orisha can be male or female. This is an important consideration in Sarduy, whose notions of culture and the sacred are closely enmeshed with his irreverent attitudes toward gender.

Before moving on to this last part of the novel, let us turn to Sarduy's parodying of Cuban politics of the 1940s. In one page, he draws on Jakobsonian linguistics, Columbus's diary, classical rhetoric, José Martí, and Afro-Cuban religious terminology. Written like a play, as different characters speak, Sarduy adds stage directions in parentheses, usually describing the emotion or tone of the character. These are often references to opera, cinematic personages, or popular song. The mix, of course, is incongruous and jarringly funny and points to several elements in Sarduy's narrative style: its lack of realism, its refusal to latch onto fixed identities (either for the "characters" or in terms of a coherent stable "message"), its ability to be in constant metamorphosis through code-switching, cross-dressing, and plain outrageousness.

The final segment, "The Entry of Christ into Havana," starts in Spain with Auxilio and Socorro looking for a vanished young lover (Mortal Pérez). The two return to Cuba, where they are seduced and "Cubanized" by a mulatto. In Santiago (eastern Cuba) they find a wooden Christ who is the incarnation of Mortal. They rejuvenate him and take him on a procession to Havana where a snowstorm has blanketed the city in white. As the wooden effigy disintegrates, the twins and the crowds are sprayed by bullets from helicopters. Christ's entry has at least a double reference: Fidel Castro's victory over Batista (1959) and James Ensor's "Christ Entering Brussels" (1898), though the ending itself bears an uncanny resemblance to Buñuel's *Exterminating Angel* (1962). Sarduy's snow imagery could be a reference to Cuban writers' fascination with snow, epitomized by Julián Casal's (1863–93) book of poems *Nieve* (Snow).

The hail of bullets and the snow blanketing Havana could be interpreted in rather apocalyptic terms, of nothingness, of blankness, of death, but I think that the twins picking up the pieces of the wooden Christ and saving them in their handkerchiefs is only the beginning of a new cycle of transculturation and transfiguration. Let us not forget that in Islamic mysticism snow is analogous to sand in being a great unifying peace, which dissolves the anxieties of existence. And Obatalá, whose color is white, is from the mountains. In Tibetan Buddhism the mountains with their snow are the locations of their sacred monasteries (this is more the case in *Cobra* and *Maitreya*). When Fernando Ortiz uses the term *transculturation*, he says that deculturation often is the first step, followed by acculturation; these steps precede a more even give-and-take between cultures. Transculturation is not some wonderful and smooth synthesis, but a historical process fraught with conquest, resistance, and bloody class and ethnic conflict. The meeting of East and West in Sarduy's work is often violent, disruptive, and calamitous. But then there is a suggestive phrase, a proliferation of language and image that is close to hope, but tempered by a wily aversion to the great metanarratives. And as a chastened *bricoleur*, he picks his way through the shards and ruins of philosophical and religious systems in order to piece together not a paradise through language but a heterotopic burst of erotic search and expenditure.

Though Sarduy begins this segment in Spain, it is peppered with references to its Arabic past. Sarduy has an entire scene that takes place at the tenth-century Madinat al-Zahra, a city-medina built by Abd Al-Rahman III.

But perhaps more significant for Sarduy is the symbolic significance of Islamic calligraphy, which he treats as the visual embodiment of revelation. "The letters, words and verses of the Quran are not just elements of a written language, but beings or personalities for which the calligraphic form is the physical or visual vessel. Hence the oft quoted saying 'Calligraphy is the geometry of the Spirit' " (Nasr, 1987, p. 18). This Quranic calligraphy is an archetype for the cosmos, amply used in architecture, the basis for a sacred geometry. Sarduy will draw on the written sign as "beings, powers, talismans," as cosmological components not only in *From Cuba with a Song* but with even greater intensity in *Cobra* and *Maitreya*, where he will often refer to this sacred writing as a tattooing of the body, textual or otherwise (see also Sarduy, 1982, pp. 68–69, on tattooing).

The spiritual life of the word is found in the poetry of the Spanish mystical poet St. John of the Cross. Spanish mysticism is closely linked to baroque painting and image-making. In fact, the ascetics and mystics often spoke of images being able to move (in all senses of the word) people to want to perform acts of faith. Ignatius of Loyola's *Spiritual Exercises* often employ visual methods and imagining techniques to grasp aspects of the faith, meditate on Christ's passion, and lead to spiritual betterment. Curiously, this ascetic re(de)nunciation of the world is combined with a fervent sensuality. As Emilio Orozco Díaz has said: "The mistrust and disillusionment come not from a negation of the world but, on the contrary, from its most intense and rushed enjoyment of it, even if shaded by the melancholy knowledge of fugacity; or by lingering on before it in order to transcend it, and discover in its concreteness and finitude the presence of spirituality and infinity" (Orozco Díaz, 1970, pp. 83–84). Sarduy treads along those horizontal and vertical axes of tension that characterize the baroque with consummate artistry. Sarduy will again turn to St. John of the Cross at the end of his life.

From Cuba with a Song could be considered a long gloss on the *son* that the title derives from ("El son de la loma"), unmasking the search for origins and beginnings of Cuban culture as delusory at best. Here I agree with González Echevarría (who has taken it from Sarduy's *Barroco*) in his appreciation that for Sarduy the origin is a trope, a figure, and often a mistake (e.g., Columbus thinking he had found the Orient). Writing, and art, then, dis-figure that origin which tries to explain everything. This is perhaps one of his most significant differences with Lezama Lima and his concept of "las eras imaginarias," particularly in light of the figure and *figura* as used by Auerbach (see Chapter 5). This dis-figuring is taken to an unusual extreme in his next novel.

If Derrida were a Cuban mulatto drag queen writing opera libretti, he could have written *Cobra* (1972). Helene Cixous said that *Cobra* is a "text twister," which means it could be seen as a reading and rewriting of many artistic, literary, and scientific texts: Kepler, Columbus's diaries, Octavio

Paz's *Conjunctions and Disjunctions* (and his poem "Blanco"), Spanish baroque painting, *The Tibetan Book of the Dead*, Lacan, Derrida, and even his very own *From Cuba with a Song*. Long before critics and writers were using terms like "writing with (or on, from, of) the body," Sarduy had published a book of essays called *Written on a Body* (1969; trans. 1989), in which he develops an erotics of writing close to Barthes's *Pleasure of the Text*. Both that book and his *Barroco* (1974) should be read as companions to *Cobra*, since both speak eloquently to Sarduy's aesthetic concerns and his philosophy of writing or *écriture*. Salvador Elizondo's *Farabeuf o la crónica del instante* (1967) is also a text that is close to Sarduy's in terms of valuing the ideographic nature of the writing process.

Cobra, the main character(?), is incessantly transforming his/her body. S/he is a transvestite dancer in the Lyric Theater of the Dolls in 1960s Paris, is also a member of a motorcycle gang, part of a group of Tibetan lamas that dress like hippies (or vice versa), has a dwarflike image of herself called Pup (also a reference to astronomy), is also, well . . . you get the idea. Cobra's ever-changing body is the metamorphosis of the text, its delirious language constantly remaking the characters and other texts. Part of this ongoing process is the constant use of drugs, remedies, poisons, cures, operations, and so on, all linked to the notion of writing. Many critics have pointed out the similarities with Jacques Derrida's essay "Plato's Pharmacy" in his book *Dissemination* (1972; Eng. trans. 1981). Though the book was published the same year as Sarduy's novel, "Plato's Pharmacy" was published in two parts, in the Parisian magazine *Tel Quel* in 1968.

Derrida focuses his discussion on Plato's *Phaedrus*, performing a close reading of the words *pharmakos, pharmakon, pharmakeus, pharmacia*. They come up in a discussion of writing: the different words, from the same root, can mean remedy, drug, cure, poison, charm, spell, magician, and scapegoat. Needless to say, such a rich association of meaning concerning writing was highly stimulating to Sarduy. But it also refers to makeup and the painting of the body. Derrida sums it up admirably:

> The magic of writing and painting is like a cosmetic concealing the dead under the appearance of the living. The *pharmakon* introduces and harbors death. It makes the corpse presentable, masks it, makes it up, perfumes it with its essence, as it is said in Aeschylus. *Pharmakon* is also a word for perfume. A perfume without essence, as we earlier called it a drug without substance. It transforms order into ornament, the cosmos into a cosmetic. Death, masks, makeup, are all part of the festival that subverts the order of the city, its smooth regulation by the dialectician and the science of being. Plato, as we shall see, is not long in identifying writing with festivity. And play. A certain festival, a certain game. (Derrida, 1981, p. 142)

Sarduy is a skilled practitioner of writing as play and from the very beginning of *Cobra* we witness a delirious description of the *pharmakon* as makeup, as body painting: Cobra takes six hours to get made up every night for her show in the Lyric Theater of the Dolls. Mixed in with his/her routines are quips about writing: "Writing is the art of ellipsis" (1995, p. 5); "Writing is the art of digression" (p. 6); "Writing is the art of recreating reality. Let us respect it" (p. 7); "No. Writing is the act of restoring History" (p. 7); "Writing is the art of disorganizing an order and organizing a disorder" (p. 9); and "Writing is the art of patchwork" (p. 12). These numerous statements refer to Sarduy's own aesthetic (particularly the one about ellipsis), but also something he questioned all the time (writing is the art of recreating reality). Sarduy would agree with this last comment if it does not imply a kind of simple-minded realism, that is, writing as mimetic device. However, if we read it so that recreating is meant as an act of creating reality anew through the word, then perhaps the phrase might not seem ironic. If for the Islamic world calligraphy "provides the external dress for the Word of God," Sarduy's ideographic passion would lead him to dress up the Void with his incandescent words. Void or emptiness in Buddhism is not the equivalent of nothing, but a nonduality of perfect *gnosis*.

In a sense, then, Sarduy claims (and not only here) that writing is a kind of transvestism. What does this mean? On an almost literal level, it means that writing is not what it appears to be, that is, it is a kind of linguistic makeup that hides a certain practice. This would be the equivalent of saying that writing is a kind of fetishism. Writing is a way of disavowal of a lack that is constantly affirmed and denied at the same time. In Freudian and Lacanian theory the lack fetishism tries to conquer is the absence of a maternal phallus. The child sees that nothingness and as a result makes substitutes for it, which simultaneously deny and affirm that lack (e.g., shoes, raincoats, gloves). Literature fetishizes desire itself (in part because it uses words, signs that always point to, but are not what they designate, so it mimics the desiring process), and Sarduy takes this to an impossible extreme. One could say that "Fetishization functions in analogous fashion to the process of hysterization: both make a part or a whole of the body a phallus. They eroticize, even give a genital meaning to non-genital parts of the body" (Wright, 1992, p. 117). Sarduy eroticizes language, but not in a phallic or logocentric fashion. In *Cobra*, this is incarnated in the lead character's castration at the hands of Dr. Ktazob.

As Enrique Márquez has pointed out, Cobra's castration is not such a bad thing. In fact, the phallus is like an injunction or a prohibition, and without one Cobra is not marked by a fixed cultural and gender identity, and thus his sexual gratification is limitless. The erotic movement, or better yet, erotic figuration, dismantles binary oppositions: "Reality and desire, taboos and norms, the lived and the expected, the body and its phantasms, all would be one . . . even the death-desire split would be harmonized and eliminated" (Márquez, 1991, p. 304). This is further driven home by the fact that his rival, a female transvestite, Cadillac, has an operation whereby a penis is grafted on and immediately she begins smoking cigars, swaggering, and acting like a pimp. Márquez further points out that this new decentered identity allows Cobra to practice all kinds of "perversions" (from sadomasochism to coprophilia) as if they were sacred events, as in Tantric feasts.

Sarduy's *Cobra* is a hysteric text if we understand the term as Lacan meant it: as the quintessential question about gender since the hysteric's vacillation between being a man and a woman calls into question the viability of being able to reduce identity to gender. Despite the suffering and anxiety of the hysteric's body, the hysteric is not repelled by her body, but by the attempts to pin it down, to accept what Lacan called the master signifier. In other words, the hysteric is a rebel, someone who speaks a certain truth that society, knowledge, patriarchy repress, and "the unsatisfied desire converts into a desire for unsatisfaction, a desire to keep our desire 'open' " (Zizek, 1995, p. 106). This questioning of gender and identity is crucial to Sarduy's fiction, and it is no coincidence that many of his characters not only cross-dress, but actually change sex, adopt different bodies, or assume new hybrid identities.

Cross-dressing, or tranvestism, does go to the heart of identity issues. In *From Cuba with a Song*, we saw how Sarduy questioned stable, fixed definitions of ethnicity, gender, and even class. In *Cobra* he pushes the limit further by incorporating Tibetan Buddhism and Tantric practices into the text. The Eastern or Chinese element was certainly present in *From Cuba with a Song*, but it was almost as a backdrop to his parody on desire and the Western fashion for Oriental erotica. Here the characters—a motorcycle gang made up of Tundra, Totem, Tiger and Scorpion—perform Tantric rites after having killed Cobra. Sarduy's tranvestism is a metaphor for transculturation because it resolutely opposes paternalistic, logocentric, and rigid thinking, especially about culture, gender, and class. In the give-and-take, new textures are created from preceding ones (Morejón), and transvestism is an extraordinary example of being other and becoming an(other), at least in Sarduy.

Many feminists have pointed out that cross-dressing can uphold masculine domination of women by its very celebration of and identification with women, which also expresses contempt. That is, at the same time that men are stepping out of their rigid gender roles they are still putting forth images of women that are ultimately misogynist: women as creatures of disguise and simulation, frivolity, obsessed with appearance, artificiality, and glamour. And beneath the skirts, as one critic put it, "the power-granting penis remains—what a relief!" (Alisa Solomon in Ferris, 1993, p. 145).

The significance of Sarduy's work on the reinvention of gender must be understood in a Latin American context. He is the first writer (aside from José Donoso's *El lugar sin límites*) to make transvestism a central element of his work in contemporary Latin American fiction. By virtue of that achievement, he was a writer that pushed gender issues to the fore. And for Sarduy it was not merely a matter of characters dressing up in drag; they truly transform themselves into new beings, demigods, singers, entrepreneurs, mystics, prostitutes, Buddhists, orishas, poets, hustlers, incarnations of the Buddha, like the cook Luis Leng in *Maitreya*, which means the Buddha of the future. None of the identities, moreover, is exclusive. In Sarduy the drag queen not only looks and pretends to be someone else but *is* someone else, refashioning oneself into a vaster collective self which is at the same time social, erotic, cosmic, and sacred. In "realistic" drag, the queen is someone else until the show ends. With Sarduy, the show never ends: there's no turning back (or straight, for that matter).

Moreover, Sarduy's textual practice is one of the most radical attempts in Caribbean discourse to dismantle the patriarchal, centered voice of a writer who seeks to impose his authority, by either reinterpreting or creating his own canon. Often we ask ourselves while reading some of Sarduy's more experimental texts: who is narrating or more so, *what* is narrating? Whoever or whatever, it affects you viscerally, it goes into your bloodstream, which brings us back to Derrida's reading of Plato: writing is magic, a cure, poison, a cosmetic, or perfume that transforms the dead letter(s) of tradition (other texts) into a carnival, a dancing theater of passion. For Sarduy the magic is the way a text can transfigure itself, like a shaman, not some kind of folksy magical realism. The cure or poison is an altered state, the handling of a substance that is so potent that it can heal or enfeeble. It literally can affect the body. The perfume or cosmetic adorns the body (textual and otherwise) to disguise its demise. Characters dissolve, die, are reborn, countries and continents are bounded in a couple of sentences, centuries are traversed in a flash, cultures are crisscrossed and rewritten with a reckless, poetic *jouissance*. In a way, Sarduy recreates Caribbean history on a planetary scale with a sassy charm, so aptly expressed by Helene Cixous: "*Cobra*'s language plays with its words the way a baby plays with his toes. Are those mine?" (Adams et al., 1974, p. 30).

Sarduy even goes as far as trying to establish a cosmic model for his baroque, eroto-aesthetics (see Gil and Iturralde, 1991, pp. 337–42, on Sarduy's cosmographic vision). In his book *Barroco* (1974) he uses the term *retombée* to refer to analogies that do not work in the normal chronological sense, as when the echo precedes the voice. In this regard he speaks of Galileo's circle and Kepler's ellipse as prefiguring the big bang and steady state models of the universe in the twentieth century. In an interview, Sarduy said he sought out the baroque through astronomy, not through the more accepted route of the plastic arts and literature. His vision of the baroque was different from Lezama's. Sarduy claims that to be baroque or neo-baroque was to "threaten, judge, and parody bourgeois economy" with its rationality, its obsession with saving. "Throw away, expend, burn away language for sheer pleasure—that's the baroque's core notion." It is a language that is nonmoralistic, noninformational, and nonutilitarian, subverting the normal order of things by not falling prey to an economy of accumulation, consumption, investment.

Platonic cosmology valued the circle as geometric representation of perfection and divinity. Sarduy says Galileo stayed within that model and showed great disdain for both figurative and rhetorical language, as well as anamorphosis (considered a perversion of perspective). Kepler's revolution changes things considerably: "The master figure is no longer the circle, with a unique center—radiant, luminous, and paternal—but the ellipse, which in contrast to this obvious focus adds a second focus, equally active, equally real, but sealed off, dead, nocturnal, the reverse of the solar yang, fructifying and absent" (Sarduy, 1974, p. 56). Sarduy then compares Kepler's ellipse to Góngora's use of ellipsis, a key rhetorical device in baroque poetics. Ellipsis is a figure of speech when parts of meaning (the signified) are eclipsed, omitted, expelled, or hidden from the symbolic universe. From here it is not a great leap to see how Kepler's ellipse and Freud/Lacan's decentered subject are linked together: "Because the subject is decentered, is pulled so to speak bifocally in two different gravitational directions, that his speech becomes elliptical—that parts of it drop into the unconscious. The unconscious in Lacan's conception [is] precisely that part of the subject's discourse which, although it regulates the subject's actions, is nonetheless not at his disposal: that part which cannot be spoken, constituted as it is by a 'failure of translation' " (Felman, 1987, pp. 66–67). Fernand Hallyn has argued differently from Sarduy in observing that Kepler did not reject the circle, also claiming that Kepler was a mannerist and not a baroque thinker (see Hallyn, 1993, pp. 203–30). Hallyn also believes that it is the oxymoron and not the ellipsis that is the tropological basis of this cosmology. (Sarduy tends to subsume metaphor, synecdoche, allusion, and metonymy as being part of the "field" of ellipsis.) For our purposes that is not the most important issue: what is germane is that Sarduy sees a theory of the subject (Lacan), a theory of the universe (Kepler), a theory of literature (baroque aesthetics/rhetoric/ Derrida), a theory of culture (transculturation, cross-dressing), and a theory of history (displacement, anti-logocentrism, and anti-patriarchy) as tropes, and that these tropes are an integral part of the formation of the Caribbean psyche. Furthermore, they speak or echo each other through what he has called a *retombée*, which is not quite the same as an analogy, in a direct correspondence. There is an oblique, sly, roundabout way that they illuminate each other, like the moving shafts of light in Caravaggio.

In *Cobra*, Sarduy goes from cosmic models to sacred texts. One of the main characters is called Pup, a miniature version of Cobra, or, as the author put it: Pup = $\sqrt{\text{Cobra}}$ (Pup is the square root of Cobra). But Pup is also known as a white dwarf, an astronomical term that refers to a dying star (formerly referred to as a "red giant") with a density of gravity so great that even the lightest objects would weigh tons. Eventually, a white dwarf shatters in a nova or supernova explosion, or it can become a black hole (Gil and Iturralde, 1991). Sarduy links his characters to these astronomical phenomena, and through his own tropes or associations (color, makeup) has them cross-dress. Almost literally he brings the stars down to shimmy on stage, in a cosmic dance that is rich in sources, from the Elizabethan theater, to Balinese dance, Spanish Golden age painting (Pup is compared to Carreño's truly grotesque portrait of a young girl called *La Monstrua*), or the Cuban rumba (Gil and Iturralde, 1991, pp. 339–40). Pup, the dwarf, might have a Hindu resonance as well. Vishnu became a dwarf to hide or to trick the demon Bali (Doniger O'Flaherty, 1975, pp. 176–79). Vishnu also expanded, growing to enormous, even cosmic proportions, again echoing astronomical phenomena. Sarduy, like most Caribbean artists, when he is not building on existing myths (radically reworking, dis- and refiguring them), creates his own.

Despite Sarduy's aversion to texts with univocal meaning, he constantly interrogates sacred texts, be they from Afro-Cuban, Tibetan Buddhist, Koranic-Sufi, or biblical traditions. His transgressive, erotic play with words and his healthy irreverence could never make him an unquestioning believer. Lourdes Gil narrates a telling incident, after Sarduy had finished writing *Cobra*. He was on a boat in the sacred Ganges River and threw a copy of *Cobra* into the river as an offering. The book came back to him. Undeterred, he threw it back in. Again it returned. This happened several times, but *Cobra* "would return like a child afraid to separate from its father." Finally, Sarduy found a stone, attached it to *Cobra*, tossed it in the water, and it sank into the depths of the Ganges. Gil correctly points out two important points: first, Sarduy was not intimidated by the first signs of the book coming back. He kept insisting, which she interprets as a quintessentially Cuban trait, that is, "to try and impose conditions on the gods," to rewrite the signs of divine interpretation (Gil, 1994, pp. 213–14). This is close to the Afro-Cuban traditions, where the orishas are like a family: they bicker and quarrel, they flirt and pray, they rely on divine intervention as well as their own wits. Sarduy enters into the sacred but not as an act of surrender, but one of revelation through rebellion.

Sarduy saw writing in all its corporeal dimensions (as a tattooing of the body) and as an activity which escapes the (de)formation of the *logos*. It was a dance of signs that echoed Nietzsche's analogue of dancing and writing, and not surprisingly *From Cuba with a Song* was translated into French as *Écrit en dansant*. The author summed it up admirably in an interview: "The writer is a *material, situated* subject and not an 'inspired' floating author. As in the Tibetan mandalas, everything explodes from the genitals and goes up to the hand. I write naked, and sometimes I dance around looking for the words, looking for them until my body turns into a language and the language on the page turns into a body, into something tangible, tactile, which dances and looks in turn" (Adams et al., 1974, p. 11). Cobra's Tibetan dance ends up in the snow-covered Himalayas, precisely where his next novel, *Maitreya*, begins.

Maitreya is inscribed as a textual practice of Tantric philosophy, a radical reappropriation of the *Bardo Thodol*, or the *Tibetan Book of the Dead*. Tantric practices embrace both the sacred and the profane, enmeshing themselves with the material world, almost grotesquely, as a means of spiritual enlightenment (West, 1994d, p. 115). Every act is carnal, shot through with desire, but equally it is a powerful cosmic symbol that leads toward an abolition of the world and the flesh, seeing these earthly manifestations as illusory masquerades of misery. As Octavio Paz says: "For Tantrism the body is a true double of the universe, which, in turn, is a manifestation of the diamondlike, incorruptible body of the Buddha" (Paz, 1969, p. 81). The Tantric subtle body is used as an instrument for meditation or concentration, gestures known as *mudras*. Sarduy writes with the body, scattering signs, a *mudra* of mutations; these *mudras* inform or inflate the text with a language of excess, both iridescent and precise, exemplifying one of Barthes's definitions of the pleasure of the text as being "that moment when my body pursues its own ideas—for my body does not have the same ideas I do" (Barthes, 1975, p. 17). Sarduy, who often wrote without his clothes on, believed in an erotics of reading and writing and practiced it to a degree that borders on unhinged rapture, trying to inscribe the body of perfection (the Buddha, nirvana) through his own words.

The Tantric tradition sees language as a verbal double of both the body and the universe, and often it does not even take a whole word: a syllable alone can become a mantra, a unit of sound that has great religious, emotional, or magical impact. A mantra is not a concept but a nondiscursive, sonorous fetish that makes the body vibrate and links it to the cosmos. The bones of the deceased master at the beginning of the novel are like mantras scattered to the wind, but instead of being a bridge between body and cosmos, the bones initiate a long series of migrations and transformations because *Maitreya* is, above all, a novel about exile.

The exile is set off by an initial limit, death. The demise of the master in the Tibetan monastery begins as a limit which will be transgressed. There is a double reference to Lezama here, both as a person (he died while Sarduy wrote the novel) and as literary catalyst and mentor in that Luis Leng (and to a lesser extent Juan Izquierdo) are both characters from *Paradiso*. In Lezama's novel, however, they are minor: in Sarduy, Luis Leng, a Cuban Chinese cook, is central, and even becomes a reincarnation of the Buddha. And why not? Cooks have become presidents.

Exile can be seen as a limit imposed by revolution, and the novel sports three major historical convulsions: the Chinese, the Cuban, and the Iranian. The monks, after a crushed uprising, will flee Tibet and Chinese domination. The Leng sisters escape through India to Sri Lanka with the new child master, the Instructor. They're joined later by their niece, Iluminada Leng, who shacks up with El Dulce (Honey Boy). The couple takes a boat from Colombo (Sri Lanka) to Cuba, where Luis Leng is born. Also born in Saguá La Grande (a nucleus of the Chinese community in Cuba) are the female twins La Divina and La Tremenda, of unknown parentage. They are likened to the *ibeyes* of Santería (Sts. Cosmas and Damian in Catholicism), the offspring of Oshún and Changó. They perform miracles and cure the sick until their first period, when their powers disappear. They become opera singers, but with the Cuban Revolution they flee to Miami with a dwarf named Pedacito, who also paints murals. There the twins become fanatical members of F.F.A., Fist Fuckers of America. When later they go to New York, one of the twins falls in love with an Iranian chauffeur. They follow the Iranian to his native land, where La Tremenda and Pedacito run a massage parlor and S/M emporium. The last stages of the revolution of the mullahs which would soon overthrow the Shah again causes them to flee, and the novel ends with La Tremenda, after giving anal birth to a strange creature with blue hair and webbed feet, starting a new cult in Afghanistan.

Even the physical attributes of characters are varied, Sarduy borrowing heavily from painting: the monks in the monastery are surrounded by Tibetan mandalas and gods depicted in Himalayan art; the Leng sisters are like Kuhn-Weber puppets; the twins are right out of Botero; Pedacito (modeled after Velázquez dwarfs) paints murals inspired by Wifredo Lam; the descriptions of the Iranian episodes have the lush, dense details of Persian miniatures. The loss and displacement of exile is compensated for by a proliferation of images, new cultural icons and beliefs, succulent, untried food, uncanny experiences that push limits to their breaking point.

Maitreya is a novel about exile and the dispersion of culture, language, and belief systems, bereft of any idea of recuperating some kind of totality or center with which to anchor one's existence. Despite this, and the novel's ambiguous ending, it is not a despairing work. One is left with a sense of expansion, of a flock of birds waiting to take flight.

Sarduy has taken the anecdote from Lezama and made it a novel, the displacement of humans due to revolution as a springboard (transmigration as transformation), of fashioning beings into new selves; he has Tantric eroticism, Sufi mysticism, and Santería ritual collide into a shimmering, exploratory tapestry that focuses on the decentering of identity, culture, time, and place.

It is a stretch to call the people in Sarduy's fiction *characters*. Often we have no physical sense of what they are like; in other instances they are deformed, monstrous, fantastic, or hybrids. They often sprout doubles; they vanish or die suddenly; they become transformed into other characters; they change gender, name, and place in a flash. If Sarduy were an orthodox believer, we could say that he concurs with Buddhist teachings that insist on seeing human development as a series of mental states (toward corruption or enlightenment) not underlined by a sense of unified self, or rather the self is a necessary illusion on the way to enlightenment. Instead, in recognizing his unorthodoxies toward virtually everything, it might be more prudent to say that his "characters" are a place where all of the signifiers of desire gravitate. They cluster together and then disperse, moving along with a kind of metonymic breathlessness. Characters, words, flock together, soar upwards.

Birds appear constantly in his work, in *Colibrí* (1984), *Cobra, Pájaros de la playa* (1993), as well as *Maitreya*. In many religions or cultures they denote the soul or the spirit, for example, the *simmurgh* of Persian and Sufi origin, a flock of thirty birds that went in quest of inner purity and the supreme being (Nasr, 1987, pp. 100–105). The *simmurgh* migrated toward India and became Garuda, Vishnu's charger and creature of the higher realms. In Christianity the dove's symbolism is a well-known spiritual sign, and in Guaraní mythology, the spirit of dead shamans speaks to apprentice shamans in their dreams through a hummingbird. Though his writing is jagged, fragmented, the humor and lightness of expression make Sarduy's words ripple and fly (West, 1994d, p. 119).

The soul has always been described in organic models, vitally linked with the body and its metaphors. Indeed Francis Huxley claims that Plato likened it to a double of the body, claiming that the soul "was fixed to the body by a multitude of small nails that made up the totality of the spirit—a sort of organic crucifixion" (Huxley, 1974, p. 62). This is reminiscent of Kongo practices, whereby *mkisi* (sculpted human figures in wood that are spirit personalities that control a particular activity or function) have nails, blades driven into them, often to hunt down and haunt a wrongdoer, or, in more benign cases, to heal (MacGaffey and Harris, 1993, p. 27). Sarduy takes the nails of the "totality of the spirit" and makes them into syllables, mantras, in order to pierce the writing body. The nails are traces, mnemonic devices, which imprint or mark the body (literally) of the author, what Sarduy called "la arqueología de la piel" ("the archaeology of skin/flesh"). And it reminds us that the mystic drive is always a spiritualizing of desire, of being part of the body of Christ, or to "obtain the perfect body [of Buddha], adorned with signs and graces" (Evans-Wentz, 1960, p. 207).

But unlike Christianity (where the soul departs the body at death), in the *Tibetan Book of the Dead* the initiation is to prepare the soul for a descent into the body, the locus of a new incarnation and life. The disciple attains mastery over death, sees it as illusion, and soars far from fear. In the words of Lama Anagarika Govinda: "This illusoriness of death comes from the identification of the individual with his temporal, transitory form, whether physical, emotional, or mental, whence arise the mistaken notion that there exists a personal, separate egohood of one's own, and the fear of losing it" (Govinda in Evans-Wentz, 1960, p. lxii).

Maitreya, with its characters suffering transformations, births, and deaths, is an exorcism of death, or better yet, a rehearsal for death in that it implies a denial of just one universe and one life for each human being; it affirms that death is only an initiation into another form of life. The body is not a tomb or a slab of flesh, but a creator and vessel for epiphanies that unchain the imagination. Lezama spoke in similar terms: "Death engenders us all anew. That infinite possibility which is in death, by becoming visible, stakes out its perishable space. Non-time, that is, the edenic, the paradisical, makes us think about life as infinite possibility that arises from death" (Lezama, 1971).

In his *Cristo de la Rue Jacob* (1987), one of his most autobiographical works, Sarduy mentions that the short pieces in the book are what he called "epiphanies," a daily occurrence is suddenly linked to the sacred, the absolute. It is a Joycean term derived from Christianity; others, like Alberto Ruy Sánchez, call it "a prose of intensities"; Paz, "our ration of eternity"; Pasolini, "the apparition of the Centaur"; Roland Barthes, "the neutral" (Ruy Sánchez, 1992, pp. 31–32). With Sarduy, it is important to retrieve an expression from his essay on the baroque, *filigrana*, or filigree. His writing could be referred to as *una escritura de epifanías en filigrana*, or a writing of epiphanies in filigree. The Spanish *filigrana* is from the Latin words *filum* and *granum*, meaning thread and grain. It designates something made with perfection, subtlety, and delicacy, or a watermark. In Cuba it is also a wild plant with rough, aromatic leaves (*lantana odorata*), flowers, and a small, pineapple-shaped fruit.

Sarduy's writing, his *escritura de epifanías en filgrana* (filigree), his finely wrought arabesques, trace a welter of cultural allusions, heterotopias, historical tropes. The sheer proliferation makes it gain texture, grow thicker, and yet the humor, the precision of his language, the supple lightness of the metaphors give it the purity of line you find in fine etchings. The words hit splitting wood like the nails driven into the *mkisi*, as if time were being sundered by a blade made of shadows (West, 1994d, pp. 120–21).

Sarduy's notion of writing has an erotic-coroporeal aspect strongly tied to different traditions, but most notably to Tantrism. Sarduy was fond of Tantric beliefs and tales, like that of Purusa and Prakriti united in transcendental intercourse, which obviously suggested more earthly variants of bliss. This is similar to the poetry of Zen master Sengai, whose verses were laced with mystical allusions, where carnal and cosmic foreplay formed a whole (see Stevens, 1990, pp. 108, 111–12).

The sexuality in *Maitreya* has this quality of playfulness to it, but often it is pure expenditure and rarely is it "fertile." Ejaculation rarely finds a womb. The release of sperm in Tantric coitus is often accompanied by the recitation of a mantra that makes the act a ritual sacrifice where *el líquido feliz* (the joyful liquid), as Lezama called it, is amorously offered to the fire (associated with the feminine). With Sarduy, though, this ritual sacrifice is ungendered and nonprocreative, and, as in Tantra, a religious violation of moral strictures. Says Octavio Paz: "Sperm in the Tantric tradition is transmuted into a divine substance that ends by becoming immaterial, either because it is consumed by the fire of sacrifice or by virtue of being transformed into the thought of illumination" (Paz, 1969, p. 91). How different, say, from Protestantism where it "engenders children, families: it becomes social and an action to transform the world" (Paz, 1969, p. 91).

But Sarduy takes it further than this. The novel includes several episodes of fisting, an act that does not include heavy genital contact. In fact, as Michel Foucault said in an interview: "Physical practices like fist-fucking are practices that one can call devirilizing, or desexualizing. They are in fact *extraordinary falsifications of pleasure*, which one achieves with the aid of a certain number of instruments, of signs, of symbols, or of drugs such as poppers and MDA . . . to make of one's body a place for the production of extraordinarily polymorphic pleasures, while simultaneously detaching it from a valorization of the genitalia, and particularly of the male genitalia" (Miller, 1993, p. 269). The hand is closed, it is a fist, more like a cone, sinking into the gluteal depths of different characters in the novel. The intensity of the act is so great that it shatters the self's notion of itself in sexuality. If one is on the receiving end, it is an act of total abandonment, of releasing any control of your body and your pleasure. (Many testimonies clearly state, for men at least, that during fisting they get neither hard nor aroused in any usual way.) It is as feminized as a man can get; the rectum is the only "canal" or source of men's fantasies of childbirth. In the case of Lady Tremendous, fisted by the Iranian chauffeur, it is a devirilizing gesture that is also germinative, since she gives anal birth to a creature, albeit somewhat deformed (it has blue hair, gigantic earlobes, and webbed feet and hands). This last characteristic bears an eerie resemblance to nuclear holocaust mutations, at the same time that it refers to Yoruba traditions, where webbed feet are a sign that a child has consumed his twin brother in the womb. Other aspects of the description of the creature seem a composite of Tibetan and Hindu myhthological figures. After the miraculous birth, the Iranian disappears, his paternity vanishing with him. The hand or fist in Sarduy: like nails driven into *mkisi*, like Plato's nails of the souls—are they instruments of ecstasy or torment, illumination or degradation, life or death? Is it a trick to turn the void into a mirror, bursting with movement, like the swirling hips and bodies that adorn some Buddhist temples, literally erotic murals of the universe? Sarduy is suggestive, but offers no sure answers. He ends the novel with these words: "Embalmed Islamic twins: thus beneath minarets, lay the dwarf and Lady Tremendous' anal son, Koranic saints joined together, buried between oil wells, listening to the sound of pigeons, their feet ciphered in gold letters. They adopted other gods, eagles. They indulged in rites until they were bored or stupefied. To prove the impermanence and the emptiness of everything" (Sarduy, 1995, pp. 272–73). It is curious that Sarduy ends the novel in Afghanistan, a sort of gateway for the Middle East, Asia, and the furthest extensions of Europe. A year after the novel was completed, the Soviets would invade (1979). Again, as in many parts of the novel, East meets West, often with catastrophic and bloody consequences. Sarduy's *Maitreya* is a relentless effort to sift through the shards of Eastern mysticism and the ideological detritus of the West. In the karmic tussling of his characters, and through a "prose of intensities," Sarduy refashions the void into a vibrant theater of signs.

Already sick with AIDS, close to the end, Sarduy wrote a series of twenty poetic prose texts called "El estampido de la vacuidad" (The Crash of the Void) in which he comments on St. John of the Cross. There is a quiet transparency, of living in a divine light that's not exempt from a feeling of loss: "Defended, walled in by silence and solitude. Last hope: not poison myself with remorse, desires for vengeance, anxiety about what's left of life or annihilation, recapitulations, or fear. Take the step forward without a scenic stage, without pathos. In the most neutral way. Almost with calm" (Sarduy, 1994a, p. 37). But a few paragraphs later he is in a much more Buddhist frame of mind: "If there is no *atman*—being, self, individual, soul—what can reincarnate after death? If there is no *brahman*—universal soul, cosmic consciousness—what do we dissolve into? Once we make the leap, how do we hear *the crash of the void*?" (Sarduy, 1994a, p. 38). Sarduy's mentor, Lezama, wrote his last poems in this kind of cross between Western and Eastern mysticism. The last poem of his posthumous collection of poetry (*Fragmentos a su imán*) is called "El pabellón del vacío" (The Pavilion of the Void). Sarduy ends his meditations at home in a kind of domestic peace or tranquility, with his library, reviewing his life, his exile, his paintings, waiting for death with a quiet acceptance and beauty. You know he wants to keep writing, but he knows that he is not Sheherezade: the game is up. But in a way—and all throughout his work—the game was always up, and many have pointed to his obsession with the mechanisms of writing and death. Instead of despairing about that relationship, though, Sarduy turned his obsession into a motive for celebration.

In one of his last poems, seven *décimas* called "Epitaphs," Sarduy rhymes *tumba* (tomb) with *rumba* (rumba) (Sarduy 1994b, p. 21). The poem contains his baroque homoeroticism, the humor and lightness of expression that make his words ripple and fly, the mystical void of St. John of the Cross and Buddhism. In those mere ten lines, Sarduy brings together the three elements of the Koranic letter: the spoken form for the ear (rhyme and rumba), the written/visual form for the eye, and the spiritual form, whose locus is the heart. Close to death, as in life, Sarduy rendered the epiphany of the body luminous, where the pleasure of the void meets the furious fire of the world, echoing Lezama's words that death "engenders us all anew."

SEVEN

Paradigms Lost: The *Manigua* of Meaning

This book began by claiming that Cuba and its history are continuously being imagined both inside and ouside the island, by its own people and by others. James Hillman speaks of the link between *eidola*, the world of image and soul, and the underworld of *skia*, or shadow. Cuba's politicians have imagined it as a sweatshop or as utopia, both equally abstract, shadowy. Cuba's artists have conjured up a magical and ancestral historical world: ideas, dreams, figurations, representations, recollection. This Orphic vision is made of specters, too. We think of specters as nonexistent, immaterial, chimeric. But just like Wifredo Lam's figures, landscapes, and totems, they have a presence that is corporeal, fiery, emerging from earth: apparitions of substance, "fleshed out" if you will. Unlike the political imagination, obsessed with control, order, and exploitation, the artists' historical apparitions prepare their entry in unexpected ways, like props pushed out at the wrong time. Sent off stage, they always come back. For Lezama, it might be the *imago* taking root in history, spawning imaginary eras. In Morejón, it is the stone with its *aché*. Sarduy's apparitions are the demons of history unleashed by transculturation. In the case of Virgilio Piñera, it is all the serfs coming back to haunt the cozy comfort of the powerful. With Carpentier, the ghost of utopia and social redemption returns like a shimmering lamp. For Dulce María Loynaz, it is the house of time, with its intimate histories. While the returning specters of these six authors are by no means exhaustive, hovering close by, as always, is José Martí, that apotheosized figure of Cuban letters and history, and no doubt the specter/spectrum of Fernando Ortiz: transculturation with its full range of colors, thoughts, rhythms, images, modes of production, is a recurring revenant (or reverie?). And always present, circling in with a swaying embrace, is Yemayá, as fountain of life and fertility, as well as indomitable spirit who metes out justice sternly but with fairness.

How has the Cuban Revolution dealt with these visions, dreams, and specters, the unruly underworld of the artist's historical imagination? Despite its centralized state, one-party political system, and definite sense of what constitutes its national boundaries, Cuba is a diasporic culture. It has managed to offer its people a narrative of its nationhood based on the conquest of dignity and social justice, from the *mambises* of the nineteenth century to the anti-Machado forces in the 1930s to the July 26th Movement that overthrew Batista. But in a vast effort to rewrite history, the Cuban Revolution has instituted a "syntax of forgetting" (see Introduction) that is costly and dangerous, one that has tried either to banish or domesticate the specters mentioned. Cuba is not alone in fashioning a totalizing national narrative, as it has tried to steer a course between utopia and tyranny. The exile, dispersion, and displacement of more than a million of its citizens has created a true "other," those who would undo that syntax, counteracting oblivion with a tenacious memory that is indispensable for the future healing of a deeply sundered society. Cuba's social and cultural imagination for the the last thirty-six years has been shaped by centripetal and centrifugal forces. The centripetal forces are well known: the establishment of a revolutionary society where nation, people, and state should be one entity, an anti-imperialism that demands complete unity and obedience, a class solidarity that views difference and dissent as treason—in short, a road to freedom paved with paranoia. The centrifugal forces are not obscure either: exile, difference (sexual, class), pluralism, and distrust.

But out of these forces that tear Cuba apart or plunge it into the unknown is the mediating influence of Cuban culture. Cuba's artistic imagination is based on human solidarity, not on governmental exhortation or coercion. Its source of continuity is neither linear and unbroken, on the one hand, nor frozen in time on the other. Its own contradictory, heterogeneous imagination is what holds hope for those who see things starkly and polarized between paranoia and freedom, terror and dream, ideology and utopia. For, as we shall see, ideology and utopia need each other.

Cuba remains a faded but still persistent mirage of some of our era's most cherished and tarnished notions: faith in progress, the goal of a classless society, the hope of offering greater material comfort for all, the ability of a society to regulate itself on the precepts of transparency, equality, and rationality. Every single one of these ideas, however, is taking a beating, and not only because of the collapse of Communism, particularly since 1989. Brought up on the dream of the "beautiful totality," Cuba's young artists, fiction writers, poets, and video/filmmakers are risking their political safety to create new tropes that are critical of the revolution's image of itself and the image it projects to the world. To the notions of a teleological course in history they speak of plurality and difference, to the hope of greater material wealth and technical progress they caution that this must be accomplished soulfully. They do not hesitate to point out that the Cuban development model is bankrupt. Instead of utopia it is heterotopia, and when they hear words like transparency, rationality, and equality they react a bit like Kundera, who warned that the only truly transparent society is a police state.

If we were to adopt Lezama's terminology, perhaps we can say that modernity was (is) an imaginary era. Communism would be the attempt to take modernity to its ultimate consequences, some would say to the point of parody. Zygmunt Bauman has made this point with great eloquence and insight:

> The fall of communism was a resounding defeat for the project of *total order*—an artificially designed, all-embracing arrangement of human actions and their setting, one that follows the rules of reason instead of emerging from diffuse and uncoordinated activities of human agents; it was also the downfall of the grandiose dream of *remaking nature*—forcing it to yield ever more of anything human satisfaction may require, while disregarding or neutralizing such among its unplanned tendencies as could not be assigned any sensible human benefit; it demonstrated as well the ultimate frustration of the ambitions of global management, of replacing spontaneity with planning, of a transparent, monitored, supervised and deliberately shaped order in which nothing is left to chance and everything derives its meaning and *raison d'être* from the vision of a harmonious totality. In short, the fall of communism signalled the final retreat from the dreams and ambitions of *modernity.* . . . With the fall of communism, the ghost of modernity has been exorcised. (Bauman, 1992, pp. 178, 180)

These words point clearly to the Enlightenment dream gone amok. In many ways capitalism embodies these same traits, but Western capitalism has perhaps avoided the extremes of this vision by virtue of having some kind of political democracy. However, in its third world variants, history has offered an appalling array of examples that combine the need for control and planning with environmental degradation, extreme inequalities of wealth, lack of political freedom, poverty, sexism, and social violence. The end of the so-called cold war has done little to ameliorate these deplorable realities.

What are some of the images that characterize that "beautiful totality," as it was expressed in earlier and more innocent times? Bauman offers three metaphors for the nature of the modern state pursuing this goal: (1) a gardening state; (2) a therapeutic/surgical state; (3) a space-managing state (ibid., p. 178). I would add two more: (4) a total visibility state; and (5) a nontemporal state. The gardening state selects "useful plants" and "exterminates the useless ones." This garden metaphor (with perhaps a sly bow to Voltaire's *Candide*) has an agricultural as well as social dimension. Despite the goal of remaking nature, the social process is equated with natural ones. Even today, in our highly technical societies, a supreme compliment is to say that someone is natural. But just as in nature there are "bad weeds," so too in society. Communist experiments with nature as productive unit have been miserable, and sometimes hilarious. Cuba has been no exception, even if it has avoided the forced collectivization and famine that took the lives of millions in the USSR of the 1930s. The "ten million ton harvest" planned for 1970 failed and caused an enormous disruption of the economy. Plans to surround Havana with a coffee belt were equally futile, and a plan to plant trees by the shores to serve as a buffer against hurricanes led to the severe erosion of the coastline. The cruel ironies of sugar monoculture are still felt, so admirably summed up by a landowner and economist of the 1940s. The first said, "Without sugar there is no nation"; the second, "Because of sugar there is no nation" (as cited in Pérez-Stable, 1993, p. 14). These statements issue a double warning, aside from the obvious point of the dangers of monoculture: that nature can not be remade to conform to society, nor can nature be a norm for society. And perhaps a third: if a nation is like a being, then it is not stable, fixed, and permanent but depends on dialogue, event, consensus, and interpretation (Vattimo, 1992, p. 11).

In the "therapeutic/surgical model," a very defined sense of what is acceptable is established, and deviations from the norm are pathologized, interpreted as a sickness or a disease. The citizens of a society are at best viewed as patients who must be tutored by their doctors (the state, the party) toward good health. As bourgeois society and capitalism are viewed as a sickness, the population under socialism and eventually Communism must transcend this ailment. Perhaps this explains socialism's obsession with athletic prowess, sports training, healthiness, and cleanliness. Under (over?) this biological determinism, of course, is an ideological message. Communism is capable of producing faster, higher-jumping, and better physical specimens than its capitalist counterparts. Curiously, it seems to mirror the productivist ethic of capitalism and its ever-growing proliferation of material goods. But as history showed, even though Communism was quite successful in producing high-quality athletes, it was clearly outmatched in the area of consumer goods. In both the remaking of nature and the building of a "healthy" society, Cubans have rallied around centuries-old calls to duty, heroism, and sacrifice which will be discussed more in depth when we examine Cuba's four codes of political discourse.

The space-managing state refers more to landscape and architecture, a model of creating and distributing space that views territory as a wasteland to be sculpted by a "unifying, homogenizing principle of harmony" (Bauman, 1992, p. 179). A Soviet book from the 1960s describes the NUS (New Units of Settlement) in terms of grids featuring three complexes: the residential, the research, and the industrial (Baburov, 1970). It clearly is an improvement over the neo-classical Stalinist architecture of previous decades, but it still reflects the totalizing impulse to order everything: production, nature, education, and culture. Cuba made similar experiments in trying to close the gap between country and city, so central to the philosophy of Communism. In some cases the efforts were successful; in many they were not, and they came at the expense of letting major cities (Havana, Santiago, Matanzas, Cienfuegos) decay, in terms of buildings, infrastructure, and historical edifices.

More important is how Cuban Communism tried to erect a total visibility state, a transparent society. This transparency has several dimensions. The first is the visibility of the source of power in a revolutionary society: the maximum leader. It is easy to regard this fact as an example of mere tyranny and move on. But the ubiquity (and omnipotence) of the leader serves to embody the unity of the people, the representation of the general will. For Fidel as maximum leader, a most significant function is to ensure that the visibility works both ways. It is not only Cubans who see the leader, but the leader (party, state, etc.) who sees them. Recall that when Fidel launched the CDRs (Committees for the Defense of the Revolution), created in the wake of an attempted coup (and a U.S. economic embargo), he told the millions assembled that he needed the Cuban people to become the protectors of the revolution, *its eyes and ears*. This visibility of each citizen, this transparency of a person's motives into the public light, creates a kind of a universality of the confessional mode. Bad weeds and sickness must be rooted out, counterrevolutionaries and hypocrites must be exposed. Building on the Catholic tradition of confession and Afro-Caribbean modes of sociability, the Cuban Revolution created its own instrument to keep the visibility always present: the CDRs. They are on every block of the country and are responsible for "antisocial behavior," criminal activity, and political dissidence. They make sure people do "voluntary labor," go to political rallies or meetings, do night watch, and so forth. To their credit, the CDRs do valuable work related to health care, construction, and other civic projects. Their efficiency has brought about, however, the opposite of what was sought: their attempt to enforce total transparency has created a total split between public life and private behavior, unleashing the hypocrisy it claims to eradicate.

The fifth image, the nontemporal state, sounds contradictory. Revolutions are constantly claiming to be historical phenomena, issuing in a new secular order. The linear logic of revolutions seems to make them totally time-bound, keeping them always on the move. But time has a peculiar relation to politics. Regis Debray said that "time is to politics what space is to geometry," especially if we understand it to be modern, non-Euclidean geometry. In times of crisis, political time moves fast; so, for example, in a month of revolution we might learn more about a society than in years of status quo. In Cuba the political time moved fast in the 1960s, but clearly it has slowed down. This is not only due to an institutionalization of the revolution, but to the general orientation of socialist societies: they are always geared toward the utopian future. As a result, they are impatient with the present and undervalue the past. They compensate in a voluntarist fury by pressing harder for the future, the upshot being that they freeze time. This is reinforced by a scientific ideology, a blind faith in progress, a thirst for destiny and a one-party state. E. R. Cioran reminds us of the words of Seneca: "The life of the insane is sad, agitated, because it's always oriented toward the future." Communist history carries some of that same madness, as in the Cuban Communist Party's slogan for its First Congress (1975) which stated, "Human beings die; only the Party is eternal."

As contradictory as it seems, nothing illustrates this better than the communist mausoleums of their great leaders: Lenin, Stalin, Mao, Ho Chi Minh, Kim Il Sung. Despite visual proof of mortality, it is as if the leader's dead body were the embodiment of the Party's eternal power. The social body, the body of doctrine, the collective body of the Party must never be allowed to decay, become "corrupt." The mausoleum itself seems to indicate its triumph over nature: its immobility, its "sacred" dimension bespeaks perfection. In these images all the models we have spoken of come together: nature, architecture/space, medical-therapeutic, visibility, and time. The "beautiful sickness" of revolution has become the "beautiful totality" of utopia in the form of a dead body, the corpse of paradigms lost.

In their intense questioning of established truths, Cubans are critically redefining many terms: nation, history, class, *cubanía* (Cubanness), race, and the relationship between art and politics. On the issue of *cubanía*, one of the tenets of the Cuban Revolution is being either discarded or substantially revised: that one must be on the island to preserve one's Cubanness. By extension, this tenet apparently holds true for Cuban art (and its artists), which is one of the most unfortunate and myopic consequences of the Cuban Revolution, as well as being historically ungrounded. Some of the greatest examples of Cuban art were created in exile: José María Heredia (1803–39), José Martí (1853–95), and the composer Ignacio Cervantes (1847–1905) are some of the prime examples in the nineteenth century. In the twentieth, Alejo Carpentier, Nicolás Guillén, Lydia Cabrera, Reinaldo Arenas, and Severo Sarduy are among the best-known examples, not to mention a series of Cuban-American artists who have flourished in exile, for example, Cristina García, Elías Miguel Muñoz, José Kozer, and Dolores Prida. At the crudest level, for example, this tenet concerning *cubanía* meant that if an anthology of Cuban literature was being edited, and a writer had left the island and was anywhere from indifferent to hostile to the revolution, s/he was not included in the book. After 1960, writers like Guillermo Cabrera Infante, Lino Novás Calvo, Lydia Cabrera, Enrique Labrador Ruiz, and Gastón Baquero would not be selected. After 1980 the list grew longer:

Heberto Padilla, Reinaldo Arenas, Antonio Benítez Rojo, José Triana, Jesús Díaz and many more. In the last few years, since 1989 and 1990, some attempts have been made at discussing and even publishing authors who had left the island, such as Lydia Cabrera, Jorge Mañach, and Lino Novás Calvo. But it is still far from being enough: Cabrera Infante and Arenas are still considered taboo. Sarduy is viewed more favorably, although it is doubtful that his work will be published in Cuba any time soon. And even more troubling is the state of the Cuban economy and the cost of imported books, which makes it extremely difficult for Cubans to purchase books unless produced locally.

Likewise, Cubans who fled the island adopted an equally defensive attitude to the utopian vision of Communism, which they defined as merely tyrannical. Some retreated into nostalgia, clinging to a pre-1959 Cuban society and culture, which they viewed as authentic and as now being destroyed by an atheistic and communist revolution. Others simply tried to fit in wherever they went, and left their *cubanía* if not behind, at least on hold. But many Cubans who came of age in exile in other countries viewed things differently. Cubans in the United States, for example, began to question their identity and culture vis-à-vis an Anglo culture with which they were familiar but which somehow did not satisfy a lingering sense of longing for knowledge of the island. This generation, growing up away from the island, yet saturated with its parents' mythic nostalgia and unremitting political rage, also began exploring why Cuba went through a revolution, a questioning aided by the context of the 1960s and the Vietnam War. They felt cut off from their Cuban heritage and experienced that separation as a terrible loss, both personally and politically. No doubt this was reinforced by the fact that from 1959 to 1977 no Cuban who had left the island had returned. Some Cuban writers and artists did go back to Cuba, seeking to build bridges, people such as Lourdes Casal and Ana Mendieta, or members of the Antonio Maceo Brigade (AMB). However courageous and welcomed these efforts were, they were still initiatives by individuals, except for the brigade. The AMB did require, however, a high degree of identification with the Cuban Revolution, even if it was critical of individual Cuban governmental policies. All of these efforts, both individual and organizational, were subject to the whims of the Cuban and U.S. governments. If relations were strained, it was almost impossible to travel to the island.

A more recent effort to build bridges between Cuban artists, intellectuals, writers, historians, and thinkers bore some fruit, in a double issue of the *Michigan Quarterly Review* (*MQR*, summer and fall 1994 issues, reprinted in book form in 1995). For the first time since the revolution, a Cuban writers' publication included a roughly even breakdown: half the contributors were in exile, the other half from the island. This is not meant to belittle previous efforts, as in the case of Edmundo Desnoes's *Los dispositivos de la flor* (1981).

But the double *MQR* issue, appropriately titled *Bridges to Cuba/Puentes a Cuba*, went far beyond the Desnoes effort because it included a much wider spectrum of political, historical, and cultural opinion. Edited by Ruth Behar, anthropologist, poet, and writer, it is an exciting compendium of essays, poems, fiction, personal narrative, memoirs, criticism, and artwork. Behar states in her introduction:

> In this second number, we extend the notion of the bridge beyond the relationship between Cuba and its post-revolutionary diaspora. In my intro-duction to the first number, I was only able to allude to the way syncretism, transculturation, and diaspora are deeply embedded in the Cuban sense of identity. Here the complex hybridness of Cuban culture is explored in greater depth and in a variety of exciting and original bridgings. Rather than starting from the assumption of Cubanness as a given, the aim is to unpack the layers of meaning which are crammed into that bulging suitcase. (Behar, 1994b, pp. 639–40)

How do you begin to unpack such an overstuffed suitcase? In continuing to explore contemporary *cubanía*, we concur with Behar's assumption that it is not a given, but instead a historical construct which must include both imagined islands.

Transculturation and syncretism are still the Cuban people's creative response to diaspora, now encompassing an increasingly dispersed and disseminated Cuban identity. *Cubanía* is intimately related to Cuban nation-alism, and its history is long and complex, beyond the scope of this discus-sion. This nationalism has been expressed at many different times and with varying degrees of virulence. As a colonial subject of Spain in the nineteenth century, it was put forth by many who wanted the island to become an independent republic: Céspedes, Agramonte, Gómez, Maceo, Martí, to name only the best known. As a U.S. proctorate under the Platt Amendment (1902–34), Cuba was nominally an independent country but still subjected to the whims of U.S. policy. Its nationalism was redefined again after 1959, wedded to a project of modernization and liberation. It also became radi-cally internationalist, tacitly recognizing the limitations of the Stalinist view that revolutionary socialism in one country (particularly in Latin America, so close to the United States) would not work. This outlook involved Cuba in guerrilla struggles in Latin America, Africa, and Asia (primarily Viet-nam). This radical internationalist nationalism had a price, which was dependency on the Soviet Union. And so in the 1990s Cuba has again had to redefine its nationalist ethos within a post–cold war climate. It probably awaits another redefinition when it comes to terms with the diasporic reality it helped create: nearly two million Cubans who are now living abroad.

It is fashionable nowadays to bash nationalism and claim in our post-modern times that it is part of our modernist past, one of the grand narratives we can dispose of, like truth, metaphysics, and religion. But it is not quite so simple. Are small, poor, underdeveloped countries and their nationalistic impulses always to be criticized because of what we see happening in Bosnia or the recent war between Iran and Iraq? Cuban nationalism, even given its excesses, has never showed itself as chauvinistic, or with imperial or expansionist pretentions. Far more significant is to see how that nationalism has been embedded within a political logic that has shown remarkable consistency.

Nelson Valdés has incisively commented on recurring themes of Cuban political discourse, which have dominated social thought on the island for at least the last two centuries. He speaks of four codes: (1) the generational; (2) morality and idealism as a lever of conduct; (3) betrayal and treason as an ever-present danger; and (4) the duty-death imperative (sacrifice and martyrdom). The generational code speaks to youth as renovator/innovator of society, taking over from the older generation, whose ideas have become stagnant, corrupt, or decadent, this latter word being laden with heavy ideological baggage. But to speak of youth as "regenerating" society is to use biological metaphors, a common enough ocurrence. It also draws on family metaphors, and this convergence of society and family equally conjures up the analogy of leadership of a generation (equals head of family) with the usual paternalistic connotations. The underlying assumption of generational metaphors, despite the differences and conflict to which they allude, is that we are a big happy family, one preferably headed by a stern father. Cuban patriarchal mores have continued throughout the revolutionary period (some would say they have been exacerbated) and are echoed by the following comment by Raúl Castro, head of the armed forces, when referring to his brother: "Fidel is our father, and father of the Revolution." In this context, the word *affiliation* takes on enormous (if not ominous) resonance. To become affiliated with the revolution (the Party, Marxism) is a filial relationship, to history and to the ruler. To affiliate is to be a member of a group, to trace an origin. This corporeal identity (biologistic, if you will) evokes the body politic, which is headed by a person who is the literal embodiment of power. This literality is closely intertwined with the visibility, transparency, and power mentioned earlier. There is nothing new in this, as it goes back to Christian theology, as well as medieval political theory about kings and their power (Ernst Kantorowicz's the king's "two bodies": individual and collective, mortal and immortal, worldly and divine). What is perhaps novel in modernity is how this concept has been recycled in twentieth-century autocratic and totalitarian regimes, using the mass media and other manipulative though noncoercive systems of persuasion to project and display a visibility of that body that is not only ubiquitous, but all-powerful. (And, of course, when persuasion fails there are more coercive ways to enforce this visibility.) It literally occupies not only a real social space, but an imaginary social space which can only be described as mythic as Lévi-Strauss spoke of myth (and more recently, music), as not only an obliteration of time, but as possessing a power that encompasses the totality of being.

It is precisely this double body of power that Virgilio Piñera so scathingly exposes in his story "The Dummy." Indeed, one could say that the four codes outlined by Valdés have received the most implacable criticism from his work. In one story, which reads as a savage parody of the "martyrdom-sacrifice" code, Piñera borders on the unthinkable: the narrator defends the eating of babies as a patriotic act, since in this fashion they will not be butchered in war.

Valdés speaks of the generational code as leading to a kind of subjectivism, making Cuban thinkers ignore the material and social consequences that come to bear on political circumstances. This "emotionalism," what writer Rolando Sánchez Mejías would refer to as the "epico-sentimental guild," has a Rousseau-ish hue to it. While most Cubans may not have read Rousseau, some of Rousseau's imagery has made its way down through Martí. According to Rousseau, the heart was the source of virtue. This can be extraordinarily problematic, if it is linked to the notion of general will, or the will of the people. Rousseau used the image of the multitude united in one body to express that general will, and Robespierre brought it to its bloodiest consequences. This definition of the will of the people means that the collective will of society will always be in conflict with individual passions because the latter are an expression of egotism, not virtue. Rousseau spoke of the *âme dechirée* (a divided soul) to speak of the tension between private passion and public virtue. Robespierre introduced this divided soul into the political sphere with a goal of total visibility. Hannah Arendt sums it up: "Robespierre and his followers, once they had equated virtue with qualities of the heart, see intrigue and calumny, treachery and hypocrisy everywhere" (Arendt, 1963, p. 96). But as Robespierre himself said: "The hunt for hypocrites is boundless and can produce nothing but demoralization" (ibid., p. 97). In Cuban terms, we could say that the search for counterrevolutionaries is endless, since everyone is capable of betraying the revolution.

Robespierre's tragic moral dilemma dovetails with Valdés's third theme of betrayal and treason. This logic of pure political commitment, building *el hombre nuevo* (the new man), pure of mind and heart, puts an enormous strain on Cuban political discourse: "The right of different political perspectives to be clearly in competition with one another has not won acceptance in Cuban politics. Like other social relations, politics seems to be based on a total, complete and absolute loyalty—towards an individual or a group of 'moral' norms. Politics, then, requires unconditional loyalty, confidence, and faith" (Valdés in Rodríguez Beroff, 1995, p. 149). Again, this treasonous motif is closely linked to generational/family metaphors and provides constant nourishment for the passion to create regimes of total visibility, in which the revolutionary sun casts no shadow where treasonous doubt can hide. Newer voices, however, are suggesting that this kind of family is dysfunctional at best, if not pernicious for the political health of a nation.

Valdés's other two themes can be summed up under the notion of heroism (morality-voluntarism and duty-death). I have often suggested that the time for heroes in Cuban history is over and have evoked that wily old Communist Bertolt Brecht himself, in his play *Galileo*, who when hearing the lament that sad is the country without heroes, retorts, "Sad is the country that needs heroes." I am not alone in voicing this opinion: Coco Fusco, Nena Torres, Ruth Behar, and others of our generation in exile have also expressed themselves in a similar vein. (I am not saying that Cubans cannot perform "heroic" deeds; but from that to "being a hero" is a large step, one as far as going from history to myth.) However, no one has expressed the danger of the hero with the devastating eloquence of Elías Miguel Muñoz in his poem "Los vaticinios" (Prophecies):

> I dislike people who predict the future,
> who announce catastrophes and miracles.
> Indolent sorcerers who claim they can invent
> tomorrow. I am not speaking of those
> who have no choice but to write.
> I'm referring to those other wizards:
> those who predict without thinking,
> who rely solely on their clairvoyance.
>
> A sorcerer once told me of an exodus
> that would become my sustenance.
> He offered details of my future routines.
> Calm and collected, highly informative,
> he described a fall, a bottomless pit,
> a bedroom-turned-theater with no exit.
> He showed me the exciting fucks
> but didn't let me see the silences,
> the betrayals.
>
> A kinder one took me by the hand.
> And stroking me as though I were his cat,
> he foretold this moment when,
> exhausted, skeptical but lucid,
> I try to remember all the prophecies.
>
> And I still wonder, as I face the deeds
> that haven't yet been written,
> if postponing myself is worth the pain.
> "Too soon to wonder about that," says the prophet.
> "Most of you poets think you're so unique,"
> he adds reproachfully.
> "You boast about your sacrifices:

how one must defer the meaning of one's life
for the sake of artistic vision.
What snobbery, what dreams of grandeur!
If you were real, you would face up to reality.
You wouldn't turn to words after each blow."

And without putting on airs
or hiding behind poetic proclamations
(most of which are worthless),
I confess to him that when it comes to heroism,
I consider myself rather small.
You see, I know the meaning of my writing:
it's home (a common place),
a bed (because poetry has never betrayed me),
my daily bread (a half-baked motif).
My justification.

Meanwhile,
what truths are the wizards announcing?
That a plague will devastate the Earth
and then a flood shall cleanse us;
that we will shed our skins, gradually;
that we will lose our voices,
our eyes, our sex.
So we can be reborn with skins of steel,
with robot voices,
with eyes only for numbers.
Born again with larger-than-life cocks.
(The "weak" genders won't survive the deluge.)

Not coral skin
(because we won't be like the sea).
Not a free voice (a myth that has
nothing to do with Defense).
But a new vision:
that of a warrior, a cybernerd,
a talk-show-host, a yuppie, a dink,
an actor, a liar, a thief.

Let it be known that I do not believe
in prophecies.
(Muñoz, 1989, pp. 53–54; trans. Muñoz)

Muñoz's poem, with its savage humor, goes to the heart of what was previously mentioned about socialism's madness of always living in the future. He debunks the utopian vision which promises all the excitement but says nothing of "the silences, / the betrayals." But the poem does much more than that, creatively riding the line between ideology and utopia, showing how they feed on each other. If ideology is the gap that must be filled between the claims that a society makes and the beliefs of its citizens, then ideology, aside from a distorting function, has an important goal of preservation and identity (of a nation, a class). But there are moments when that order (which ideology has put forth or narrated) seems inadequate, even fleeting. That is where utopian thinking can move societies forward, by offering alternatives, by at least advancing an ideal, no matter how unattainable; because, as Paul Ricoeur says, "A society without utopia would be dead, because it would no longer have any project, any prospective goals" (Ricoeur, 1986, p. xxi). Muñoz's poem evokes the stark reality of our condition—an unshakable contingency—but assumes it with a kind of restless patience. If utopia seems to foresee the future with unambiguous clarity, then "history that can be foreseen is no longer history" (Heller, 1993, p. 51). Instead it has become prophecy. By rejecting utopia as prophecy, the poet is closer to Richard Kearney's definition of the utopic: "The utopian horizons of social imagination are open-ended goals which motivate a free variation of possible worlds. They are not pre-established goals or predetermined. They are tentative, provisional, fragile. The universality of the *u-topos* derives from the fact that it is the possession of no one and the possibility of everyone" (Kearney, 1991, p. 219).

Muñoz is able to speak of betrayals and silences so convincingly because he shared that vision of the "beautiful totality." Equally poignant is his understanding of poetry and its relationship to politics, but without belittling it (by placing it beneath social concerns) or inflating it through a kind of art-is-all narcissism. Kant equated poetry with the productive imagination (to some degree, then, utopic) as opposed to a merely reproductive imagination (ideology). The poem, or the work of art, is utopian not because it offers a detailed blueprint of a perfect society, but because it allows us a perspective to see the poverty of the given; it is disruptive, a breaking through of reality (Ricoeur, 1986). This breaking through is a recreation of reality; it helps us think from somewhere else, creating a sacred site (sight?) for new understanding.

But in his poem Muñoz is equally sanguine about capitalism's promise of a bigger, better, and more efficient future, mostly through the promise of technology and science. His lucidity and caution still leave a door open for future visions and alternatives, but they will no longer be bought at the price of collective constraint or a rampant individualism that reinforces conformity. There is a fleeting vision of hope by subtraction, by not giving into the seduction of false redemption. In Greek, apocalypse means "revelation." Muñoz suggests that revelation can happen without one's having to be "burnt by the sun."

One of the silences Muñoz speaks of has been the voice and power of women and their role in Cuban history. This will constitute one of the thoroughly new aspects of Cuba's future, with its own tropes and its own confrontation with ideological and utopian thinking. Can we speak about a "women's time" for Cuba? What might that be like? Julia Kristeva, in her essay "Women's Time," speaks about a concept of nation that now seems to be outdated, one characterized by economic homogeneity, historical tradition, and linguistic unity. All of these criteria have been opened up by economic interdependence as well as a symbolic complexity in terms of tradition and language. In Cuba's case the economic interdependence has always had an element of dependence on colonial or foreign powers (Spain, the United States, the USSR). Cuba's linguistic unity is changing with its diasporic culture that is also writing, thinking, and expressing itself in English. It is no longer acceptable, if it ever was, to assume that the work of Cristina García, Oscar Hijuelos, Robert G. Fernández, Elías Miguel Muñoz, or Carmelita Tropicana is any less Cuban by being in English. The historical tradition is also being pluralized, made more inclusive by those who have not previously spoken or have been completely marginalized (women, gays, war veterans, Afro-Cubans).

Kristeva also speaks of temporality in terms of gender, with linear, progressive time, defined by productivity and obsessiveness with conquering and power, as male-oriented. She evokes Nietzsche's distinction between cursive (linear) and monumental time, which transcends national boundaries, linking up with a wider temporal dimension akin to Lezama's imaginary eras. Monumental time is either cyclical or biologistic, and some feminists have tried to draw a positive source of strength from this kind of time without turning women into a kind of archetype, devoid of historicity. Too often, Cuban history, its national symbols, its goals, have been defined in cursive time, as an airtight tradition or as prophecy. Some of the chapters of this book have been dedicated to exploring a historicized version of this monumental time, particularly the ones on Nancy Morejón and Dulce María Loynaz (and to a lesser extent Lezama and Sarduy). Will this "new time" (women's and beyond) speak of *jouissance*, create and describe new forms of power, propose a new way of valuing intersubjectivity, move away from models of domination and mastery, view human development as a dialectic of autonomy and mutuality? Possibly, and some of the writers in this book either directly or indirectly suggest these possibilities for an imagined Cuban future.

In the chapter on Morejón I spoke of the *manigua*, the Taíno word referring to a place with dense vegetation, consisting of shrubs, bushes, and lianas. The *manigua* is a landscape where there was a "natural profusion of confusion," a locus of escape from oppression and a new spot from which to begin a life of freedom. If we compare it to the colonial model of the square with a plaza and its important buildings (symbolically and politically), perhaps the *manigua* will seem chaotic. But it is not; instead it is a more flexible place than the plaza, one that must be both respected as it is, but also shaped for its new purposes of freedom. It is a signifying space as well, which, if indicative of monumental time, does not need everlasting monuments. Ultimately, it is a *manigua* of meaning, where the goals, identity, and images of Cuban history will be interpreted and contested—and peopled with the *figuras* to be fulfilled in the future, as mentioned in the discussion of Lezama. This *manigua*, with its delicate and intricate ecology, is not being opposed to the city or constructed environments. Traditionalists will perhaps see the *manigua* as an Arcadian retreat, revolutionary modernists as a guerrilla *foco*, and postmodernists would liken it to a rhizome. But actually the vision being proposed is more modest. It is closer to how Leszek Kolakowski sees the cultural role of philosophy, not as something that delivers or possesses the truth, but as a quest for truth, a quest that allows us to "build the spirit of truth, and this means to never let the inquisitive energy of mind go to sleep, never to stop questioning what appears to be obvious and definitive. . . . Philosophers neither sow nor harvest, they only move the soil" (Kolakowski, 1990, p. 135). This moving of soil is not busywork: by allowing the soil to breathe, we find old roots that needed to be unearthed and new ones that will be discovered.

We are not opposing "natural" to "artificial," or nature and society. Lezama, Morejón, and Loynaz have shown us that that kind of thinking is limited and superficial in understanding Cuban history and culture. Instead it speaks to the paths that have already been taken in the course of Cuban history, as well as the many that still beckon in the future. In that quilt of possibilities we can visualize that homecoming through otherness, best nurtured by the watchful eyes of Elegguá (Eshu), as Nancy Morejón reminds us. Orisha of the crossroads, at the intersection of different times, the plurality of his *aché* is also a paradigm of different perspectives and visions, and holds the key of our potentialities. Also a trickster, with a penchant for mendacity, he ultimately gives his life by telling the truth. As Robert Farris Thompson reminds us: "Eshu the prince devoured the truth by lying, never sacrificing, heedless of the damage done, and paid for his arrogance, when he finally told the truth, by dying. Thus in the Afro-Cuban myth Eshu devours himself but once again returns when proper sacrifice, centered upon a piece of stone, is made. The story of Eshu is an intricate retelling of the Yoruba belief that the highest form of morality is sharing and generosity—the strongest talisman to hold against jealousy" (Thompson, 1984, p. 22). The *manigua*, then, is a locus of questioning and where knowledge takes root (literally, sometimes), the breaking of new ground for different kinds of production: economic, social, symbolic, numinous. The *manigua* presents a thicket where meaning runs deep and where history can be swallowed whole, to be brought back by a propitiation that must be made of contingency, myth, generosity, memory, and metaphor.

Let us recollect some final images of that *manigua*. First, in the spirit of knowledge through otherness, we turn to one that is geographically far away. The beginning of Wagner's *Twilight of the Gods*, the fourth and last opera of his Ring Cycle, features three Norns handling the chord of destiny, with which they weave time. They are the daughters of Erda, goddess of wisdom and the earth, and represent the past, the present, and the future. They surround the Yggdrasil, the World Ash Tree, quite withered. From the tree a fountain streamed forth, that of wisdom. They yearn for a lost harmony, brought about by Wotan's actions. In order to obtain wisdom he gave up the use of one eye. In addition, Wotan took a piece of the tree to make a spear on which he inscribed the laws and from which he derived the power to rule. But that caused the tree to lose its power and dry up the fountain of wisdom. As the Norns try to wrap the chord or rope around the rocks, it snaps or breaks. Finally, in despair, they return to Erda and sink into the earth. A Jungian interpretation will, of course, point out that Wotan's ignorance of the earth's wisdom is also a repression of the feminine, of his anima, and ultimately a destructive act. This is borne out by the opera's end where Wotan and Valhalla perish in flames, as the sacrificial act for a new beginning.

It would be tempting and perhaps too easy to read a literal meaning of this ending of the Ring Cycle into current Cuban history. Instead, in the spirit of Fernando Ortiz, and seeking in the dying tree from the Old World the inventiveness of the New, I would instead offer the following counter-point: there is a knowledge, a subjectivity, and a history embedded in Cuba's official history that is being explored and has not fully blossomed—that of women, of gays and lesbians, war veterans, and Afro-Cubans. That knowledge is very close to the poetics described by Gaston Bachelard in the epigraph at the beginning of this book: "We are never real historians, but always near poets, and our emotion is perhaps nothing but an expression of poetry that was lost." It also derives from our understanding of air, water, and earth as a constant, renewable source of knowledge (a *manigua*). Consider Bachelard's words on roots and trees:

> As a dynamic image, the roots assume the most diverse powers. It is both a sustaining force and a terebrant force. At the border of two worlds, the air and the earth, the image of the root is animated paradoxically in two directions, depending on whether we dream of a root bearing to heaven the juices of the earth, or of a root going to work among the dead, for the dead. . . . A root is always a discovery. . . . The tree is everywhere at once. The old root—in the imagination there are no young roots—will produce a new flower. The imagination is a tree. It has the integrative virtues of a tree. It is root and boughs. It lives between earth and sky. It lives in the earth and in the wind. The imagined tree becomes imperceptibly the cosmological tree, the tree which epitomizes a universe, which makes a universe. (Bachelard, 1987, pp. 84, 85)

This description of the tree and its analogy to the imagination has a suggestive correspondence with the *ceiba* tree in Cuba, another New World symbol with ancient configurations. The *ceiba* is considered sacred by whites, blacks, santeros (or not), as well as the Chinese. Humans are not supposed to cut the tree down without making the proper offerings. The *ceiba* is so sturdy that neither lightning nor hurricanes are capable of destroying it (Cabrera, 1992, p. 149). It is sacred in the Afro-Cuban tradition of Santería, being both a life force and containing the souls of the dead as well. It is known as the Mother Ceiba and referred to as the tree of the Virgin Mary. Lezama refers to it in *La expresión americana*, along with the *ombú* tree as a historical tree.

In rewriting Wagner's scene for three Antillean Norns born in Cuba, we can invoke Yemayá, Oshún, and Oyá, the three great female orishas of Santería, who rule over the Cuban psyche: Yemayá, who gave birth to the river, the orishas, and all that lives; Oshún, Yemayá's sister, orisha of love, celebration, sensuality; and Oyá, impetuous and sometimes violent, who rules over lightning, the winds and storms, as well as cemeteries. She helped Changó escape from jail and often accompanied him in battle. These three orishas guard the *ceiba* tree and make not only the dead speak, but the living as well. Like the three Norns who thread time and its roads, they invoke Elegguá.

Maybe the three Norns—but much more so Yemayá, Oshún, and Oyá—seem to come together in Carmelita Tropicana's performance piece *Milk of Amnesia*, which is a kind of ongoing conversation with Cuban history's dead and living spirits as she painfully reconstructs the memories shattered by exile. She crosses genders and borders in a kind of exorcism which is always mixed with Cuban *choteo* (poking fun) par excellence, as if to exemplify Gianni Vattimo's idea of freedom "as a continual oscillation between belonging and disorientation." This is hilariously evoked in two different episodes, one in which she becomes a horse during colonial times, another when she turns into a pig during the current "Special Period." As if turning Lezama's "animistic (and animalistic?) counterpoint" inside out, Carmelita's memory trances evoke the pain of the "syntax of forgetting," but with enormous humor and compassion. The horse complains of having the hairs of his tail used to make shirts, but these humiliations are small compared to the genocide of the indigenous population that he has witnessed. The pig remembers having a family photograph taken with a baseball cap on, an innocent foretaste of his ultimate fate as a *lechón asado*, or a roast pork sandwich. At one point Carmelita shadowboxes with a strung-up pig figure, a rich metaphor for the demons and passions of history that always seem to elude our grasp.

Carmelita's oscillation between belonging and disorientation is translation in overdrive, as if to say, "there are no facts, only interpretations." She seems constantly to question from where she speaks: here, there, nowhere, from women's time, queer time? Perhaps she is a *figura* under the shade of a *ceiba* tree, traversing the *manigua* of meaning, knowing that more than a journey, or a path, it is a bridge to the past that must be constantly reinvented, so that history will not be "the most dangerous product evolved from the chemistry of the intellect." If the path or the bridge is to speak to the future (or in the future), it must embrace tropes that fashion the act of tolerance "that creates the imaginative province where no one owns the truth and everyone has the right to be understood."

CODA

Living Tropes, Living Hopes

I, too, am a living trope of Cuban history. As a writer, I have sought to create my own "open gnostic space" or *manigua*. As in Bachelard's root and tree imagery, there is a vertical flowering toward heaven and a seeping into the earth to "work among the dead." Perhaps the space should be called the "tree of tangled destinies," one that spans three homelands (Cuba, Puerto Rico, the United States), two languages, and as many mytho-aesthetic realms as there are continents. At our first of many stops, in Houston, Texas, I lost my Spanish, which was a way of losing my history, my sense of *cubanidad*. If, as George Steiner said, "History, in the human sense, is a language net cast backwards," by "rediscovering" my Spanish, language then became a way of re-collecting history, allowing me truly to inhabit my past and my future. I now write poetry and fiction primarily in Spanish, and journalism, essays, personal narrative, and criticism in both languages. Each medium offers a containment for the tension of its unifying metaphors in a different way. While for Lezama the symbolic generativity of the "animistic counterpoint" offered a method for historical interpretation, for me the dialectics of lost and found language, nation, and history have become a strategy for survival.

The island's history is my family's history, first in my grandparents' generation as immigrants to the island, later as exiles after the revolution. As a child of almost six, I witnessed the entry of Fidel Castro into Havana, interpreted by almost everyone as an omen of hope. I also saw the hope turn to frustration, bitterness, and rage. And later, in exile, while sympathetic to many of the revolution's aims, I also witnessed the terrible pain of separated families, cold war rigidities from both sides of the Florida straits, and a sense of loss aggravated by so many missed opportunities. As tempting as it was to forget, it was an impossible task for any considerable stretch of time. Cuba's presence is overwhelming: the island will not let you forget. I would not go so far as to describe myself as being tattooed by history, like Cuban poet and fiction writer Rolando Sanchez-Mejías, but at the same time Cuba has exerted a pull that is dangerously close to being an obsession.

In the previous chapter I analyzed a poem by Elías Miguel Muñoz, "Prophecies," from his book *No fue posible el sol* (It Wasn't Possible to Have the Sun). There is an affinity between Muñoz's poem and a recent text I wrote about Cuban music. Written for a Cuban magazine published in Madrid while I was in the midst of preparing this manuscript, it offers a deconstruction of the hero in the spirit of Sarduy's notion of transcultura-tion as cross-dressing. The translation is a free one, trying to echo some of the wordplay found in the original Spanish.

"Island Arias: La política e mobile"

One of the first Cuban operas was titled "The Devil Contrabandist (Smuggler)," from 1840. Prophetic because you have to be a little of both to survive on the island during what is euphemistically called the "special period." But let's follow the example of Saumell (and his unstaged opera *Antonelli*) and propose a current-imaginary opera; one we can cull from Beethoven (at least the name): *Fidelio*. Maybe we can bring it up to date and call it *Fides Fiddles with History*. A rescue opera no doubt. Besides, we can build on a Cuban tradition of transvestism: remember that Leonor (in the Beethoven opera) dresses as a man, going under the name of Fidelio, to rescue her imprisoned husband Florestan. I nominate Reinaldo Arenas as the central character, dressed as Obatalá. Why not? His *Color of Summer* reads like a libretto for an opera, and the sheer (and queer) quantity of characters, choruses and extreme liberties taken with believability put it on the Pharaonic scale of *Aida*. Arenas imper-sonates Fidel in order to rescue his jailed lover (called Rococo), who is a jaguar that during the day looks like Lezama and at night like Virgilio. The prison is built in the form of a pineapple. But, as chance would have it, the head of state visits the prison that day, bringing about the encounter of the two Fidels. Naturally, each accuses the other of being an impostor. Who is more faithful (or is it fi(s)tful)? A judge is needed to ascertain the highest degree of fidelity: Raúl Castro is brought forth, dressed as *vedette* Rita Montaner. With a Wag-nerian touch, the two sing arias longer than El Comandante's speeches, leaving the audience and the other characters in a deep sleep. With the somnolent air still heavy with snoring bodies, a ghost appears à la Macbeth: General Ochoa. Like a bolt, he strikes Fidel with a blow of his machete, surer than the aim of Ogún. Arenas and his lover get married with Severo Sarduy performing the ceremony, and Raúl-Rita Montaner (now contrite) sings a blessing aria while the chorus builds rafts from old Soviet Marxist-Leninist manuals. Curtain drops. Follow the *lieder*. (West, 1996)

This segment was written as a playful comment on Cuban politics, perhaps conjoining its highly charged emotionalism with operatic outrageousness and a dose of Cuban *choteo*. But a closer look begins to reveal many of the themes and issues brought up in this book: transculturation, gender and identity, the specters of history, exile and homecoming (through otherness), the island's yearning for freedom, affiliation and filiality, loyalty and patriotism, faithfulness to one's roots and ideas.

Why is Arenas chosen as the "protagonist" of my imaginary opera? In part, no doubt, because his own life appears as unbelievable in many ways as most opera plots. But also because his life and work (not a distinction he drew very clearly) are still an unfinished chapter in recent Cuban history, literary and otherwise. There is an element to Arenas which I think has made him "indigestible" on both sides of the divide and is summarized by Abilio Estévez who quotes him: "The world and I are at war." His war was against all types of conformity, and in this regard he was spiritually close to Virgilio Piñera, his mentor (the other was Lezama). Arenas had the rare ability to depict both the greatness and squalor of what it means to be Cuban, but usually in the most unflattering of ways. Estévez puts it thus: "Reinaldo Arenas damns us and we come to love him, as we love the demon who saves us by showing us the frightful sight of our own lives" (in Behar, 1994b, p. 867).

At some level my Cubanized *Fidelio* is a parable of betrayal and reconciliation. The betrayal-treason code discussed by Valdés is seen at least twice: in Arenas trying to impersonate the body of power (Fidel) and in the ghost of Arnaldo Ochoa, trusted general who has "betrayed" the revolution and who many see as himself betrayed by the revolution. When the two Fidels confront each other, of course, there must a contest to demonstrate their authenticity. If Arenas "betrays" his disguise, he loses. At one level, Arenas as "other" is a double of what he despises, reinforced by the fact that Arenas dresses like the orisha Obatalá. But at another level, being able to impersonate the body of power is a definition of democracy. That is, the possibility of any citizen being able to assume the body of power is what constitutes a democracy (the seat of power is empty and is assumed by each new elected president).

Clearly all the impersonating going on in this sketch points to the double life of Cuban society, so admirably and humorously illustrated in the recent film *Fresa y chocolate* (Strawberry and Chocolate). Nancy (Mirta Ibarra), for example, is in charge of the CDR (neighborhood vigilance) for their block. Ostensibly someone who is faithful to Marxism, she is constantly praying to St. Barbara (Changó in Santería), trades on the black market (at that time a punishable offense), and is the first to warn people about turning up the radio so that certain conversations can take place.

These Cuban images of cross-dressing contain both a historical and gender dimension which are inextricably linked and which try to navigate that tension between ideology and utopia, particularly if the latter is understood as said before, as being "tentative, fragile, provisional, and open-ended." Obviously, the thought of Raúl Castro dressed as Rita Montaner is absurd, but it signals the desire to move beyond the warrior mentality of Cuban society and its revolution, which in this instance it shares with Santería. So is the marriage of Reinaldo Arenas at the end, which, literally speaking, is ridiculous, made even more so by casting Severo Sarduy as the priest (he was not only openly gay but a Buddhist as well). This image of reconciliation is a dream, unrealizable, and not only because Arenas and Sarduy have died of AIDS, but also because a traditional betrothal as image of reconciliation is clearly not sufficient or accurate as a trope. Despite a certain harmony or resolution, it is not a completely happy ending.

Beethoven's opera is about marriage just as Cuba's tropes and traditions are wedded to history, to faithfulness, and loyalty to one's roots. The opera is also about freedom, but in the Cuban version it is not just political freedom, but economic, social, reproductive, sexual, and racial freedom as well. The ending by no means describes a perfect marriage: as Elías Miguel Muñoz says, it has been made up of "silences and betrayals." This marriage of deprivation is both a displacement and an uncertainty, a kind of bereavement. As Cioran says: "The more we are dispossessed, the more intense our appetites and illusions become."

The intensity of appetites and illusions of dispossession is one of the major threads that I chronicled in my recent book of poems, *Dar nombres a la lluvia / Finding Voices in the Rain*. To a degree, the poems are a conversation with many of the authors discussed in this book. Through the audacious imagery of these writers, I began to understand Cuban history in a novel way, particularly with the work of Carpentier, Lezama, and Sarduy. Their proximity and their distance to the island allowed me to comprehend that images have their history and at the same time can shape history. The first part of the book is subtitled "Hi(stories) of the Image." It builds on mythologies of different cultures (Afro-Caribbean, Chinese, Arabic, Greek), as well as the techno-mythic machine known as the movies. The first section, drawing on a baroque eroto-aesthetics of writing, is not only a celebration of a rediscovered language and history, but an active engagement with a literary tradition that began with Spain's Golden Age of Literature and has been redefined and recreated by Caribbean writers in the twentieth century (Lezama, Césaire, Sarduy). In contrast, the more declarative style for the second half is titled "Images of History." Again, gathering sustenance from my own lived history as well as authors from Martí to Morejón, the second half of the book explores either how history creates images of itself or how we do so through memory. "O Tempora! O Mores!," the last poem, seeks to synthesize historical with writerly concerns under the rubric of a philosophical meditation on a film by Chris

Marker, *Sans soleil* (Sunless). Marker's 1982 film is an experimental documentary with a haunting magical aura to it, depicting unforgettable scenes about war and loss, memory and hope, culture, tradition, myth, and belief. With footage from Japan, Guineau-Bissau, and France, it is structured as a series of letters sent to and read by the unnamed narrator. The sense of distance and separation, which resonated with my own exile experience, is softened by the incantatory effect of a multilayered narrative that freely and poetically shifts spatial and temporal realities. The film constantly questions how images can represent history, culture, even happiness, and as such is a metaphor for memory as recollection, in the Hegelian sense.

Toward the end of the poem I question the ability of names or images to portray the true horrors of history. The two passages are near each other but not immediately contiguous:

> Horror has a face but no name
> As long as it's a face that remains as image,
> > we will place it with others in a never-ending gallery
> > still as a collected butterfly,
> > and in the mausoleum we'll domesticate it,
> > surgically remove it from time.

> History/horror
> > We give it a name to make it memory
> > Bergen-Belsen, Tuol Sleng, Little Big Horn, Panzós, Sumpul
> > As long as it has a name we can retrieve it
> > in the vain hope that it will illuminate history,
> > which, if named time and again, might become a sort of primer.

> . . . .

> All those images could be my memory
> All those images could be the clasped hands of a devout person
> > praying ceaselessly to the rhythm of life
> > as one might buy the paper on the way to work
> Could be that crayfish that bit me as a boy
> Could be that light/wreath that falls between two trees.

> That scent
> mingling autumn and spring,
> the earth's inclination intoxicating the sparrows
> > From this sponge that could be fire
> > and the bark's next outbreak of fever
> > the resting of the branch drunk with arrows
> > now light   now spike of grain

> > The image, that first step toward passion
> > > and ruin.

(West, 1995, pp. 131, 133; trans. Mark Schafer)

The conclusion of the poem evokes an image that is both an ending and a beginning, a recurring theme in the book, one that suggests the sly and unpredictable movements of history. It encourages a reworking of Bachelard's phrase as follows: we are never real poets but always near historians, and both our wonder and our despair are an expression of history (and poetry) that reemerge, like the shifting border of light and shadow, embroidering the abyss. If Cuba's history echoes an Orphic dismemberment, our tropes make us more whole; poetry is a re-membering, affording us the numinous and difficult serenity of the *manigua*. From the manigua, trope and nature, philosophy and history sing their memory and image. Like a great *ceiba* tree, it outwits and outlasts the unheeding and forgetful night.

APPENDIX

Cuban History: An Overview

THE COLONY AND THE REPUBLIC, 1492–1958

Cuba is the longest and largest island of the Caribbean, its shape often compared to a *caimán*, a smaller version of the crocodile. In area it is equivalent to the state of Pennsylvania, but in terms of length it stretches a distance comparable to going from Jacksonville, Florida, to Houston, Texas. The island has a curent population of ten and a half million. The original inhabitants of Cuba were the Siboneyes, followed by two principle migrations of Arawak indians: the Sub-Taínos and the Taínos. When Columbus arrived in 1492, the island's inhabitants were mostly Sub-Taíno (90 percent). The estimated numbers of the indigenous population at the time of the Conquest were about 112,000, though estimates vary from 16,000 to 600,000.

The Siboney civilization was not as developed as the Arawak. They tended to build camps instead of settlements, and they divided their nomadic existence into two areas: those by the sea, bays, or swamp and those among the cliffs and ravines, often living in caves. The name Siboney appears to be derived from the Arawak words *siba* (cave) and *eyerí* (man). Their economy was simple, based on hunting and gathering, but most of their food came from the sea. They shared property, sporadically used fire, and traveled on foot, having no beasts of burden. Little is known of their cultural or religious practices or language. The latter tongue was different from Arawak, because the Spanish colonizers who could speak to the Taínos could not converse with the Siboneyes. Most of the Siboneyes were displaced by Arawak migrations in the eastern part of Cuba.

The Taínos belonged to the language group of speakers of Arawak, meaning "meal" or "cassava eater." The staple of their diet was yucca (or cassava), though they also grew other crops—sweet potatoes, corn, tomatoes, pineapples, peanuts, many kinds of fruits and berries—and caught various types of fish and shellfish. At the time of the Spanish Conquest they were in the Neolithic period (they used ax heads of polished stone, but did not use metal as instruments); however, they were extraordinarily skilled in sculpture, ceramics, and basket weaving. In addition they were remarkably talented with cotton and other fibers for making hammocks, nets, ropes, cord, mats, and mattresses. Their social organization was based on a *cacique* (chief), who ruled over the *nitaínos* (a higher class) and the *naborias* (workers). Recent archaeologcal evidence (from Puerto Rico) has revealed more than fifteen instances of women being Taíno *caciques*.

The Taínos had a religious cosmology, believing in supernatural deities that lived in the sky, such as Yocahú (the Supreme Maker) and Juracán (god of destructive winds), the source of the word *hurricane*. Their myths, stories, and traditions were passed on and retold in ceremonial dances called *areytos*, held in a plaza or *batey*. These plazas or courts also were the place of their ball games, played by ten to thirty players and vitally linked to religious beliefs of sacrifice and fertility. Some archaeologists point out the similarities between Mayan/Mesoamerican beliefs and practices and that of the Taínos. To name only a few: the belief in twin gods, the myth of the flood, the ball game played by both, in which the losers were part of a sacrifice (but not always), their association of owls with death and frogs with rain. There was indeed contact between the civilizations over several centuries.

The Spanish, however, were more interested in shinier objects, mainly gold, and put the Taínos to work extracting it, with many dying from overexertion and mistreatment. Some Spanish priests, such as Bartolomé de Las Casas, energetically denounced these practices, in particular when he traveled with the Pánfilo de Narvaez expedition to Cuba in 1512. Whether or not one views Spanish colonization as genocide because of how complete the annihilation of indigenous cultures was in the Caribbean, it should not obscure the following fact: the majority of the Taínos died from unknown diseases brought by European settlers. Even a trivial example shows how seemingly innocuous behavior can have devastating consequences. The presence of unpenned pigs, cattle, goats, horses, and other animals brought by the Spanish colonists was calamitous. These untended beasts fed on grasses and on the crops of the Taínos, causing immense ecological damage. This caused hunger and malnutrition, and in many instances whole villages had to move. Infanticide and suicide became widespread, becoming one of the main causes of death, as described by Las Casas and others. Said one Spanish officer: "There were days in which they were all found hanging, with their women and children, fifty households of the same village."

Goldfields and mines were exhausted quickly in Cuba, which paralleled the decimation of the indigenous population, which by 1519 was at 19,000, then down to 7,000 by 1531. After that, the *encomiendas* were dedicated to animal husbandry and sugarcane production, introduced into Cuba from the Canary Islands in 1515. By the 1550s, most of the Taíno population had been wiped out (only 3,000 were left), paving the way for the introduction of a greater number of slaves brought from Africa. (Black slaves had already been brought to the island, but even as late as 1650 were only one out of every six inhabitants.)

The Taíno legacy, however, was important to the future societies of the Caribbean. Many foods that were unknown to the colonialists are still part of the Cuban diet: yucca, *yautía*, sweet potato (*batata*), *guanábana*, *mamey*, and peanuts (*maní*). Maize and tobacco, though originally from other Mesoamerican cultures, were introduced via the Antillean islands to Europe. Canoes (also a Taíno word), *bohíos* (the thatched huts where people lived) and hammocks (*hamaca*) were elements of Taíno society that persisted for centuries (or still do). Many Taíno names are still used for names of cities, towns, and rivers: Maisí, Baracoa, Canimar, El Caney, Mayabeque, Ariguan-abo, Camagüey. The Spanish language has more than three hundred words that are of Arawak origin: *canoa* (canoe), *cacique* (chief), *caimán* (crocodile), *manigua* (bush), *tiburón* (shark), *huracán* (hurricane), *tabaco* (tobacco), and *caoba* (mahogany).

Cuba's importance dwindled when more gold was found elsewhere. Because of its strategic location, Cuba benefited indirectly by being the point from which all expeditions set out for Mexico and Central or South America. By and large, it was a population that was transient, but slowly the population and the economy grew. Sugar, as in most of the Caribbean, was an important crop, but Cuba could not compete with Saint Domingue (Haiti), by far the world's leading producer. In fact, economic activity was centered on cattle raising and tobacco, which, because of its high price, prompted many small farmers to produce greater quantities, often selling it illegally. The concept of illegal sales must be understood in the context of Spanish economic policy: it was illegal for colonists to trade with people who were not members of the Spanish crown. Spain's rivals—mostly France, England, and Holland—also attacked its ships and looted them. The pirating and competition were intense and led to the English taking over Havana in 1762 for ten months. Although the British left, the aftermath was economic liberalization and a substantial growth in Cuban production and trade.

What kind of society was Cuba as a Spanish colony? If conceived as a pyramid, the top would be occupied by the colonial administrators and officers, followed by the clergy and the military, comprising the most powerful sectors. They would be followed by the *criollos* (Creoles), mulattoes, free blacks, and slaves, who made up the majority of the population but were not very powerful (except the *criollos* to a limited degree). Political power was centralized on the island, to keep people from rebelling against the crown as well as to provide unity in fighting against other European colonial powers. Political absolutism was the norm, under the leadership of the Spanish monarchy religious dogmatism was strict, and the economy was tightly controlled. Despite considerable racial mixing, the persistence of slavery and the suppression of African beliefs and languages show that racism was not only widespread but dangerous to the physical and spiritual well-being of slaves. The average life of a slave after being brought from Africa to the New World was ten years. Given these political, economic, and social limitations, it is not surprising that Cuban society, like most Caribbean nations, was ill-suited for change, modernization, or innovation.

In 1774, Cuba had a population of 172,000: 56 percent were white, 21 percent were free nonwhites, and 23 percent were black slaves. Though the percentage of black slaves was much lower than in French and British Caribbean possessions (where these figures ranged from 75 percent up), it was still much higher than in the Dominican Republic and Puerto Rico. As a result of the slave insurrections (1791) and resulting independence of Haiti (1804), Cuba became an important sugar-producing country, and this meant the greater importation of slaves. By 1841, 43 percent of Cuba's population were black slaves. Its growing sugar economy also reflected the importance Spain gave to the island. This was partly due to the fact that it was the only former Spanish colony in Latin America not to achieve independence (except Puerto Rico) by the 1830s. When Latin American countries achieved liberation from Spain, they abolished slavery; and by this time, the British and the French had also abolished slavery in the Caribbean.

By the early nineteenth century, no doubt inspired by the success of independence struggles in Latin America, voices for Cuban independence became more vocal, such as those of José Aponte (1812) and José María Heredia, the poet, in 1823. Both were part of conspiracies that failed, as did the attempt by Andrés Manuel Sánchez and Francisco Agüero, who led an unsuccessful uprising in 1826. They were followed by Narciso López, whose two attempts in 1850 and 1851 fizzled. López favored independence from Spain but wanted Cuba to be part of the United States. Those who favored this option were called annexationists, and the majority of the Cuban creole elite favored this option (or remaining a colony of Spain). This seems curious since the creole elite had many grievances with Spanish merchants over economic policy, which severely curtailed the profitabilty of Cuban exports. The explanation is not obscure: the creole elites owned slaves and knew independence meant abolition. Since at that point (1820s to the 1850s) the United States still practiced slavery, annexation seemed like a good option to the Cuban creole elite. The great bulk of slaves in Cuba were brought there after 1791. From 1512 to 1763, 60,000 slaves were brought into Cuba, but between 1790 and 1864, the figures are staggering: the estimates vary between 650,000 and 832,000. Slaves and free nonwhites made up half the population of Cuba. Both Spain and the creole elite were alarmed at this, and Madrid encouraged European immigration to "whiten" the Cuban population mix. Many Spaniards fleeing newly independent Latin American countries wound up in Cuba. Naturally, they favored continued colonial rule. (As black slave figures began to decline, Cuba imported Chinese indentured servants, which from 1847 to 1874 totaled nearly 125,000. By 1959, the Chinese population of Cuba was estimated to be between 17,000 and 20,000.)

The independence forces grew under the aegis of excellent spokespeople like José Antonio Saco (1779–1855), José de la Luz y Caballero (1800–1862), and Félix Varela (1787–1853), all intellectuals, philosophers, and educators. But it was a new generation of Cubans born in the nineteenth century who were to provide the leadership of a more solid independence and revolutionary movement: Carlos Manuel de Céspedes (1819–74), Antonio Maceo (1845–96), Ignacio Agramonte (1842–73), and Máximo Gómez (1840–1905), who was Dominican. By far the most brilliant was José Martí (1853–1895), an extraordinary writer, poet, and journalist, an inspiring orator and a tireless advocate for the Cuban independence cause.

In 1868, Carlos Manuel de Céspedes and others led the "Grito de Yara." Céspedes freed his slaves, proclaimed Cuban independence, and with his co-conspirators drew up a constitution several months later known as La Constitución de Guáimaro (April 10, 1869). This first great independence war was called La Guerra de los Diez Años (The Ten Years War), lasting from 1868 to 1878. It was a long, bloody conflict, costing hundreds of thousands of lives and millions in property damage, and severely crippling the productive capacity of the country. It left a festering wound in the island between pro-independence and pro-Spain forces, between the rich and the poor, and also between blacks and whites. For Spain, Cuba was one of two colonial outposts left in Latin America (Puerto Rico was the other). Though it had declined from its imperial glory of the sixteenth century, for Spain, Cuba was still considered a prized possession whose prestige far outweighed its economic importance. One important positive outcome of the war was that slavery was finally abolished in 1886.

José Martí was too young to have been a major player in the 1868 uprising, though as it wore on, he played a role in exile, first in Spain, then in Latin America. Finally, in New York, where he spent many years (1881–95), he campaigned, fundraised, and rallied Cubans toward independence. Along with Gómez, Maceo, and Calixto García, Martí initiated a new struggle for independence in 1895. Though Martí was killed early on (May 1895), the struggle continued and was quite successful, despite a further setback with the death of Maceo in 1896. Overall, the war continued to favor the Cuban patriots, but again it looked like a protracted struggle. This changed abruptly when, in 1898, the U.S. battleship *Maine* was blown up in Havana harbor. The United States blamed the Spanish, who denied responsibility, but by April 1898 both countries had declared war on each other, and the United States intervened militarily, defeating the Spanish in a few months.

Cuban freedom fighters had waged three wars in thirty years. They wanted a country politically and economically free of Spain; they had fought for the abolition of slavery and had given blood to forge a nation in which they could live in peace without the intervention of foreign powers. Martí had warned his compatriots that Cuban independence was not only threatened by the Spanish but by the designs of U.S. expansionism. His political acumen in seeing future developments was borne out by subsequent events.

The United States ruled Cuba directly from 1898 to 1902 with a military government. Though Cuba achieved formal independence as of May 20, 1902, the Platt Amendment, passed by the U.S. Congress, gave the United States the right to intervene in Cuba whenever it thought its interests were in peril. Furthermore, the United States also leased a military base in the eastern part of the island, known today as the Guantánamo Naval Base; it is still under U.S. control. These issues are a humiliating reminder to Cubans of U.S. control over their affairs.

The Platt Amendment was abrogated in 1934 after dictator Machado was overthrown. From 1902 to 1959 the Cuban political system had been relatively democratic, plagued with periods of tight control (1929–33 and 1952–59). Despite a progressive constitution in 1940, most civilian governments had been marked by corruption, inefficiency, and nepotism, undergirded by dramatic social and economic injustice. One of the key figures in this period was a sergeant who later became General, Fulgencio Batista. For a quarter of a century (1934–59) he dominated Cuban politics either directly or behind the scenes. He was president from 1940 to 1944, and in this first period was esteemed to be an apt and respected leader. He then withdrew from public office but was always a significant player behind the scenes. As subsequent governments (1944–52) proved inept, Batista stepped in again. Seeing that his appointed candidate would lose the 1952 elections, he engineered a coup d'état. For the first few months, not much changed, but then his regime grew more repressive, often killing its political opponents. Some disgruntled sectors of society felt that Cuba would not change pacifically. Among them was a young lawyer, Fidel Castro. On July 26, 1953, Castro and about 150 followers attacked the Moncada Barracks in Santiago, Cuba, hoping to establish a base for resistance and ultimately spark an uprising in the general population. It failed, with many killed or jailed. Castro was among the imprisoned, and in his defense speech, over two hours long, he laid out the ills that beset Cuban society. The speech, called "History Will Absolve Me," spoke of "el tiempo muerto" (dead time), the six months of the year when cane workers are unemployed, the 5 percent of the rural population that eats meat, the lack of proper sanitary conditions (running water, health care), the large numbers of Cubans who cannot read or write (about 25 percent). Castro eloquently bemoaned the dismal expectations of a one-crop country (sugar constituting 85 percent of exports) dependent on one country, the United States. He denounced the vast social and racial inequalities in the country, stated that they needed to be addressed, and that there was a need for political democracy. Though his speech was a sensation, Castro was jailed, only to be released by an amnesty in 1955. By the following year, from Mexico, he and 82 followers launched an invasion by boat, landing in Oriente province. They began a guerrilla struggle against the Batista government, under the banner of the July 26th Movement. Their popularity grew, and in a little over two years they defeated the Batista dictatorship. They were also favored by a pro-democratic climate in the western hemisphere that was rejecting military dictatorships like that of Trujillo in the Dominican Republic (1930–61), Pérez Jiménez (1953–58) in Venezuela, Rojas Pinilla (1953–57) in Colombia, and Alfredo Stroessner (1954–) in Paraguay.

Cuba in the 1950s, despite being a poor, underdeveloped nation, was among the more prosperous of Latin American countries. It had a fairly evolved industrial base, a more than adequate road system, excellent communications, and a growing, if erratic, economy. Why would this relative prosperity lead to a revolution? Part of this is explained by what Castro referred to in his "History Will Absolve Me" speech. The economy was growing, but there was high unemployment; the political system, with censorship, repression, and corruption, had made the Batista regime extremely unpopular. Social inequality between classes was great, and this generated expectations and resentment among the poor. And Cubans, a very nationalistic people, saw major sectors of their society in U.S. hands (including Batista himself), not to mention a tourist industry viewed as an American playground. More critical voices denounced the vices of tourism more emphatically and called Cuba "the whorehouse of the Caribbean." Cubans' frustrated nationalism, so admirably expressed by Martí, was given eloquent form in the leadership of Fidel Castro, whose oratorical skills border on genius. Castro was able to gather the support of all major sectors of society to overthrew the Batista tyranny. Most Cubans welcomed the triumph of the Cuban Revolution, with the hope of establishing the Constitution of 1940, a pluralistic, liberal document. Little did they know that the storm of history would soon turn their world inside out, with greater force than any hurricane.

THE CUBAN REVOLUTION, 1959–PRESENT

The triumph of the rebel forces in 1959 was not just the overthrow of a corrupt and repressive government (i.e., Batista's rule), but a radical attempt to install an anti-imperialist, nationalist, and popular (or revolution-ary) government. Its anti-imperialism sought the creation of a country that was free of the dictates of major powers, which meant the United States and the Soviet Union. As nationalists the Cubans wanted the affairs of the nation primarily to advance the economic, social, political, and cultural welfare of its own populace. In a popular or revolutionary government the Cubans wanted a government that would enact policies to help the poor, create jobs for the unemployed, provide education and health care for all, eradicate racism, and promote the economic and social advancement of women.

The Revolution quickly enacted major social legislation: it decreed land reform, urban reform, and other types of laws that addressed issues of economic justice. Its increasingly nationalistic stance antagonized and wor-ried the U.S. government. When Fidel Castro's July 26th Movement took power, U.S. companies in Cuba controlled 40 percent of raw sugar produc-tion, 90 percent of telephone, light, and power services, half the public railways, and 25 percent of all bank deposits. The United States suspended the sugar quota (the amount of sugar that it guaranteed to buy from Cuba every year) in 1960. When U.S.-built oil refineries refused to refine Soviet oil, the Cuban government nationalized these properties and later all U.S. properties, valued at $1 billion. Cuba then expropriated all large firms or industries in the country. The United States responded with an embargo, prohibiting any U.S. company or individual from doing business with Cuba. The embargo, in different forms, still persists.

Tensions increased and the United States broke off diplomatic relations with Cuba (1961). In the meantime, the U.S. government, the CIA, and Cuban exiles hostile to Castro planned the military overthrow of his gov-ernment. In April 1961 they landed at Playa Girón (the Bay of Pigs), with roughly 1,700 men. They were to establish a beachhead that would then spark uprisings in the rest of the country. The plan was a failure, with most of the troops defeated and captured within seventy-two hours. Cubans, with their nationalism inflamed even more by these events, rallied behind Fidel, who took advantage of this support and declared the Cuban Revolu-tion socialist. Several months later he would openly declare himself a Marxist-Leninist, reaffirming his adherence to Communism. By then, Cuba had drawn much closer to the Soviet Union in order to boost its economy. During this first period of the radicalization of the revolution (1959–63), many Cubans fled the island (approximately 300,000), since it was still legal to do so and the United States openly welcomed them.

Castro was suspicious of the United States and sought indisputable weapons of defense to ensure that Washington would not invade Cuba again. The USSR responded with its military might and installed nuclear missiles on Cuban soil. When U.S. reconaissance confirmed the presence of nuclear weaponry on the island, the U.S. government responded with outrage. Cuba proved stubborn in not wanting to withdraw the missiles, and from October 16 to 28, 1962, the world lived on the brink of a possible nuclear showdown between the United States and the USSR over Cuba. Khrushchev, the Soviet president, backed down after strong pressure from President John F. Kennedy and withdrew the missiles, despite the angry protestations of Fidel Castro. In exchange for the withdrawal of the missiles from Cuba, the United States agreed never to attack Cuba militarily and to remove missiles on Turkish soil aimed at the Soviet Union.

Despite the peaceful resolution of the crisis, relations between the United States and Cuba grew worse. In 1964 the Organization of American States (OAS) requested that all its members sever economic and diplomatic ties with Cuba; all did so except Mexico. Cuba responded angrily, claiming that U.S. pressure was behind the move, and called the OAS the "United States Ministry of Colonies." Part of it had to do with Cuba's support for Latin American guerrilla movements, many of which were later to become part of OSPAAL, an organization dedicated to the solidarity of peoples in liberation struggles in Africa, Asia, and Latin America. OSPAAL was founded in January 1966 in Havana. By then, Che Guevara, Fidel's right-hand man and premier guerrilla warfare strategist, was fighting in the mountains of Bolivia, where he had gone to establish a continental base that could fan the flames of revolution throughout South America. Guerrilla movements were active in Guatemala, Venezuela, Peru and Bolivia, as well as several African countries (Angola, Mozambique, Guinea, South Africa), and, of course, the war in Vietnam was escalating daily. All of these liberation movements were opposed by the U.S. government, who saw Cuban support, if in many cases only moral and/or political, as major contributors to "subversion and communist infiltration."

A "revolutionary offensive" launched by Castro in 1968 nationalized some 55,000 small businesses in Cuba. Except for some private farmers (around 20 percent of rural landowners), all economic activity in Cuba was placed in state hands. In fact, it was part of an ideological hardening that began in 1965 with the creation of the UMAP (Units to Assist Military Production). The UMAP was originally set up to imprison armed counter-revolutionaries who had taken up arms against Castro in the Escambray mountains from 1962 to 1966. But by early 1966 those anti-Castro forces had either surrendered or been killed. The UMAP became political internment camps with harsh conditions. Rapidly the ranks of the UMAP swelled with dissidents of all kinds, be they political opponents, homosexuals, young people with long hair, or others whose behavior was considered "anti-so-cial." The UMAP were closed down in 1967 (some claim 1969) as a result of an alleged visit by Castro himself, who found the conditions deplorable and inhumane. Despite their closure, the Cuban system still had ways to punish political dissidence, either through incarceration or closely supervised hard labor (mostly cutting cane).

In 1968 the Soviet Union invaded Czechoslovakia. Despite regretting the need to take the action, Fidel Castro defended the invasion, saying that it saved Czech socialism. This marked a turning point in Cuban-Soviet relations, which at the time of the invasion were uneven because of what the Cubans perceived as a lack of Soviet revolutionary enthusiasm in backing liberation struggles in the third world. Fidel Castro then took this opportunity to draw closer to the Soviets and at the same time launched a new offensive: a ten million-ton sugar harvest for 1970.

The harvest was not only to be an economic barometer of Cuba's production potential, but also a show of political will, a triumph of revolutionary consciousness, to prove socialism's superiority over capitalism. It was also to serve as a springboard to help Cuba overcome its underdeveloped status. In 1970 Cuba had its largest harvest ever, 8.5 million tons, but it was far short of the goal. But more disastrously, many other workers from other sectors of the economy were used to make the harvest "successful." It left the Cuban economy in disarray, and this marked a second crucial moment in Soviet-Cuban relations. After this failure, the Soviets insisted their aid be tied to a more organized planning method based on the Soviet model. Many technicians, economists, engineers, and planners came from the USSR to make this happen, and in 1972 Cuba joined the Council of Mutual Economic Assistance (COMECON), the socialist bloc's version of the Common Market. Cuban economic policy during the first decade of the revolution had been improvised, marked by political exhortations (revolutionary mobilizations) and a call to selflessness and sacrifice (purely moral incentives). The ideas of Ché Guevara espoused in "Man and Socialism in Cuba" were to give way to Soviet planning manuals: the Cuban Revolution was headed for a phase of institutionalization.

In some areas, though, revolutionary fervor did not let up, as when Cuba sent troops to Angola (1975) in order to stop the advance of South African troops. This action and subsequent military successes played a key part in ensuring Angola's national sovereignty, as well as paving the way for the end of apartheid in South Africa. In 1977, under President Jimmy Carter, Cubans began returning to their native land to visit for the first time after seventeen years. It is estimated that from 1977 to 1980 hundreds of thousands of Cubans in the United States visited family and relatives. In that period Cuba released 3,000 political prisoners and their families, who emigrated mostly to the United States. Some say these visits, with family members bringing to the island cash and consumer items not readily available to Cubans, helped precipitate the Mariel Crisis of 1980, when more than 120,000 emigrated from Cuba in a little over two months.

During the 1980s the Cuban economy grew at a respectable rate of 5 percent a year. After a quarter century, Cuba led most Latin American countries in health care indicators: it had the lowest infant mortality rate, a high life expectancy, plus universal and free coverage for the entire population. Many third world students from Africa and Latin America were studying at Cuban schools, and many Cuban professionals and medical personnel were serving abroad. Cuba was also buoyed by the Sandinista triumph in Nicaragua (1979) and the New Jewel Movement in Grenada (1979), both becoming close allies. The Cubans reciprocated by helping out the Sandinistas and the Grenadians in terms of education, health care and the training of their respective armies.

But not all was well. By 1986 a rectification campaign was instituted to try and curb waste, excess bureaucracy, and corruption, all too familiar evils in a centrally planned economy. The year 1989 turned out to be crucial. That summer Cubans were to witness the trials of several high-ranking Cuban officials and military personnel on charges of corruption and drug smuggling. Among them was General Arnaldo Ochoa, a popular figure and brilliant military strategist who had won major battles in Angola. He had won the highest titles: Hero of the Cuban Republic and the Máximo Gómez Order, First Degree. Ochoa was found guilty not only of these charges but also of treason and was executed by firing squad. It was a sad moment and one that shocked many Cubans, because as implicated as he was in some charges, everyone knew that Ochoa was breaking the law with the knowledge and consent of higher-ups. They knew Ochoa was a scapegoat, and this further undermined people's credibility in the government.

But more trouble was to follow: in the fall of 1989 several communist governments fell in Eastern Europe (East Germany, Poland, Hungary, Czechoslovakia, and Rumania). Soon afterwards, in February 1990, Cuba's principal friend in Latin America, the Sandinistas, were defeated in elections.

The loss of socialist bloc support was disastrous. Cuba conducted 90 percent of its trade with COMECON countries. The loss was soon felt in the Cuban economy; shortages were more frequent, and many products and medicines simply vanished from Cuban shelves. Even the Soviet Union started to draw back on its commitments to Cuba, and after the failed coup in 1991, and with the subsequent presidency of Boris Yeltsin, Russian largesse has ended. The magnitude of Soviet aid had allowed Cuba to achieve what few poor third world countries could even dream of. Cuba had an economic system with virtually no unemployment, whereas most underdeveloped countries have from 20 percent to 60 percent of their populations without work. They had built an educational system that was comprehensive and had eradicated illiteracy. The health system was not only free to all but preventative and able to deal with even sophisticated medical problems; it was widely praised by the World Health Organization. Cuba even exported doctors to Africa. The Cuban sports system was also very effective and achieved international renown. Politically, Cuba was a player on the world stage, being active in the nonaligned movement, by its involvement in southern Africa, Central America, the Caribbean, as well as being an active voice in the United Nations.

These achievements must be weighed against the drawbacks. Cuba has a particularly closed political environment, with a one-party state (the Cuban Communist Party is the only legal political party in the country). Fidel Castro is the indisputable leader, and while there are established political institutions, his charismatic leadership and his *caudillista* style define the country irrevocably. Political dissent (not just specific criticism of a certain policy) is dealt with harshly, and human rights activists are often jailed, beaten or deported. The other alternative is leaving the country, which many have chosen to do. Censorship of the press is widespread. While freedom of religion is now more widely respected, for many years it could adversely affect Cubans, particularly in terms of university admission or certain job opportunities. While more lax nowadays, personal liberties such as changing jobs or pursuing a certain career of study were more restricted for decades. And because of U.S. hostility toward Cuba, the government diverts important resources to defense, which has made Cuban society more militarized, often in subtle ways. In terms of the economy, many consumer goods are scarce, and for thirty years there has been a rationing system. Shortages of items such as rice, cooking oil, and meat are constant. Centrally planned economic policy has caused much waste, inefficiency, and lack of initiative on the part of workers, with a resulting low productivity. For example, Cuba has a sophisticated biotechnology industry with considerable exports, but cannot produce ballpoint pens or a decently functioning telephone system. Cuban wages are very low, but many social goods are free (health, education, sports, and so on) or extremely cheap (rent, phone, electricity, water).

With the loss of Soviet support, many of the achievements of the revolution are being eroded. Medicines are in short supply, schools are more limited, and many factories have closed down or are functioning at 20 percent capacity. As a result, unemployment is up, possibly as high as 10 to 15 percent. Fuel shortages have made Cubans revert to using bicycles as a main means of transportation, but with poor diets, a hot tropical climate, and often long distances to cover, it can mean great hardship. Many are feeling discontent, which was dramatically shown in July and August 1994, when tens of thousands of rafters tried to brave the waters and sharks and make it to Florida, or at least be picked up by the U.S. Coast Guard and be taken to U.S.-owned Guantánamo Naval Base in southeastern Cuba.

The Cubans call this recent downswing "the special period." The government, attempting to liberalize economic matters somewhat, has decriminalized the holding of dollars and has allowed the opening of private produce markets to alleviate food shortages. This has improved the Cuban diet, but dollars are needed to make purchases in these markets, and not everyone has the same accessibility to dollars. Clearly much else needs to be done, since the Cuban economy has probably contracted by at least half in the last five years. Deals and joint ventures with many European, Latin American, and Japanese firms are a hopeful sign. The economic future of the country is clearly going toward market measures while still trying to retain the social gains of the revolution. This juggling act has had mixed success, perhaps because little real change has ocurred in the political realm. When the communist governments of Eastern Europe fell in 1989, many predicted Cuba would soon follow. Yet eight years later, Fidel Castro is still in power, defying all odds. Cuba's political future remains uncertain as it continues in the grip of a cold war mentality, abetted by U.S. hostility (and recalcitrant sectors of the Cuban exile community) on the one side and Cuban intransigence and dogmatism on the other.

SELECTED READING

Cuban History—General

Abel and Torrents, eds. (1986). *José Martí, Revolutionary Democrat*. Duke University Press: Durham, N.C.

Aguilar, Luis E. (1974). *Cuba 1933: Prologue to Revolution*. W. W. Norton: New York.

Bonachea and San Martín (1973). *The Cuban Insurrection: 1952–1959*. Rutgers University Press: New Brunswick, N.J.

Farber, Samuel (1976). *Revolution and Reaction in Cuba, 1933–1960*. Wesleyan University Press: Middletown, Conn.

Foner, Philip (1972). *The Spanish-Cuban-American War and the Birth of American Imperialism*, 2 vols., International Publishers: New York.

Foner, Philip (1977). *Antonio Maceo*. Monthly Review Press: New York.

Guerra, Ramiro (1952). *Historia de la nación cubana*, 10 vols. Havana.

Marrero, Levi (1972–86). *Cuba, economía y sociedad*, 12 vols. Editorial Playor: Madrid.

Moreno Fraginals, Manuel (1978). *El ingenio*. 3 vols. Editorial Ciencias Sociales: Havana. (Abridged English version: *The Sugar Mill*. Monthly Review Press: New York.)

Moreno Fraginals, Manuel (1983). *La historia como arma*. Editorial Crítica: Barcelona.

Ortiz, Fernando (1995). *Cuban Counterpoint: Tobacco and Sugar*. Duke University Press: Durham, N.C.

Perez, Jr., Louis (1986). *Cuba under the Platt Amendment, 1902–1934*. University of Pittsburgh Press: Pittsburgh.

Pérez, Jr., Louis (1988). *Cuba: Between Reform and Revolution*. Oxford University Press: New York.

Pérez de la Riva, Juan (1978). *El barracón: Esclavitud y capitalismo en Cuba*. Editorial Crítica: Barcelona.

Schroeder, Susan (1982). *Cuba: A Handbook of Historical Statistics*. G. K. Hall: Boston.

Thomas, Hugh (1971). *Cuba or The Pursuit of Freedom*. Harper & Row: New York.

The Cuban Revolution

Azicri, Max (1988). *Cuba: Politics, Economics and Society*. Pinter Publishers: London.

Benglesdorf, Carollee (1994). *The Problem of Democracy in Cuba*. Oxford University Press: New York.

Cardenal, Ernesto (1974). *In Cuba*. New Directions: New York.

Domínguez, Jorge (1978). *Order and Revolution*. Harvard University Press: Cambridge, Mass.

Domínguez, Jorge (1989). *To Make a World Safe for Revolution: Cuba's Foreign Policy*. Harvard University Press: Cambridge, Mass.

Franqui, Carlos (1985). *Family Portrait with Fidel*. Vintage: New York.

Leo Grande et al. (1989). *The Cuba Reader*. Grove Press: New York.

Mesa-Lago, Carmelo (1981). *The Economy of Socialist Cuba*. University of New Mexico Press: Albuquerque.

Mesa-Lago, Carmelo (1994). *Historia económica de Cuba socialista*. Alianza Editorial: Madrid.

Oppenheimer, Andrés (1992). *Castro's Final Hour*. Simon and Schuster: New York.

Pérez-López, Jorge F. (1995). *Cuba's Second Economy: From behind the Scenes to Center Stage*. Transaction Publishers: New Brunswick, N.J.

Pérez-Stable, Marifeli (1993). *The Cuban Revolution: Origins, Course, and Legacy*. Oxford University Press: New York.

Timmerman, Jacobo (1992). *Cuba: A Journey*. Vintage: New York.

On Fidel Castro

Lockwood, Lee (1969). *Castro's Cuba, Cuba's Fidel*. Vintage: New York.

Matthews, Herbert L. (1970). *Fidel Castro*. Simon and Schuster: New York.

Szulc, Tad (1988). *Fidel: A Critical Portrait*. Morrow: New York.

Immigration and Cuban-Americans

Behar, Ruth, ed. (1994). "Bridges to Cuba." *Michigan Quarterly Review*, Part 1, vol. 33, no. 3; Part 2, vol. 33, no. 4.

Boswell, T., and Curtis, J. (1984). *The Cuban-American Experience: Culture, Images and Perspectives*. Rowmann & Allanheld: Totowa, N.J.

Casal, Lourdes, and Hernández, A. (1975). "Cubans in the U.S: A Survey of the Literature." *Cuban Studies/Estudios cubanos*, vol. 5, no. 2.

Olson, James, and Olson, Judith (1995). *Cuban Americans: From Trauma to Triumph*. Twayne Publishers: New York.

Pérez-Firmat, Gustavo (1994). *Life on the Hyphen: The Cuban-American Way*. University of Texas Press: Austin.

Torres, María de los Angeles (1988). "From Exiles to Minorities: The Politics of Cuban Americans." In *Latinos and the Political System*, ed. F. Chris García. University of Notre Dame Press: Indiana.

Uriarte, Miren, and Cañas, Jorge, eds. (1984). *Cubans in the United States*. Center for the Study of the Cuban Community, Inc.: Boston, Mass.

Bibliography

Acosta, Leonardo (1981). *Música y épica en la novela de Alejo Carpentier*. Editorial Letras Cubanas: Havana.

Adams; Cixous et al. (1974). "Focus on Cobra." *Review*, Center for Interamerican Relations: New York.

Agosín, Marjorie, ed. (1994). *These Are Not Sweet Girls: Poetry by Latin American Women*. White Pine Press: Fredonia, New York.

Alciato (1985). *Emblemas*. Ediciones Akal: Madrid. Edition and commentary by Santiago Sebastián.

Arendt, Hannah (1990/1964). *On Revolution*. Penguin Books: New York.

Arias, Salvador, ed. (1977). *Recopilación de textos sobre Alejo Carpentier*. Serie de Valoración Múltiple, Casa de las Américas: Havana.

Aristotle (1968). *Poetics*. Prentice Hall: Englewood Cliffs, N.J. Edition and commentary by O. B. Hardison, Jr. Translated by Leon Golden.

Armstrong, A. H., ed. (1970). *The Cambridge History of Later Greek and Early Medieval Philosophy*. Cambridge University Press: Cambridge.

Auerbach, Eric (1959). *Scenes from the Drama of European Literature*. Meridian Books: New York. Translated by Ralph Manheim.

de Azúa, Félix (1983). *La paradoja del primitivo*. Seix Barral: Barcelona.

Bachelard, Gaston (1964). *The Poetics of Space*. Beacon Press: Boston. Translated by Maria Jolas.

Bachelard, Gaston (1983). *Water and Dreams*. Dallas Institute of Humanities and Culture: Dallas. Translated by Edith Farrell.

Bachelard, Gaston (1987). *On Poetic Imagination and Reverie*. Spring Publications: Dallas. Translated by Colette Gaudin.

Bachelard, Gaston (1988). *Air and Dreams*. Dallas Institute of Humanities and Culture: Dallas. Translated by Edith Farrell and C. Frederick Farrell.

Barthes, Roland (1973). *El grado cero de la escritura*. Siglo XXI: México City. (Spanish translation of *Writing Degree Zero*, 1967.)

Barthes, Roland (1975). *The Pleasure of the Text*. Farrar, Straus, Giroux: New York. Translated by R. Howard.

Baudrillard, Jean (1981). *El sistema de los objetos*, 6th ed. Siglo XXI: Mexico City.

Bauman, Zygmunt (1992). *Intimations of Postmodernity*. Routledge: New York.

Behar, Ruth, ed. (1994a). "Bridges to Cuba/Puentes a Cuba, Part I." *Michigan Quarterly Review*, vol. 33, no. 3.

Behar, Ruth, ed. (1994b). "Bridges to Cuba/Puentes a Cuba, Part II." *Michigan Quarterly Review*, vol. 33, no. 4.

Behar, Ruth, ed. (1995). *Bridges to Cuba*. Ann Arbor: University of Michigan Press.

Behar, Ruth, and Suárez, Lucía (1994). "Two Conversations with Nancy Morejón." *Michigan Quarterly Review*, vol. 33, no. 3, pp. 625–635.

Bejel, Emilio (1990). *José Lezama Lima, Poet of the Image*. University of Florida Press: Gainesville.

Benítez Rojo, Antonio (1992). *The Repeating Island*. Duke University Press: Durham, N.C.

Benjamin, Jessica (1988). *The Bonds of Love*. Pantheon: New York.

Benjamin, W. (1977). *The Origin of German Tragic Drama*. Verso: London. Translated by John Osborne.

Bhabha, Homi K. (1994). *The Location of Culture*. Routledge: New York.

Bolívar Aróstegui, Natalia (1990). *Los orishas de Cuba*. UNEAC: Havana.

Bowie, Andrew (1993). *Schelling and Modern European Philosophy*. Routledge: New York.

Bradley; Beatty; Long, eds. (1967). *The American Tradition in Literature*. Vol. 1. W. W. Norton: New York.

Brenner, Philip, et al., eds. (1989). *The Cuba Reader*. Grove Press: New York.

Briggs, John C. (1989). *Francis Bacon and the Rhetoric of Nature*. Harvard University Press: Cambridge, Mass.

Brophy, Brigid (1988). *Mozart the Dramatist*. Da Capo Press: New York.

Butler, Judith (1987). *Subjects of Desire*. Columbia University Press: New York.

Cabrera, Lydia (1992). *El monte*. Ediciones Universal: Miami.

Calderón de la Barca, Pedro (1974). *El gran teatro del mundo*. Ediciones Cátedra: Madrid.

Canetti, Elias (1994). *The Agony of the Flies*. Farrar, Straus, Giroux: New York.

Cardoso, et. al., eds. (1995). "Cuba, siempre Cuba: Entrevista con Víctor Fowler." *Dactylus* (Austin, Tex.), no. 14, pp. 9–20.

Carpentier, Alejo (1963). *Explosion in a Cathedral*. Farrar, Straus, Giroux: New York. Translated by John Sturrock.

Carpentier, Alejo (1989). *El siglo de las luces*. Ediciones Cátedra: Madrid. Critical edition by Ambrosio Fornet.

Cassirer, Ernst (1953). *Language and Myth*. Dover Publications: New York. Translated by Susan K. Langer.

Chao, Ramón (1984). *Palabras en el tiempo de Alejo Carpentier*. Editorial Argos Vergara: Barcelona.

Chiampi, Irlemar (1980). *O realismo maravilhoso*. Editora Perspectiva: São Paulo, Brazil.

CILCA (Centro de Investigaciones Literarias de Casa de las Américas) (1971). *Interrogando a Lezama Lima*. Editorial Anagrama: Barcelona.

Cixous, Helene (1991). *Three Steps on the Ladder of Writing*. Columbia University Press: New York. Translated by Sarah Cornell and Susan Sellers.

Collingwood, R. G. (1960). *The Idea of Nature*. Oxford University Press: New York.

Cooper, J. C. (1978). *An Illustrated Encyclopedia of Traditional Symbols*. Thames and Hudson: London.

Curtius, Ernst Robert (1956). *European Literature and the Latin Middle Ages*. Princeton University Press: Princeton, N.J.

Dallmayr, Fred (1993). *The Other Heidegger*. Cornell University Press: Ithaca, New York.

Daly, Peter M. (1979). *Literature in Light of the Emblem*. University of Toronto Press: Toronto.

Debray, Regis (1983). *Critique of Political Reason*. Verso: London.

Derrida, Jacques (1981). *Dissemination*. University of Chicago Press: Chicago. Translated by Barbara Johnson.

Derrida, Jacques (1994). *Specters of Marx*. Routledge: New York.

Desmond, William (1986). *Art and the Absolute*. SUNY Press: Albany, N.Y.

Díaz-Plaja, Fernando (1960). *Griegos y romanos en la Revolución Francesa*. Revista de Occidente: Madrid.

Dollimore, Jonathan (1991). *Sexual Dissidence: Augustine to Wilde, Freud to Foucault*. Oxford University Press: Oxford.

Doniger O'Flaherty, Wendy, trans. (1975). *Hindu Myths*. Penguin Books: London.

Dupont, Florence (1989) "The Emperor God's Other Body." In M. Feher, ed., *Fragments for a History of the Human Body, Part Three*. Zone Books: New York.

Eagleton, Terry (1981). *Walter Benjamin or Towards a Revolutionary Criticism*. Verso: London.

Eagleton, Terry (1990). *The Ideology of the Aesthetic*. Basil Blackwell: Oxford.

Eagleton, Terry (1991). *Ideology*. Verso: London.

Eagleton, Terry, et al. (1990). *Nationalism, Colonialism, and Literature*. University of Minnesota Press: Minneapolis.

Echeverría, Bolívar, ed. (1994). *Modernidad, mestizaje cultural, ethos barroco*. UNAM: Mexico City.

Eliade, Mircea (1976). *Occultism, Witchcraft and Cultural Fashions: Essays in Comparative Religion*. University of Chicago Press: Chicago.

Evans-Wentz, W.Y. (1960). *The Tibetan Book of the Dead*. Oxford University Press: London.

Felman, Shoshana (1987). *Jacques Lacan and the Adventure of Insight*. Harvard University Press: Cambridge, Mass.

Ferris, Lesley, ed. (1993). *Crossing the Stage: Controversies on Cross-Dressing*. Routledge: New York.

Filoramo, Giovanni (1990). *A History of Gnosticism*. Basil Blackwell: Oxford. Translated by Anthony Alcock.

Foucault, Michel (1977). *Discipline and Punish: The Birth of the Prison*. Pantheon: New York. Translated by Alan Sheridan.

Foucault, Michel (1984). *The Foucault Reader*, ed., Paul Rabinow. Pantheon: New York.

Fowler, Víctor (1993). "Poesía joven cubana: de la maquinaria al ontologismo goticista." *Journal of Hispanic Research*, vol. 2, pp. 249–68.

Franqui, Carlos (1980). "The Island of Cuba." In Philip Brenner et. al., eds. *The Cuba Reader*. Grove Press: New York, 1989.

Frye, Northrop (1983). *The Great Code*. Harcourt Brace Jovanovich: New York.

Gadamer, Hans-Georg (1976). *Hegel's Dialectic: Five Hermeneutical Studies*. Yale University Press: New Haven. Translated by P. C. Smith.

Gadamer, Hans-Georg (1986). *The Relevance of the Beautiful and Other Essays*. Cambridge University Press: New York.

Gadamer, Hans-Georg (1991). *Plato's Dialectical Ethics*. Yale University Press: New Haven.

Gadamer, Hans-Georg (1993). *Truth and Method*. Continuum: New York.

Gassier, P., and Wilson, J. (1971). *The Life and Complete Works of Francisco Goya*. William Morrow & Co.: New York.

Gellrich, Michelle (1988). *Tragedy and Theory: The Problem of Conflict since Aristotle*. Princeton University Press: Princeton, N.J.

Giacoman, Helmy, ed. (1970). *Homenaje a Alejo Carpentier*. Las Américas: New York.

Gil, Lourdes (1994). "Los signos del leopardo o la seducción de la palabra." In *Lo que no se ha dicho*. Ollantay Press: New York, pp. 208–16.

Gil, Lourdes, and Iturralde, Iraida (1991). "La visión cosmográfica en la obra de Severo Sarduy." *Revista Iberoamericana* (Pittsburgh), no. 154, pp. 337–42.

Gillespie, Michael Allen (1984). *Hegel, Heidegger, and the Ground of History*. University of Chicago Press: Chicago.

González Echevarría, Roberto (1977). *Alejo Carpentier: The Pilgrim at Home*. Cornell University Press: Ithaca, N.Y.

González Echevarría, Roberto (1983). *Isla a su vuelo fugitiva*. Ediciones José Porrúa Turanzas: Madrid.

González Echevarría, Roberto (1987). *La ruta de Severo Sarduy*. Ediciones del Norte: Hanover, N.H.

Grosz, Elizabeth (1992). "Voyeurism/Exhibitionism/The Gaze." In Elizabeth Wright, ed., *Feminism and Psychoanalysis: A Critical Dictionary*. Basil Blackwell: Cambridge, Mass.

Guilhaumou, Jacques (1989). *La langue politique et la revolution française*. Klincksieck: Paris.

Hallyn, Fernand (1993). *The Poetic Structure of the World*. Zone Books: New York.

Hegel, G.W.F. (1956). *The Philosophy of History*. Dover Publications: New York. Translated by J. Sibree.

Hegel, G.W.F. (1975). *Hegel's Aesthetics: Lectures on Fine Art*. Oxford University Press: Clarendon. Translated by T. M. Knox.

Hegel, G.W.F. (1977). *Phenomenology of Spirit*. Oxford University Press: New York. Translated by A. V. Miller.

Heller, Agnes (1993). *A Philosophy of History in Fragments*. Basil Blackwell: Oxford.

Hroch, Miroslav, and Skybova, Anna (1990). *Ecclesia Militans: The Inquisition*. Dorset Press: Frankfurt.

Hughes, Geoffrey (1988). *Words in Time*. Basil Blackwell: Oxford.

Huxley, Francis (1974). *The Way of the Sacred*. Doubleday: New York.

Huyghe, René (1962). *Art and the Spirit of Man*. Harry Abrams: New York.

Ichikawa, Emilio (1994). "La metáfora del ajiaco." *Proposiciones* (Havana), Año 1, no. 2.

Inwood, Michael (1992). *A Hegel Dictionary*. Basil Blackwell: Cambridge, Mass.

Jaeger, Werner (1945). *Paideia: The Ideals of Greek Culture*. Oxford University Press: New York. Translated by Gilbert Highet.

Johnson, Galen, ed. (1993). *The Merleau-Ponty Aesthetics Reader*. Northwestern University Press: Evanston, Ill.

Jonas, Hans (1963). *The Gnostic Religion*. Beacon Press: Boston.

Junco Fazzolari, Margarita (1979). *Paradiso y el sistema poético de Lezama Lima*. Fernando García Gambeiro: Buenos Aires.

Karmel, Alex (1972). *Guillotine in the Wings*. McGraw-Hill: New York.

Kearney, Richard (1984). *Dialogues with Contemporary Continental Thinkers*. Manchester University Press: Manchester.

Kearney, Richard (1991). *Poetics of Imagining*. Harper Collins Academic: London.

Kelly, George A. (1972). "Notes on Hegel's 'Lordship and Bondage.' " In Alasdair MacIntyre, ed., *Hegel: A Collection of Critical Essays*. Doubleday: New York, pp. 189–217.

Kerman, Joseph (1956/1981). *Opera as Drama*. Greenwood: Westport, Conn. (A reprint of the Knopf edition of 1956.)

Kleist, Heinrich von (1989/1810). "On the Marionette Theatre." In Ferenc Feher, ed., *Fragments for a History of the Human Body, Part One*. Zone Books: New York.

Kojeve, Alexandre (1991). *Introduction to the Reading of Hegel: Lectures on the "Phenomenology of Spirit."* Cornell University Press: Ithaca, N.Y. Translated by James H. Nichols, Jr.

Kolakowski, Leszek (1990). *Modernity on Endless Trial*. University of Chicago Press: Chicago.

Koselleck, Reinhart (1985). *Futures Past: On the Semantics of Historical Time*. MIT Press: Cambridge, Mass.

Kristeva, Julia (1986). *The Kristeva Reader*, ed. Toril Moi. Columbia University Press: New York.

Lacan, Jacques (1977). *Écrits: A Selection*. Norton: New York. Translated by Alan Sheridan.

Lacan, Jacques (1981). *The Four Fundamental Concepts of Psychoanalysis*. Norton: New York. Translated by Alan Sheridan.

Lash, John (1993). *Twins and the Double*. Thames and Hudson: London.

Lefebvre, Georges (1962). *The French Revolution: From Its Origins to 1793*. Columbia University Press: New York.

Lefebvre, Georges (1964). *The French Revolution: From 1793 to 1799*. Columbia University Press: New York.

Leppert, Richard (1996). *Art and the Committed Eye*. Westview Press: Boulder, Colo.

Levine, S. J., trans. (1995). *Cobra/Maitreya*. Dalkey Archive Press: Normal, IL.

Lezama Lima, José (1970). *Tratados en La Habana*. Editorial Orbe: Santiago, Chile.

Lezama Lima, José (1971). *Introducción a los vasos órficos*. Seix Barral: Barcelona.

Lezama Lima, José (1981). *Imagen y posibilidad*. Editorial Letras Cubanas: Havana.

Lezama Lima, José (1988). *Paradiso*. Colección Archivos: UNESCO, España (Spain).

Lezama Lima, José (1993). *La expresión americana*. Fondo de Cultura Económica: Mexico City. Critical edition by Irlemar Chiampi.

Lledó, Emilio (1992). *La memoria del logos*. Taurus: Madrid.

López Valdés, Rafael (1985). *Componentes africanos en el etnos cubano*. Editorial Ciencias Sociales: Havana.

Lowith, Karl (1949). *Meaning in History*. University of Chicago Press: Chicago.

Loynaz, Dulce María (1993a). *Antología lírica*, ed. María Asunción Mateo. Espasa Calpe: Madrid.

Loynaz, Dulce María (1993b). *Dulce María Loynaz: Premio de Literatura Miguel de Cervantes—1992*. Ministerio de Cultura: Madrid.

Loynaz, Dulce María (1993c). *Ensayos literarios*. Ediciones Universidad de Salamanca: Salamanca.

Loynaz, Dulce María (1993d). *Jardín: novela lírica*. Editorial Letras Cubanas: Havana. (Originally published 1951.)

Loynaz, Dulce María (1993e). *Poesías completas*. Editorial Letras Cubanas: Havana.

MacGaffey, Wyatt, and Harris, Michael D. (1993). *Astonishment & Power*. Smithsonian Institution Press: Washington, D.C.

MacIntyre, Alisdair (1972). *Hegel: A Collection of Critical Essays*. Doubleday: New York.

Manceron, Claude (1989). *La Révolution Française: dictionnaire biographique*. Renaudot et Cie.: Paris.

Márquez, Enrique (1991). "*Cobra*: de aquel oscuro objeto del deseo." *Revista Iberoamericana* (Pittsburgh), no. 154, pp. 301–7.

Márquez Rodríguez, Alexis (1970). *La obra narrativa de Alejo Carpentier*. Ediciones de la Biblioteca de la Universidad Central de Venezuela: Caracas.

Márquez Rodríguez, Alexis (1982). *El barroco y lo real maravilloso en Alejo Carpentier*. Siglo XXI: Mexico City.

Merleau-Ponty, Maurice (1962). *The Phenomenology of Perception*. Routledge: London. Translated by Colin Smith.

Merleau-Ponty, Maurice (1964). *The Primacy of Perception*. Northwestern University Press: Evanston, Ill. Various translators.

Merleau-Ponty, Maurice (1968). *The Visible and the Invisible*. Northwestern University Press: Evanston, Ill. Translated by Alphonso Lingis.

Miller, James (1993). *The Passion of Michel Foucault*. Simon and Schuster: New York.

Mistral, Gabriela (1971). *Selected Poems of Gabriela Mistral*. Johns Hopkins University Press: Baltimore. Translated by Doris Dana.

Moi, Toril (1985). *Sexual/Textual Politics*. Routledge: London.

Molinero, Rita (1989). *José Lezama Lima o el hechizo de la búsqueda*. Editorial Playor: Madrid.

Morejón, Nancy (1979). *Parajes de una época*. Editorial Letras Cubanas: Havana.

Morejón, Nancy (1982). *Nación y mestizaje en Nicolás Guillén*. UNEAC: Havana.

Morejón, Nancy (1985). *Where the Island Sleeps Like a Wing*. The Black Scholar Press: San Francisco. Translated by Kathleen Weaver.

Morejón, Nancy (1986). *Piedra pulida*. Editorial Letras Cubanas: Havana.

Morejón, Nancy (1987). *Para el ojo que mira de Manuel Mendive*. Ministerio de Cultura/Museo Nacional: Havana.

Morejón, Nancy (1993). *Paisaje célebre*. Fundarte: Caracas.

Morejón, Nancy (1995a). "Towards a Poetics of the Caribbean." Paper presented at Wellesley College Conference on Caribbean Women Writers, April 20, 1995.

Morejón, Nancy (1995b). "Poetics." Unpublished talk given at the University of Missouri, April 26, 1995.

Mumford, Lewis (1963). *Technics and Civilization*. Harcourt, Brace & Jovanovich: New York.

Mumford, Lewis (1970). *The Myth of the Machine*, vol. 2. Harcourt, Brace & Jovanovich: New York.

Muñoz, Elías Miguel (1989). *No fue posible el sol*. Betania: Madrid.

Nasr, Seyyed Hossein (1987). *Islamic Art and Spirituality*. State University Press: Albany, N.Y.

Nietzsche, Friedrich (1990). *Twilight of the Idols/The Anti-Christ*. Penguin: London. Translated by R. J. Hollingdale.

Orozco Díaz, Emilio (1970). *Manierismo y barroco*. Ediciones Anaya: Salamanca.

Ortega, Julio (1991). *Una poética del cambio*. Editorial Ayacucho: Caracas.

Ortega y Gasset, José (1981). *Meditación del pueblo joven y otros ensayos sobre América*. Alianza Editorial: Madrid.

Ostriker, Alicia S. (1986). *Stealing the Language: The Emergence of Women's Poetry in America*. Beacon Press: Boston.

Outka, Gene (1972). *Agape: An Ethical Analysis*. Yale University Press: New Haven.

Parker, Noel (1990). *Portrayals of Revolution*. Southern Illinois University Press: Carbondale.

Parkes, Graham, ed. (1990). *Heidegger and Asian Thought*. University of Hawaii Press: Honolulu.

Paz, Octavio (1969). *Conjunciones y disyunciones*. Joaquín Mortiz: Mexico City.

Pérez-Firmat, Gustavo (1989). *The Cuban Condition*. Cambridge University Press: Cambridge.

Pérez Sarduy, Pedro, and Stubbs, Jean (1993). *Afro Cuba: An Anthology of Cuban Writings on Race, Politics, and Culture*. Ocean Books: Melbourne. (Nancy Morejón's article is called "Race and Nation.")

Piñera, Virgilio (1955a). "Ballagas en persona." *Ciclón* (Havana), vol. 1, no. 5, pp. 41–50.

Piñera, Virgilio (1955b). "Los Siervos." *Ciclón* (Havana), vol. 1, no. 6, pp. 9–29.

Piñera, Virgilo (1956). "La mente cautiva." *Ciclón* (Havana), vol. 2, no. 4, pp. 64–66.

Piñera, Virgilio (1987). *Un fogonazo*. Editorial Letras Cubanas: Havana.

Piñera, Virgilio (1988). *Cold Tales*. Eridanos Press: Boulder, Colo. Translated by Mark Schafer.

Piñera, Virgilio (1989). *René's Flesh*. Eridanos Press: Boston. Translated by Mark Schafer.

Piñera, Virgilio (1990). "La vida tal cual." *Unión* (Havana), no. 10, año 3.

Plato (1985). *The Collected Dialogues*, ed. Edith Hamilton and Huntington Cairns. Princeton University Press: Princeton, N.J.

Preminger, Alex (1974). *Princeton Encyclopedia of Poetry and Poetics*. Princeton University Press: Princeton, N.J.

Ragland-Sullivan, Ellie (1987). *Jacques Lacan and the Philosophy of Psychoanalysis*. University of Illinois Press: Urbana.

Rawson, Philip (1973). *The Art of Tantra*. New York Graphic Society: Greenwich, Conn.

Rich, Adrienne (1993). *Adrienne Rich's Poetry and Prose*. W. W. Norton: New York. Critical edition by Barbara Charlesworth Gelpi and Albert Gelpi.

Ricoeur, Paul (1965). *History and Truth*. Northwestern University Press: Evanston, Ill. Translated by Charles A. Kelbley.

Ricoeur, Paul (1976). *Interpretation Theory: Discourse and the Surplus of Meaning*. Texas Christian University Press: Fort Worth.

Ricoeur, Paul (1977). *The Rule of Metaphor*. University of Toronto Press: Toronto.

Ricoeur, Paul (1986). *Lectures on Ideology and Utopia*. Columbia University Press: New York.

Ricoeur, Paul (1991). *From Text to Action*. Northwestern University Press: Evanston, Illinois. Translated by Kathleen Blamey and John B. Thompson.

Rodríguez, Evangelina, and Tordera, Antonio (1983). *Calderón y la obra corta dramática del siglo XVII*. Tamesis: London.

Rodríguez, Ileana (1994). *House, Garden, Nation*. Duke University Press: Durham, N.C. Translated by Robert Carr and the author.

Rodríguez Beroff, Jorge (1995). *Cuba en crisis*. Editorial Universidad de Puerto Rico: Río Piedras, Puerto Rico.

de Rougemont, Denis (1983). *Love in the Western World*. Princeton University Press: Princeton, N.J. Translated by Montgomery Belgion.

Ruy Sánchez, Alberto (1992). *De cuerpo entero*. Ediciones Corunda, UNAM: Mexico City.

Sánchez Mejías, Rolando (1994). *Derivas I*. Editorial Letras Cubanas: Havana.

Sarduy, Severo (1967). *De donde son los cantantes*. Editorial Joaquín Mortiz: Mexico City.

Sarduy, Severo (1967/1993). *De donde son los cantantes*. Ediciones Cátedra: Madrid. Critical edition by Roberto González Echevarría.

Sarduy, Severo (1970). *Escritos sobre un cuerpo*. Editorial Sudamericana: Buenos Aires.

Sarduy, Severo (1972). *Cobra*. Editorial Sudamericana: Buenos Aires.

Sarduy, Severo (1974). *Barroco*. Editorial Sudamericana: Buenos Aires.

Sarduy, Severo (1978). *Maitreya*. Editorial Seix Barral: Barcelona.

Sarduy, Severo (1982). *La simulación*. Monte Avila: Caracas.

Sarduy, Severo (1987). *El Cristo de la Rue Jacob*. Edicions del Mall: Barcelona.

Sarduy, Severo (1994a). "El estampido de la vacuidad." *Vuelta* (Mexico City), no. 206, pp. 36–38.

Sarduy, Severo (1994b). *Epitafios*. Ediciones Universal: Miami.

Sarduy, Severo (1994c). *From Cuba with a Song*. Sun and Moon Press: Los Angeles. Translated by S. J. Levine.

Sarduy, Severo (1995). *Cobra/Maitreya*. Dalkey Archive Press: Normal, IL. Translated by S. J. Levine.

Sartre, Jean Paul (1956). *Being and Nothingness*. Simon and Schuster: New York. Translated by Hazel E. Barnes.

Shah, Idries (1971). *The Sufis*. Doubleday: New York.

Sheldon-Williams, I. P. (1970). "The Philosophy of Icons." In Armstrong (1970), pp. 506–17.

Showalter, Elaine (1985). *The New Feminist Criticism: Essays on Women, Literature and Theory*. Pantheon/Random House: New York.

Silverman, Kaja (1983). *The Subject of Semiotics*. Oxford University Press: New York.

Silverman, Kaja (1992). *Male Subjectivity at the Margins*. Rutledge: New York.

Simón, Pedro, ed. (1970). *Recopilación de textos sobre José Lezama Lima*. Casa de las Américas: Havana.

Simón, Pedro, ed. (1991). *Dulce María Loynaz: valoración múltiple*. Casa de Las Américas: Havana.

Solé, Jacques (1989). *Questions of the French Revolution*. Pantheon: New York

Starobinski, Jean (1982). *1789: Emblems of Reason*. University Press of Virginia: Charlottesville.

Stevens, John (1990). *Lust for Enlightenment: Buddhism and Sex*. Shambala: Boston.

Suárez-Galban, Eugenio, ed. (1987). *José Lezama Lima: el escritor y la crítica*. Taurus: Madrid.

Taylor, Charles (1992). *The Ethics of Authenticity*. Harvard University Press: Cambridge, Mass.

Thomas, Hugh (1973). *Cuba: la lucha por la libertad*. Grijalbo: Mexico City.

Thompson, Robert Farris (1984). *Flash of the Spirit*. Vintage: New York.

Touraine, Alain (1995). *Critique of Modernity*. Basil Blackwell: Cambridge, Mass. Translated by David Macey.

Vattimo, Gianni (1991). *The End of Modernity*. Johns Hopkins University Press: Baltimore.

Vattimo, Gianni (1992). *The Transparent Society*. Johns Hopkins University Press: Baltimore.

Valdés, Nelson (1995). "La cultura política cubana: entre la traición y la muerte." In Rodríguez-Beroff (1995).

Verene, Donald Philip (1981). *Vico's Science of Imagination*. Cornell University Press: Ithaca, N.Y.

Verene, Donald Phillip (1985). *Hegel's Recollection: A Study of Images in the "Phenomenology of Spirit."* SUNY Press: Albany, N.Y.

Vico, Giambattista (1988). *On the Most Ancient Wisdom of the Italians*. Cornell University Press: Ithaca, N.Y. Translated by L. M. Palmer.

Vitier, Cintio (1970). *Lo cubano en la poesía*. Instituto del Libro: Havana.

West, Alan (1994a). "Dystopia latina." *Village Voice* (New York), May 1994, Voice Literary Supplement.

West, Alan (1994b). "Revising Cuba: A Report from Havana." *Boston Phoenix*, no. 76, August 1994, Phoenix Literary Section.

West, Alan (1994c). "Virgilio Piñera: una ética de redención en el fracaso." *Crítica*, no. 59, pp. 27–38.

West, Alan (1994d). "Inscribing the Body of Perfection: Adorned with Signs and Graces. Thoughts on Severo Sarduy's *Maitreya*." In *Lo que no se ha dicho*. Ollantay Press: New York, pp. 115–24.

West, Alan (1995). *Dar nombres a la lluvia/Finding Voices in the Rain*. Ediciones Verbum: Madrid. Translated by Alan West and Mark Schafer.

West, Alan (1996). "Sones peregrinos." *Encuentro de la cultura cubana* (Madrid), no. 2.

White, Hayden (1974). *Metahistory: The Historical Imagination in Nineteenth Century Europe*. Johns Hopkins University Press: Baltimore.

White, Hayden (1978). *Tropics of Discourse*. Johns Hopkins University Press: Baltimore.

Whitman, Walt (1902). *Collected Works of Walt Whitman, Vol. I*. G. P. Putnam's & Sons: New York.

Williams, Raymond (1966). *Modern Tragedy*. Stanford University Press: Stanford, CA.

Williams, Raymond (1983). *Keywords*, 2nd ed., rev. Oxford University Press: London.

Winner, Langdon (1979). *Autonomous Technology: Technics-out-of-Control as a Theme in Political Thought*. MIT Press: Cambridge, Mass.

Winnicott, D. K. (1971). *Playing and Reality*. Penguin Books: London.

Wolfe, Gary K. (1979). *The Known and the Unknown: The Iconography of Science Fiction*. Kent State University Press: Kent, Ohio.

Wood, Allen W. (1990). *Hegel's Ethical Thought*. Cambridge University Press: New York.

Wright, Elizabeth, ed. (1992). *Feminism and Psychoanalysis: A Critical Dictionary*. Basil Blackwell: London.

Xirau, Ramón (1987). "Lezama Lima o de la fe poética." In Suárez-Galbán, 1987, pp. 339–58.

Zambrano, María (1993). *El hombre y lo divino*. Fondo de Cultura: Mexico City.

Zizek, Slavoj (1989). *The Sublime Object of Ideology*. Verso: London.

Zizek, Slavoj (1995). *The Metastases of Enjoyment*. Verso: London.

Index

About the Author

ALAN WEST is Professor of Spanish at Babson College. A Cuban-born writer, he is author of *Being America, Roberto Clemente: A Baseball Legend*, and *José Martí: Man of Poetry, Soldier of Freedom*. His most recent book of poems is the bilingual *Dar nombres a la lluvia/Finding Voices in the Rain*. West has translated the works of Elena Poniatowska, Luis Rafael Sanchez, Rosario Ferré, and Nancy Morejón.